Benjamin Heim Shepard, Mark J. Noonan
Brooklyn Tides

Benjamin Heim Shepard is a professor of Human Services at New York City College of Technology, located across the street from Brooklyn Bridge in the epicenter of a rapidly transforming downtown Brooklyn. Much of Shepard's scholarship is based on the ethnographic study of social services and social movements in New York. He is the author/editor of many books, including *Rebel Friendships, The Beach Beneath the Streets* and *From ACT UP to the WTO: Urban Protest and Community Building in the Era of Globalization*.

Mark J. Noonan is professor of English at New York City College of Technology. He is author of *Reading the Century Illustrated Monthly Magazine: American Literature and Culture, 1870-1893* (Kent State UP, 2010) and co-editor of *The Place Where We Dwell: Reading and Writing About New York City* (2012). His current book project is entitled *City of Print: New York and the Periodical Press*.

BENJAMIN HEIM SHEPARD, MARK J. NOONAN
Brooklyn Tides
The Fall and Rise of a Global Borough

[transcript]

Bibliographic information published by the Deutsche Nationalbibliothek
The Deutsche Nationalbibliothek lists this publication in the Deutsche National-
bibliografie; detailed bibliographic data are available in the Internet at
http://dnb.d-nb.de

© 2018 transcript Verlag, Bielefeld

All rights reserved. No part of this book may be reprinted or reproduced or
utilized in any form or by any electronic, mechanical, or other means, now
known or hereafter invented, including photocopying and recording, or in any
information storage or retrieval system, without permission in writing from the
publisher.

Cover layout: Maria Arndt, Bielefeld
Cover illustration: © Caroline Shepard
Typeset by Mark-Sebastian Schneider, Bielefeld
Printed and bound in Great Britain by Marston Book Services Ltd, Oxfordshire
Print-ISBN 978-3-8376-3867-7
PDF-ISBN 978-3-8394-3867-1

City of the sea! City of hurried and glittering tides!
City whose gleeful tides continually rush or recede, whirling in
    and out, with eddies and foam!

Walt Whitman, "City of Ships" (1865)

Coney Island Presents—by Benjamin Shepard

Table of Contents

Acknowledgements | 11

Prologue
Brooklyn Is Expanding: Introductory Notes on a Global Borough | 15
    A Global Space | 24

Chapter one
Global Brooklyn: A Prehistory | 35
    Consolidation | 51

Chapter two
Chants Undemocratic | 59

Chapter three
Community, Migration, Displacement | 77
    Migration | 78
    Community and Constant Flux | 79
    Displacement | 80
    An Eviction Defense | 82
    Movements Against Displacement and a Reoccurring Wound | 87
    Flatbush Equality | 89
    From Migration to Home | 92

Chapter four
Toxicity | 95
    Water | 96
    Redlining and Land Use | 99
    East River School | 101

Chapter five
Fighting Police Brutality in Global Brooklyn: From Ferguson to NYC | 117
    Broken Windows | 118
    Bushwick, 2007 | 119
    October 2014: "Hands Up! Don't Shoot," Black Lives Matter, and the Ferguson Verdict in NYC | 120
    Strange Fruit Hanging | 125
    Decolonize NYC | 129

Chapter six
The World City and the Space of Neighborhoods:
The Battle of Brooklyn | 139
    Rezoning and the Battle over the Waterfront | 141
    Rallying to Preserve and Protect Carroll Gardens | 145
    Walmart Out of East New York | 147
    Supporting Bikes Over Cars in Prospect Park | 151
    Coney Island, the Fall and Rise, or Demise of Local Businesses | 157

Chapter seven
Of Tempests and Storms:
Super-Storm Sandy and Climate Chaos in Global Brooklyn | 165
    Energy Bikes, Mutual Aid, and Autonomous Power | 177
    Adapting to Change | 179

Chapter eight
Community Gardening, Creative Activism,
and the Struggle for Open Space | 185
    Garden Planning and Outreach | 187
    Creating the Nothing Yet Garden and the Fight for Green Open Space | 188
    Lacking Open Space: The Case for Nothing-Yet Community Garden | 191
    Spring Bulldozers | 196
    HPD List | 199
    Save the Garden, Save New York: Community Gardens in Danger Ride 2015 | 199

Chapter nine
Rethinking Jay Street and the Downtown the City Forgot:
Lost Between Double-parked Cars and Ugly Buildings | 209
    The Rezoning of Downtown Brooklyn | 213
    Rethinking Jay Street | 216

Epilogue
The Global Street | 227
    Beyond Gentrification | 233
    Slow Down Brooklyn | 236
    A Return to the Water | 244

Endnotes | 251

The Authors | 281
    Photographer | 282

Acknowledgements

Figure 1: "Mark Noonan and Benjamin Shepard on a walking tour along the waterfront, July 2010." Photo by Caroline Hellman.

Drifting through the Brooklyn Tides, we've encountered friends, supporters, storytellers, photographers, anti-consumer advocates, marching band performers and renegade community gardeners. In their own ways, each supported an image of Brooklyn, New York as a space where stories expand and clash into one another, allowing new ideas to grow. Special thanks go out to Bill Talen; Savitri D and Lena (who reminded us there are still secret places, doors leading to hiding places under the boardwalks of Coney Island); the Public Space Party and its heroes; Imani Henri; and everyone who ever declared, "Hands Up Don't Shoot,"

or stepped into the streets, volunteered at an Occupy Sandy event, or spoke out at a community forum about this ever-changing borough.

Many of these characters offered distinct support for this project. A few of these include Caroline Hellman and Greg Smithsimon, both of whom offered critical appraisals of the text early on that helped point us to where the project needed to go. Our anonymous readers furthered the process. When I was first thinking about writing about Brooklyn, Greg suggested I delve into the literature on global cities. This story grew out of that suggestion. Caroline, in turn, suggested Brooklyn Tides both as a title and a concept.

Almost a decade ago, we both participated in a grant at New York City College of Technology called "Water and Work on the Brooklyn Waterfront." Many of the supporters and participants of that project (Richard Hanley, James Reid, Robin Michals, Peter Spellane, and Stephen James) helped inform this project over the subsequent decade. Other scholars of the waterfront, including Joshua Freeman and Marta Effinger-Crichlow, also helped inspire the book as did our many students at City Tech over the years.

Bill Weinberg and Ian Landau both read through the manuscript, offering copy edits and suggestions to improve the text.

We want to acknowledge every poet of the waterfront, every dreamer who imagined a new space here, whose prose looked to make sense of this ever-changing space.

Caroline Shepard's photos come as close to anything to capturing this feeling. Thank you for that. Ten years ago when we came back from California, you and I started talking about the stories of the Brooklyn Tides. Thanks for being there with me for them, bike riding along the waterfront through the years.

The images of the space only grew from there. José Parlá, Robin Michals, Erik McGregor, Brennan Cavanaugh, and Barbara Ross generously added to this picture, donating photographs to the book.

Portions of the stories found in these pages first found their way into print through various publications including *Working USA: A Journal of Labor, Socialism and Democracy, Theory in Action, Play and Ideas*, and the *Norman Mailer Review*.

Like Benjamin's *Berlin Childhood around 1900*, this was our Brooklyn diary, an homage to stories about a space hashed out over pints at Barbes as Slavic Soul Party played, after union meetings at Bijan's, the Brooklyn Inn, or the Montero Bar, where the conversation began.

This project has been about a love affair with a space where Woody Guthrie found a bit of a home on Mermaid Avenue. It's about a borough that Lawrence Ferlinghetti captured so well in his *A Coney Island of the Mind*, a circus-like book where poems seep from the street clashes and insurrectionary possibilities of the everyday. As Ferlinghetti pointed out in his "Populist Manifesto No. 1",

Poetry still falls from the skies
into our streets still open.
They haven't put up the barricades, yet,
the streets still alive with faces,
lovely men & women still walking there,
still lovely creatures everywhere,
in the eyes of all the secret of all
still buried there,
Whitman's wild children still sleeping there,
Awake and walk in the open air.

Reading these words, it's not hard to imagine the bard referring to his old home and a summer in Brooklyn:

>   when they closed off the street
>   one hot day
>   and the
>   FIREMEN
>   Turned on their hoses
>   and all the kids ran out in it....

Figure 2: "View of the Montero Bar on Atlantic Ave." Photo by Benjamin Shepard.

Prologue
Brooklyn Is Expanding: Introductory Notes on a Global Borough

Written with Greg Smithsimon

Figures 1 and 2: "Brooklyn, USA." Photos by Benjamin Shepard.

This book concerns tides: tides of people, tides of development, tides of industry, tides of power, and tides of resistance. Brooklyn, once a city, then a borough, and now a brand, illustrates the tensions that arise between the local and the global in a given place. The ebb and flow of these dynamics can be witnessed on the street as well as in the many seminal books and films set in Brooklyn and concerned with its unique status as both a distinctive place and an ever-evolving imaginative space evoking a wide range of associations and emotions. We witness these dynamics, for example, in Woody Allen's film *Annie Hall* (1977).

In an early scene, the protagonist, Alvy, is seen as a child in a doctor's office in Coney Island in the 1940s. The doctor asks Alvy why he is depressed.
"It's something he read," explains Alvy's Mom.
"Something he read, huh?" asks the doctor.
"The universe is expanding," explains Alvy with his head down.
"The universe is expanding?" asks the doctor.
"Well, the universe is everything, and if it's expanding, some day it will break apart and that would be the end of everything!" Alvy posits.
"What is that your business?" notes his Mom with exasperation, turning back to the doctor. "He stopped doing his homework!"
"What's the point?" explains Alvy.
"What has the universe got to do with it?" his Mom chimes in. "You're here in Brooklyn! Brooklyn is not expanding!"[1]

As the scene ends, the camera zooms out from the Coney Island roller coaster, the Cyclone, with an image of Marilyn Monroe, as if in a film, blurred within the iconic landscape of this amusement park for the people. The meaning of this shot is as rich and complicated as Alvy's adolescent psyche. Monroe, of course, remains the quintessential icon of glamour. Her marriage to Arthur Miller gave the playwright a heavy dose of Hollywood glitz to accompany his Brooklyn accent. Though Monroe often claimed she wanted to retire in Brooklyn, the couple's polar personalities ensured the marriage would be brief. The grit of Brooklyn and the glamour of Hollywood did not pair off easily. The scene reminds us of the extent to which places, like celebrities, constitute a system of semiotics and often contending associations. Raised in a part of Brooklyn that remains both an actual and mythological space, Alvy, accordingly, confesses to having a hard time differentiating between reality and fantasy and, for the remainder of the film, despairs of ever finding himself on solid ground.

But Alvy's anxiety was not without reason: Brooklyn was literally expanding and, throughout the 1950s, would experience its most transformative decade as tides of newcomers arrived, while another human wave, largely white and middle-class, left for the suburbs. Existentialism was in the air in post-war Brooklyn, a strange feeling that nothing was ever going to be quite the same again after the world war which brought so many away and back. Outside global forces were at work as well, as many returning soldiers and their families moved out to the borough.

The city of Brooklyn had been contending with waves of people and change long before the mid-twentieth century. Whitman says as much in his poem "City of Ships," written in 1865:

City of the world! (for all races are here;
All the lands of the earth make contributions here;)
City of the sea! City of hurried and glittering tides!
City whose gleeful tides continually rush or recede, whirling in and out, with eddies and foam!
City of wharves and stores! City of tall façades of marble and iron![2]

Hurried and whirling tides are what Brooklyn—"city of wharves and stores"—and Manhattan—"city of tall façades of marble and iron"—have in common. At the same time, the city across the river has always felt like something very, very far away. Globalization and mercantilism, war and environmental change, have also felt like faraway notions. Nonetheless they were still felt. The incoming tides were, consequently, not always gleeful, for Brooklyn was often at the mercy of outside forces. The Dodgers were to depart in the 1950s in an example of what a global marketplace and local powerbrokers with alternate ambitions can do to a local space; this was only after the team had helped integrate baseball, offering a feel-good narrative replaced by a sense of emptiness which would last decades. From the nineteenth century into the twentieth, Brooklyn was always part of something larger, something global, with which it was both connected and seemingly disconnected, displacing residents like its beloved baseball team.[3]

It was hard to expunge the feeling that the borough was seldom at the center of things. "When I was a child I thought we lived at the end of the world," explains Alfred Kazin in his 1951 book, *A Walker in the City*. "It was the eternity of the subway ride into the city that first gave me this idea." Brooklyn was almost all periphery. Like present-day Los Angeles, it seemed to go on forever, especially on the long subway ride he describes, from the East River, beneath the Brooklyn Bridge, past Borough Hall and Prospect Park, out to Canarsie. "We were of the city but somehow not in it," he confesses. "We were at the end of the line. We were the children of immigrants who had cramped at the city's back door, in New York's rawest, remotest, cheapest ghetto, enclosed on one side by the Canarsie flats and on the other side by the hallowed middle-class districts that showed the way to New York."[4]

Kazin's concerns about his life in the city are familiar to many. "The anxiety of our era has to do fundamentally with space," argues Michel Foucault in his essay, "Of Other Spaces, Heterotopias." Spaces are not mere containers, even as they can sometimes entrap people, when there are no doors for exit or entry. For Foucault, they are places involved with sets of relations that give them meaning.

"In other words," he writes, "we do not live in a kind of void, inside of which we could place individuals and things ... we live inside a set of relations that delineates sites which are irreducible to one another.... Our epoch is one in which space takes for us the form of relations among sites."[5] The "form of relations," of which Foucault speaks, take shape through our interactions within the time we spend walking the streets, riding the subway, sitting on stoops, or hanging out in public space, where we make new friends and discover other spaces.[6] It even takes shape within Brooklyn's relationship with its Manhattan neighbor. Manhattan is most often considered a place for work, while Brooklyn is seen as a place of residence—though even this is changing. The city is shaped by our interactions within these spaces, and the social relations amongst the tides of people filling them. Waves of people, economic systems, and stories shape the borough. Increasingly, Brooklyn is a place where difference finds space between bike rides, bridges, brownfields, block parties, foreclosure-defense street actions, communities of resistance, and community gardens created by and for the people here. Here we dance with marching bands, celebrate the legacies of Michael Jackson and Prince at Fort Greene Park, visit Coney Island, or simply hang out on Brooklyn's lively streets and in its many watering holes and restaurants. Here, heterotopias take shape, day and night, through interactions with a mix of people across class and ethnic lines.

These are spaces of otherness, with countless ebbs and tides between who's coming and who's going.

Figure 3: "A scene from Bike Kill, an annual underground bike party, in Bushwick." Photo by Benjamin Shepard.

Flowing through this book are the stories of community gardeners, agitators, artists, students, and local residents trying to find a place to live, of those like Kazin, who felt on the outside, while contending with the clash of bodies and forces of the city "beyond." They are the narratives of those lost on the subway. It is the Brooklyn which has long had to cope with alienation, low-wage jobs, inadequate housing, police violence, the possibility of deportation, incarceration, and stop-and-frisk policing. As depicted in fictionalized stories such as *A Tree Grows in Brooklyn*, *Death of a Salesman*, and *Do the Right Thing*, as well as in real life, Brooklyn is filled with those longing for greater respect and upward mobility. It is a very distinct local place. Yet, as Alvy understood well, it has always been connected to something much, much larger that is in constant flux. This is a place where global forces always seem to have the upper hand. But it is also a place where people organize and build their own commons. Here, communities rise and fall, and rise again. Instead of the same old thing, citizens have learned to ride the tides, forging their own distinctive livable globalized space.

Figure 4: "Sunset Park." Photo by Caroline Shepard.

Hovering over these conversations is the concern that it may all be too late. The condominiums popping up everywhere, skyrocketing rents, ugly buildings overlooking Brooklyn Bridge Park, rampant police abuses, hospital and independent bookstore closings lend credence to this conclusion. This specter of failure has always been a part of life here. General George Washington famously lost the Battle of Brooklyn, retreating into the fog rather than face British troops who outnumbered his. The events of August 27, 1776 have often been recognized as a moment of losing a battle but ultimately winning a war. Instead of following conventional rules of engagement, Washington led his troops West through the fog, past the marsh that would become the Gowanus Canal, to the East River, where they fled to safety.[7] Sometimes you have to retreat and pick your battles. That is the story of this book, of battling titans, the British troops, even capitalism itself. You are not always going to win, but you are going to retreat, rope-a-dope, elude opponents, in the fight to preserve something truly special. We see it today in the streets of Brooklyn from Bed-Stuy to Prospect Park and Coney Island. This is a book about lots and lots of small battles that amount to large wins.

Figure 5: "A Day in the Life of Sunset Park." Photo by Caroline Shepard.

This trend can be found in the advancing and receding waves of people and history. To the western-most edge of Long Island have come successive tides of people—Native American, Dutch, English, African-American, Irish, German, Italian, Swedish, Hispanic, Caribbean, and Asian. For thousands of years, Brooklyn was home to the Leni Lenape, who followed prey in the forests and, in the summer, settled near shellfish-rich waters. Their vanquishers, the Dutch, used axes and tidal mills to clear and drain the land to establish farms that would supply agricultural products first for themselves, then for the British, then for the Americans following the Revolutionary War. In the nineteenth century, Brooklyn was flooded with people following tides of work—handling products and raw materials, building ships, tunnels, and bridges, and manning the warehouses and factories that would subsidize the Empire City across the river. Settling in working-class, immigrant communities, Brooklyn residents would continue to experience successive tides of dramatic change. Between the rise and fall of the Brooklyn Navy Yard, the Great Migration of African Americans from the South from 1910-70, the slum-clearing policies of Robert Moses, the red-lining of real estate companies in the 1950s, the gentrification of the last two decades, the compulsive re-zoning of mayors Bloomberg and de Blasio, the rising waters of Super-Storm Sandy in the fall of 2012, and waves of young people clogging the streets with their hands in the air, declaring, "Hands Up, Don't Shoot," and "Black Lives Matter" in the fall of 2014, Brooklyn has endured countless tides. The pattern is long in the making. So is the literature on this global borough and its persistent questions.[8]

Figures 6, 7, and 8: "Images of a changing borough from Clinton Hill to Crown Heights." Photos by Caroline Shepard.

A Global Space

Scholarship on global cities has identified the distinctive roles that places like New York, Paris, Tokyo, London, Los Angeles, and Chicago play in the global economic system. However, most studies of the new role of these "global cities" focus on downtown, the financial district, the multinational financial institutions, and the white-collar employees who work there.[9] Far less emphasis has been placed on the contributions of the large numbers of working-class immigrants and their transnational culture, the armies of service industry workers who sustain the financial industry and its executives, the reduced social contract working people are offered in the neoliberal global city, and the precariousness of this new economic order for most workers. Their experience propels Global Brooklyn. Writing on global cities has rarely undertaken a sustained examination of the periphery of the global city, even though it makes up the vast majority of the city in terms of population, lived experience, and space. global Brooklyn wakes the city up in the morning, provides the labor power that gets it through its day, and puts it to bed at night. Its diverse communities are also rich sources of global cultural production, even while residents face some of the most severe consequences of the neoliberal policies generated by the global city. On a day-to-day basis, its residents cope with a neoliberal political ideology that protects private property interests, drives down wages, advocates the privatization of social resources, and protests regulatory frameworks that hinder free market values. "[U]neven development inherent in neoliberal entrepreneurial economic development strategies favor ... concentrated capital at the expense of the poor and middle classes," notes Brooklyn sociologist Alex Vitale.[10] Those on the margins of this global borough feel the squeeze, as inequality increases.[11] Over and over again, the development of cities seems to mold a polarization, dividing classes, creating pockets of urban poor, who are increasingly restricted."[12]

In a departure from previous studies, *Brooklyn Tides* considers globalism's effects on these local populations, placing particular emphasis on the agency people have to act and challenge the structural constraints the global city imposes. *Brooklyn Tides* addresses the question of what it means to live in a global city for the millions of residents who experience the benefits and costs on a daily basis. Is there the possibility of another type of urban experience in the glare of globalization? How do local people find space for autonomy while contending with the tides of neoliberal urbanism crashing in around them? These questions churn through this study of the ebbs and flows of Brooklyn's tides.

To answer these questions, we consider the literature and history of Brooklyn as well as the efforts of activists who have sought to have an impact on this space.[13] The early chapters consider Brookyn's past, while the latter half of the book addresses current struggles. Living up to Walt Whitman's adage that Brooklyn can be a "City of Friends," we trace the stories of past resistance to groups of contemporary activists combating police brutality, fighting for bike lanes and community gardens, opposing big-box stores, and forging a sustainable city. While many suggest that there is no space for agency in the era of globalization,[14] these efforts suggest that Brooklyn can be a place where actors successfully take on inequality and police brutality, while emphasizing a more livable model of sustainable urbanism. Building on the principles of participant observation, these later chapters borrow from the perspective of local activists (including one of the co-authors of this book, Benjamin Shepard) to suggest there is still room for regular people to have a larger impact on globalized cities.[15] Along the way, we trace the workings of anti-gentrification activist Imani Henry, of cyclists Keegan Stephan and Monica Hunken, anti-consumer activist Reverend Billy (a.k.a. Bill Talen) and his Church of Stop Shopping, artists Robin Michals and José Parlá, as well as groups such as Right of Way, Public Space Party, Occupy, Equality Flatbush, and Transportation Alternatives to trace an alternative story of global Brooklyn. This book does not consider the struggles of every activist or campaign in this borough; rather it focuses on a small group of artists and activists taking on the challenges of the globalization churning through the streets of their neighborhoods. Through their efforts, each suggests that there are things everyone can do to create a livable city. This is a vision of a just, sustainable city, supported by mutual aid and friendship, not high poverty rates and escalating cycles of police brutality to discipline the masses.

Still, why study Brooklyn? Just as every global city has a business district, every global city has a Brooklyn. Whether they are called outer boroughs, *banlieues*, peripheries, suburbs, or shanty towns, these are the vast districts, much larger than the center-city home of power and wealth, which provide the labor for the global city. Just as each city's downtown is different because of the individual roles each city plays in the global financial economy, so, of course, every "Brooklyn" is unique, shaped by its distinctive history, the residents' responses to globalization's demands, the particular composition of its immigrant communities, and the cultural production that takes place in each borough. While no book can do justice to every facet of globalization across this borough, *Brooklyn Tides* examines the stories of everyday residents of Brooklyn to understand some of the most significant features of New York's most famous working-class, immigrant, and service-industry suburb.

Brooklyn has coped with the ravages of displacement and deindustrialization for decades. In its most desperate decade, over half a million people moved out of the borough.[16] The borough lost tens of thousands of jobs.[17] Between the infusions of financial capital, economic development, cultural redefinition, and accompanying homogenization, its neighborhoods were being remade in front of our eyes.[18] Within the last decade, rapid gentrification has made parts of the borough sites of luxury living, work, and recreation. Today, its renovated waterways are being filled with high-rise condos. Much of this development is supported by the legacies of red-lining, foreclosures, police brutality, sky-rocketing rents, and hyper-policing of public space.[19] In order to ensure this better business climate for urban growth and development, New York's brand of urban neoliberalism has cultivated intricate public policies and policing approaches aimed at maximizing social control of public spaces, including "closed-circuited video surveillance systems, anti-homeless laws, and gated communities."[20]

Today, its citizens revel in the borough's vast cultural resources but lament patterns of displacement and uneven development which follow such patterns of urban flux.[21] While many newer residents bring affluence, for much of the borough New York's fiscal crisis of the 1970's never ended. The borough continues to endure persistent unemployment and loss of work for the lower and middle classes.[22] The story of global Brooklyn also demonstrates the power of global capital and the processes of cultural erasure, as homogenization robs local spaces of their color.[23] Nonetheless, while the forces of top-down globalization steamroll communities, Brooklyn is hanging on, and even fighting back. Down the same Coney Island boardwalk where local actors fought a wrecking ball aimed at making way for franchise and new condo developments, Brighton Beach offers a pulsing Brooklyn immigrant and cultural mix, adding to the neighborhood's rich history. Each day, countless communities here counter social controls with movements aimed at spurring a vital and progressive urbanism.

As a global borough, Brooklyn contends with both cultural erasure and expansion. Like many urban geographies, Brooklyn's public spaces, its waterways, its spaces for work and play, have become sites of contestation that seek to navigate lurching changes.[24] After all, for much of the nineteenth century, Brooklyn was an agricultural community, transformed by the region's industrial development in the post-bellum period. As late as 1879, it provided much of the region's vegetable production. Four decades later, little was left of this once flourishing agricultural economy or the rural communities it helped sustain. This history raises the question: is urban development an inevitable component of industrialization?[25] Could the agricultural base of Brooklyn's past have survived the residential real estate development with some foresight? This is a question well worth asking. Brooklyn's transformation from rural economy into a dense urban center took shape in response to both technological innovation and a seemingly blind faith in free markets which made farmland prohibitively expensive. Still, questions about costs and benefits, what was lost and gained from what Marc Linder and Lawrence Zacharias term "irrational deagriculturization" grip global Brooklyn. Any number of values were stifled when the borough paved over a once vibrant agricultural terrain. Facing a rapidly changing landscape, can this "agricultural dissolution" be reversed here? Some suggest the answer is affirmative. Urban farms are making a comeback in Brooklyn. The largest of these, Brooklyn Grange, produces over

40,000 lbs. of organically-grown vegetables, grown on rooftops in the Brooklyn Navy Yard. According to Paul Lightfoot, the chief executive of Bright Farms, "Brooklyn ... has now become a local food scene second to none. We're bringing a business model where food is grown and sold right in the community."[26]

For such initiatives to become a sustained reality, policy makers must support a host of progressive ideas, particularly the right to open space. Of course, such thinking challenges cities to question a dominant paradigm which views economic development and community needs as opposites.[27] They need not be. Others follow a different road along a seemingly unsustainable path toward hyper-development. Over the dozen years of the Bloomberg era here, space was rezoned—a third of the city—to make way for more sky-scrapers, gentrification, blandification, and inevitable displacement. And the process continues today.[28]

Here, all that is solid melts into air.[29] Marx was willing to note that capitalism does amazing things, yet he was appalled by the human cost.[30] Still, negative development is not all inevitable. Throughout *Brooklyn Tides*, we consider the social, cultural, and ecological costs of such patterns, while suggesting there could be a different route for a global city. Could this be a space where regular people fight off what look like inevitable tides? Just as the Native Americans, for a brief spell in the 1650s, resisted the Dutch, and brownstone owners in Brooklyn Heights in the 1950s protected their neighborhood from demolition by Robert Moses, the borough's past suggests there might be other paths for such a global space.[31] Is it possible for this global borough to follow a path toward a more sustainable urbanism? This account of Brooklyn's past and present insists that the future of the borough remains in the hands of the people who live here.

* * *

"Take me to this place known as Brooklyn!" Allan Swann orders his host, Benjy, in Richard Benjamin's 1982 film *My Favorite Year* about 1950's television. "Where is it?" he asks. Played by Peter O'Toole, this Errol Flynn-like film star is escorted to a place which feels like the end of the world from its Manhattan neighbor. There he meets Benjy's Jewish mother, her Filipino husband, former boxer Rookie Carroca, and the rest of his outlandish tribe, as well as most of his neighbors in the apartment building. The building, teeming with quirky eccentrics, welcomes Swann as a hero.[32] For Michel Foucault, a heterotopia is a space for difference; a space for otherness; a welcoming space for long-time residents and newcomers, insiders and outsiders, such as the tribe Swann encounters.[33] Can the same be said of Brooklyn today?[34]

Sometimes marketed as a Manhattan suburb, is it a space of difference or has it become something more digestible? Long a borough of immigrants and mixed races, a reverse migration has set in. Many residents are simply displaced while even long-time home-owners have chosen to leave. As Spike Lee laments about his historically black neighborhood of Fort Greene, increased real estate values have caused many locals to sell out: "Black people by droves [are] moving to Atlanta, they're moving to North Carolina ... They're selling their houses and I don't blame them. I can't say to them, 'you can't sell your house' ... What we need is affordable housing for everybody ... Brooklyn Heights is the most expensive neighborhood. Then you got Park Slope, Fort Greene, Cobble Hill, Clinton Hill and then, you know, it works like this... the rents get cheaper the further away you go from Brooklyn. And the reality is, after the sand on Coney Island, it's the motherfucking Atlantic Ocean. So, where you gonna go?"[35] Despite increased rents, the space does, however, remain a draw for writers and those working in creative industries.[36] Today, many see their Manhattan neighbor as the outer borough. The tides of people, work, resistance, and flux continue.

Figures 9, 10, and 11: "Street party in Spike Lee's Fort Greene." Photo by Brennan Cavanaugh.

Figure 12: "Sign at Summer 2013 rally on the Brooklyn Bridge protesting hospital closures. Recalling the famous Post headline announcing President Gerald Ford's refusal to save NYC from bankruptcy in the '70s, this sign is a reminder of how government officials still view the needs of Brooklyn's local residents as somehow distant, removed from more central concerns." Photo by Benjamin Shepard.

Figures 13, 14, 15: "Scenes of a man fishing and a waterfront in transition."
Photos by Caroline Shepard.

In 2004, Brooklyn's Red Hook neighborhood lost its last shipping dry dock to make way for an Ikea store.[37] The end of the shipping industry coincided with patterns of home foreclosures and the closures of community hospitals and libraries. Today, many worry that Brooklyn is losing its soul to rampant real estate speculation and displacement to make way for sameness rather than difference. Others suggest Brooklyn is finding its center again, even as it loses itself from time to time. It's a bit of sacrilege to talk baseball here, given the infamy of the Dodgers' lamented departure. Yet, it wasn't the Dodgers who left, so much as it was Robert Moses who would not welcome them into a home at Flatbush and Atlantic, the space where basketball and trendsetting now takes shape. Jason Collins was the first openly gay player in the league who played for a brief while for the Brooklyn Nets, his jerseys selling as blows against homophobia, just like Jackie Robinson jerseys once served as emblems of anti-racism.[38] Prior to the completion of the Barclays Center, there'd been a lot of years of Brooklyn being lost to cars and Robert Moses' vision of urban dystopia. But many of us are still here, telling stories, taking pictures, cheering for our new teams, organizing, and remaking lost objects.

In December 2014, Prince William and his wife Kate Middleton, came to Brooklyn to take in a Nets game at the team's stadium named after a British bank. With "Black Lives Matter" protests swirling outside, they arrived for the second half of the game. During warm-ups, Lebron James and his team-mates wore "We Can't Breathe" t-shirts. The local press would note that British royalty have not always been welcomed here, just miles from the scene of the first battle of the Revolutionary War to take place after the signing of the Declaration of Independence, the Battle of Brooklyn.[39] In the same location, new battles have emerged in the on-going fight for justice and equality.

These experiences of parks and places, gardens lost and found and remade—this is perhaps the making of a more abundant narrative, in which we beat back the inevitable feeling of loss which so often envelops those of us who live here. Perhaps, just perhaps, we are moving somewhere else beyond a last exit. Still, to what end? How does this space cope with the tides of neoliberal urbanism rapidly transforming it? How has it coped with them? These questions churn through this story of the Brooklyn Tides.

Figure 16: "Bedford-Stuyvesant Rubinstein staircase." Photo by Caroline Shepard.

Figure 17: "*Kids playing in Brooklyn Bridge Park along a waterfront in transition.*" *Photo by Benjamin Shepard.*

Chapter one

Global Brooklyn: A Prehistory

> "Glaciers move in tides. So do mountains. So do all things."
> John Muir, unpublished journal entry, Aug. 21, 1872[1]

Looking across the East River from the vantage point of the Brooklyn Heights Promenade, one glimpses Brooklyn's geological and human ebb and flow across time. Not too long ago the park below was deserted in advance of the flood Hurricane Sandy was about to bring. Global climate change is a factor that once altered the region's geographical contours, and it clearly will do so again. Like the East River, the history of Brooklyn is tidal: in its uses, connotations, and public perception. The borough has provided a safe harbor for some and a place of danger for others; it has been the site of local and national industry but also inordinate pollution; it has undergone demographic shifts that alternately promoted community and public access and exclusivity and privilege.

Globalization, at the center of many of these changes, is not easily defined. Roland Robertson refers to it as "the compression of the world and the intensification of consciousness of the world as a whole." Over time, the rise of international communications, advances in transportation and technology, and the formation of nation-states and corporations have caused the world to become "a single place" in which thoughts and actions are increasingly interrelated. Though integrated, the world remains a diverse field of individuals, groups, and ideologies that contend with each other even as globalization "dissolves the autonomy of actors and practices in the contemporary world order."[2] Inherent in these dynamics is an ongoing, open-ended process in which universalism (sameness) contends with particularism (difference) on unequal footing. Inevitably, so it too often seems, the local comes to be subsumed by larger corporate and/or statist forces. Local traditions, once lost, can even be repackaged by marketers in a global market in which "difference" sells. Junior's restaurant in Downtown Brooklyn is an example of this process, known as "glocalization."[3] Though the owner recently refused to sell his flagship restaurant to investors, this local eatery famed for its cheesecake and 1950s decor now has additional locations at Times Square, Grand Central Terminal, and Foxwoods Casino in Connecticut.[4]

Holding out against global forces has never been easy. In 1828, a Mrs. Duffield owned precious land that was eventually to become the Fulton Mall, where Junior's now stands. The new township of Brooklyn had wanted to survey her property, but Mrs. Duffield refused. One day, while she was across the East River in Manhattan, surveyors secretly snuck onto her property. Before long, a main thoroughfare, named Duffield Street, passed by her house and the rest, one can say, is history. Or, to be more precise, an early chapter in the history of global Brooklyn.[5]

Figure 1: "A Walking Path Made of Glacial Erratics in Prospect Park." Photo by Mark Noonan.

From its beginnings as a Dutch outpost, Brooklyn has long felt the effects of globalization. This chapter discusses this history with an emphasis on how global change has often been met with tides of resistance. Obscured by history, the triumphs of localized resistance to larger global forces, whether in the form of labor strikes, peaceful protests, the formation of alternative spaces and communities, or simply the refusal to "sell out" to salivating speculators, remain the exception rather than the rule. Nonetheless, such resistance reminds us that collective endeavors for the common good and livable urban space remain possible, a central premise of *Brooklyn Tides*.

Long before tides of people came to Brooklyn, there came a tide of ice. Approximately two million years ago, the first of many sheets of glacial ice made its way down along the North American continent, covering mountaintops, deepening valleys, and carving out lake basins and riverbeds. The last ice sheet, known as the Laurentide, stretched across most of Canada, covered the Great Lakes region, and reached present day New York City, before beginning to recede some 22,000 years ago. A record of this last tide of ice remains visible in striated grooves on outcroppings of Fordham Gneiss, Inwood Marble, and Manhattan Schist throughout New York City. Grooves were also left behind in the many boulders, known as glacial erratics, found today in New York City's many parks. In Brooklyn and on Long Island, two massive accumulations of glacial debris—the Ronkonkoma and the Harbor Hill moraines—mark the terminal edges of where the Laurentide ice sheet stopped, retreated, then re-advanced before receding again. Though blasted and smoothed out by humans in the last few centuries, the hills and ridges of "the broken land," as Native Americans once called Long Island, are captured in Anglo-Dutch place names such as Brooklyn Heights, Cobble Hill, Park Slope, and Bay Ridge.[6]

Contained by the Harbor Hill Moraine, run-off from the melting and retreating ice created an extensive lake system across present day New York and Long Island until rising water levels breached a mile-wide gap now known as the Verrazano Narrows. This cataclysmic event would leave New York's upper bay drained for thousands of years, establishing a habitat well-suited for woolly mammoths, mastodons, bison, musk oxen, giant beavers, and saber-toothed tigers, as well as the Clovis people who followed and hunted these now-extinct prey.[7] As the climate warmed, sea levels rose and water again poured into the bay, creating numerous inlets, marshes, and sand bars, as well as the East River that winds around Hell's Gate and eventually pushes out into Long Island Sound, itself a former glacial lake. Technically speaking, New York Bay is not a bay at all but a drowned estuary, and the East River a tidal strait of fairly recent origin on the geological timeline. The geological history of this region foreshadows a characterization of the landscape that remains true to this day: ever-changing.

Human migrations, first on foot from Asia across the Bering Strait, then on ships from Europe across the Atlantic, and lately behind the wheels of U-Haul trucks from Manhattan, have also affected the region as well as the destinies of prior occupants—a cycle of development and displacement all too familiar to those who consider themselves "native" to Brooklyn. The true natives, of course, were the Leni Lenape, who settled along the Atlantic seaboard some 12,000 years ago. By the time of European discovery in the 1500s, approximately 16,000 inhabitants were residing in Lenapehoking, as the region extending from Delaware to Long Island was then called by the various Lenape tribes. Thirteen bands, numbering about 6,000, lived on Long Island alone, including the Montauk, the Shinnecock, the Unquachaug, the Secatogue, the Massapequa, the Merrick, the Rockaway, the Canarsee, the Matinecock, the Nissequogue, the Setaukets, the Corchaug, and the Manhanset.[8]

Figure 2: "A Tree in Bay Ridge." Photo by Caroline Shepard.

Part of the Algonquian language group, the Leni Lenape, referred to as "the Grandfathers" by other tribes and "the Delaware" by Europeans, worked cooperatively with each other to fish, hunt, and farm. As cultivators of crops, the Lenape used an ecologically advanced slash-and-burn system. The men would cut down trees, set fire to the underbrush, then mix the ashes with the soil. The women would then plant seeds of corn on small mounds between stumps. When the stalks began to grow, squash and beans were also planted, which used the corn stalks as natural poles to climb up (a practice community gardeners have again learned to utilize).[9] The "three sisters," as they were known, were planted in fields across Manhattan as well as in present-day Downtown Brooklyn (where the bustling Fulton Mall now operates). Dutch colonists were impressed by the advanced agricultural techniques of Native Americans and the volume of their production. "They raise so much corn and green beans," wrote one settler, "that we purchase these from them in fully laden yachts and sloops."[10] These native New Yorkers also grew a type of tobacco (*Nicotina rustica*) that, unlike the type introduced by the English in Virginia, needed very little attention.[11]

This first tide of inhabitants never completely disappeared as several small reservations remain on Long Island. Their legacy, however, is most evident in the toponymy of the city. Native American names have been retained in places such as Manhattan, the Rockaways, and the Gowanus Canal, linguistic traces of what historians now contend to be the first stage of globalization: the period of discovery and colonization. For Janet L. Abu-Lughod, global interdependence and consciousness of the world as a whole preceded the advent of capitalist modernity. She locates its first cycle from the founding of the colonies to around 1820. In her view, of all early American cities, "only New York figured in this earliest historic cycle, which was so critical in establishing that city's dominance on the eastern seaboard."[12]

For the Lenape, the first sign that their world was about to expand and transform was the arrival of the Italian explorer Giovanni Da Verrazzano in New York Bay on July 8, 1524. Sailing in a ship named *The Dauphine*, Verrazzano came in search of the legendary Northwest Passage, a route that would lead to the silks and spices of the East Indies. He writes how, upon entering the waterway that now bears his name, he and his crew discovered "a very pleasant situation among some steep hills, through which a very large river, deep at its mouth [the Narrows], forced its way to the sea," through which "any ship heavily laden might pass, with the help of the tide, which rises eight feet." He found the land on its banks [Brooklyn and Staten Island] densely populated with inhabitants "dressed out with the feathers of birds of various colors" who raised "loud shouts of admiration." Passing into the bay, the natives greeted his ship with "thirty or more of their small boats, from one shore to the other, filled with multitudes who came to see us."[13] Verrazzano would not stay long, however, and regretted that "a violent contrary wind" forced him "to leave this region which seemed so commodious and delightful, and we supposed must also contain great riches, as the hills showed many indications of minerals."[14]

Hoping to provide the information his benefactor, Francis I, would like to hear, Verrazzano speaks to the potential commercial advantages the port might offer. His description of the Native Americans, too, suggests that they will be of great use, being in his view both friendly and simple. What's most striking about this passage, however, is what Verrazzano's Eurocentrism tends to dismiss: that the people he encounters are sophisticated traders in their own right, hardly the naïve tyros he portrays. Indeed, the thirty or so boats that came out to greet *The Dauphine* were part of a fleet of well-built watercraft, some a "full forty feet in length" that the Leni Lenape had long used to build a far-flung inter-tribal trading network."[15] As archeologists now know, the Lenape not only built trails for trade and commerce throughout Long Island and Manhattan and New England, but relied on extensive water and land routes to reach the Great Lakes region, Meso-America, and the Caribbean.[16]

The New York region would not be explored again until by Europeans until 1609, when an Englishman by the name of Henry Hudson, sailing for the Dutch East India Company, brought his 80-ton Dutch galliot, the *Half Moon*, to anchor in Jamaica Bay near present day Coney Island. Neither Hudson nor his predecessor found the Northwest Passage. But what Hudson *did* discover in his subsequent explorations made Dutch investors excited nonetheless. Rather than the silks and spices of the East, Hudson had found a land teeming with beavers. Along with tobacco, beaver pelts were to be America's first global product and the economic backbone of what was to become New Netherland.[17]

Hoping to better organize and oversee the fur trade, in 1621 the Dutch established New Netherland under the jurisdiction of the newly formed West India Company (WIC). The ostensible aims of WIC were two-fold: to make profits and prevent trade monopolies by the New World colonies of Catholic Spain. In 1624, the company created a set of regulations and conditions for settling New Netherland, called the "Provisional Orders." The company offered families willing to settle a degree of personal freedom as well as interest-free loans (for livestock and farm tools) and, most importantly, land. In exchange, settlers would help acquire beaver pelts, sell them to the company at set prices, and "obey and carry out without any contradiction" all company orders.[18] Unlike the English colonists of New England who were relatively free to rule and worship as they pleased, these proto-New Yorkers were already fully under corporate control.

Also unlike the English, the Dutch believed that land in the New World did not simply belong to the discoverer, but that it had to first be purchased from the Native Americans and subsequently utilized. According to the now familiar story, in 1626, Peter Minuit made his famous purchase of Manhattan from the Canarsee Indians for trinkets and goods valued at 60 guilders, the equivalent of $24.[19] Throughout the 1620s and 1630s, land in Brooklyn would go to the Dutch for similar prices. In June of 1636, 15,000 acres around today's Flatlands was purchased for the site of Fort Amersfort. In the same year, a 930-acre parcel known as Gowanus, today's Red Hook, was purchased. In 1637, Joris Jansen De Rapalje purchased land "in the bend of the Marechkawieck," i.e. Wallabout Bay, named after the Walloons who first settled there. In 1638, the governor of New Amsterdam bought, for his own use, Newtown Creek (today's Greenpoint) as well as all of present-day Bushwick and Williamsburg for "eight fathoms of duffels, eight fathoms of wampum, twelve kettles, eight chip-axes and eight hatchets and some knives, beads, an awls."[20]

Chapter one: Global Brooklyn: A Prehistory   41

Figures 3 and 4: "Bushwick, Brooklyn Today." Photo by Caroline Shepard.

What appears to have been a horrendous deal for the Native Americans fails to take into account the fact that Native Americans were pleased to exchange European knives, iron pots, and beads for land that was so widely available. They felt similarly about the exchange of readily available skins for European goods. Each side, in essence, thought they were getting the better end of the deal. Yet, it's also clear that the natives did not realize that "selling" land meant not being able to continue to use it for themselves.[21]

In a *Description of New Netherland*, Adrian Van der Donk depicts Native American understanding of land ownership as follows:

Of all the rights, laws, and maxims observed anywhere in the world, none in particular is in force among these people other than the law of nature or of nations. Accordingly, wind, stream, bush, field, sea, and riverside are open and free to everyone of every nation with the Indians not embroiled in open conflict. All those are free to enjoy and move about such places as though they were born there.[22]

Figure 5: "Gowanus Houses. Formerly the land of the Carnarsee."
Photo by Mark Noonan.

The Dutch viewed property laws differently. Their windmill construction across Manhattan and Long Island broadcast this different worldview in no uncertain terms. Long associated with the Dutch, windmills were used in the homeland to dredge and keep water out of areas below sea level. They were also used to saw wood, mill corn, and grind flour. All of these purposes were put to good use in New Netherland. But more than just a tool for survival, windmills were symbols of innovative technology, economic prowess, and land ownership—the hallmarks of modern civilization.

It was inevitable that the permanent settlements of the Dutch were to cause conflict with Native American tribes. While the first decade of settlement saw Natives and the Dutch colonists live in close proximity to each other in relative peace, tensions emerged in the 1640s, leading to full-scale war. The initial catalyst for dissension was Governor Keift's decision in September of 1639 to levy a tax "in peltries, maize, or wampum," on tribes who lived in the vicinity of Fort Amsterdam. Hard-pressed for money, the Company claimed that the Indians around Manhattan should pay for the protection the Dutch gave them against their enemies. The local tribes, however, refused to pay for what they neither asked for nor were provided with. In an early version of the Boston Tea Party, a group of Raritan warriors tried to capture a sloop that had been sent to trade with them but were driven off. One month later, the Dutch accused the Raritans of stealing hogs from a farm on Staten Island. When the natives refused to make restitution, Keift sent out a party of Dutch soldiers who tortured and killed the chief's brother, killed several others, then burned the tribe's corn fields.[23]

Border warfare ignited as Native American tribes across the region united to combat the encroachment of a force intent on usurping land and controlling its people. According to one settler's account, "the enemy continually rove around in parties, night and day, ... killing our people not a thousand pace from the Fort; and things have now arrived at such a pass, that no one dare move a foot to fetch a stick of fire wood without an escort."[24] In February of 1644, however, the great Canarsee chief Penhawitz was finally captured, his entire force vanquished near the village of Hempstead.[25]

Worn out by a war in which thousands of Indians and Dutch settlers lost their lives and property, the two sides agreed to a peace settlement in August 31, 1645. Not entirely eradicated, the Indian population would continue to decline and live as impoverished, second-class citizens into the eighteenth century. They would also find themselves landless. For, just one month after the war ended, a deed signed by three sachems formally ceded all remaining Long Island land, from Gowanus to Coney Island, "for the behoof of the noble Lords, the Managers of the Incorporated West India Company."[26]

Figure 6: "Flatbush Dutch cemetery." Photo by Caroline Shepard.

Looking out across the East River from the Brooklyn Heights Promenade, one notices a legacy of Native American know-how: kayaks, free to use by tourists and local residents who have come to spend the day at Brooklyn Bridge Park. How this waterway was first wrested from the native inhabitants is an important narrative thread in the larger annals of the Brooklyn waterfront, its successive tides of inhabitants and uses. It tells us how a once-thriving population was displaced by a formidable tide of settlers who wanted what they had for themselves; it tells us how Native Americans did not give up their land quietly and offered stark resistance.[27] In today's age of pressing environmental concerns, it reminds us of the dangers we have put ourselves in by vanquishing rather than co-existing with and learning from these ecologically balanced peoples.

Today, the original home of the Canarsee is the site of the Gowanus Houses. It is one of the largest public housing projects in Brooklyn and so crime-ridden that, up until his arrest in 2014, "even the project's most violent gang leader wore a bulletproof vest for protection."[28] Gowanus Canal, once a crystal-clear creek named after Chief Gowanes, is also nearby. A dumping ground for chemicals and other pollutants, this inky, noisome waterway is now known locally as "Lavender Lake." Long recognized as toxic and hazardous, in 2013 it was finally designated an EPA Superfund site and will cost taxpayers $400 million to clean.[29]

The more one contrasts globalization's past and present, the more evident it becomes that tidal cycles have a way of repeating themselves. The Dutch, for example, would cede the land to the British in 1664, who in turn would lose the region to American colonists following the Revolution. While the Revolutionary War is generally understood as a fight for equal rights, it remains a blight on the legacy of our Founding Fathers that not all Americans were given their rights following Independence. The most egregious example of this was the African Americans. In 1626, the first of many waves of enslaved blacks from Africa and the Caribbean arrived to New Netherland, to be sold in what would become "the region's premier slaving port."[30] Many were put to work locally; their hands literally built the wall of Wall Street. They swept the floors, cooked the meals, washed the clothes, and tended the children in white households. They cut the firewood, caulked the boats, drove the wagons, and tended the gardens—all without pay. At the time of the Revolution, African Americans in Brooklyn constituted thirty percent of its population, employed primarily in agricultural work. According to E.A. Livingston, "In 1790, roughly 40 percent of all white families in Kings County owned at least one slave, making Kings the largest slaveholding county in New York State."[31] Many African Americans would remain enslaved, mostly working on farms until 1827, when slavery was finally banished.

One revealing account of the life of a Brooklyn slave comes to us in the form of an autobiography by John Jea. Born in southern Nigeria, John was captured as a child and shipped to America in 1773. Sold to the Terhune family of Flatbush, he worked as a field hand until attaining his freedom at the age of 16, owing to his conversion to Christianity and attainment of literacy. He later worked as a ship's cook and itinerant preacher, publishing in 1800 *The Life, History and Unparalleled Sufferings of John Jea, the African Preacher*. In it, he reveals just how difficult life was for the unfree of Brooklyn. As he writes,

Our labour was extremely hard, being obliged to work in the summer from about two o'clock in the morning, till about ten or eleven o'clock at night, and in the winter from four in the morning, till ten at night... We dared not murmur, for if we complained ... they flogged us in a manner too dreadful to behold; ... and often they treated the slaves in such a manner as caused their death, shooting them with a gun, or beating their brains out with some weapon, in order to appease their wrath, and thought no more of it than if they had been brutes: this was the general treatment which slaves experienced.[32]

Particularly ironic is Jea's recollection of the rejoicing in Brooklyn after a victory by American troops. As he writes, sympathizers of the patriot forces "expressed their joy by the ringing of bells, firing of guns, dancing and singing, while we poor slaves were hard at work."[33]

Even after emancipation, life for African Americans was arduous. As Craig Wilder writes, freedom merely "destroyed a mode of persecution, it did not extinguish the benefits of exploitation, nor did it limit white people's power to decide the fate and place of black Americans ... black Brooklynites were particularly vulnerable as the nation matured to capitalism. The Civil War ended slavery, not the class struggle."[34] Wilder's *A Covenant with Color: Race and Social Power in Brooklyn* is filled with examples of labor segmentation and racial exclusion throughout Brooklyn's history, focusing on the workings of power to create a second-class citizenry. Even as industry began to boom along the banks of the East River following the Civil War, for example, blacks were continually kept out of factory work or skilled apprenticeships.

Despite stark challenges, African Americans in nineteenth-century Brooklyn managed great accomplishments. Particularly notable was the exclusively black community created by James Weeks, known as Weeksville. An ex-slave from Virginia, Weeks bought a plot of land once owned by the Lefferts family, the largest Brooklyn slaveholders in colonial times. He encouraged a group of African-American land investors and political activists to create a village, a haven where African Americans could live safely in a community based on progressive ideals. By the 1850s, the village, located in today's Crown Heights, had over 500 residents, churches and businesses, its own school, an orphan asylum, a cultural center, and an elder hostel. It also printed one of the first African American newspapers, the *Freedman's Torchlight,* and served as a safe zone for endangered African Americans, fleeing the violence of New York's draft riots in 1863.[35] Weeksville served as a model for the kind of corrective black counter-public W. E. B. Du Bois describes in *Black Reconstruction in American 1860-1880*. Here, a black community of resistance and autonomy felt connected to the world, perhaps more than the nation.[36] Such sentiments are not unfamiliar for global Brooklyn.

Other ethnic communities were also developing in an increasingly global Brooklyn owing to an explosion in immigration. In 1845, Alsatian Jews moved to Grand Street in Williamsburg. They established their own synagogues and soon the area would become a bustling orthodox community. European-born Jews would eventually spread out across Brooklyn, setting up dry goods stores, tailor shops, hat factories, and entering the slaughterhouse business to provide kosher meat across Kings County.[37] In 1865, Abraham Abraham and Joseph Wechsler opened a clothing store in the center of Brooklyn's bustling mercantile district on Fulton Street, the beginnings of the famed A&S (Abraham and Straus), a local symbol of Jewish-American success.[38]

Chapter one: Global Brooklyn: A Prehistory   47

Figure 7: "Weeksville Today." Photo by Caroline Shepard.

Figure 8: "Fulton Street Today." Photo by Caroline Shepard.

Following the Great Potato Famine in 1846, over 50,000 Irish immigrants poured into New York, many of whom crossed the East River into Brooklyn. For employment, the women worked as servants and cooks, while the men provided the cheap labor source that would build Brooklyn. They dug the Gowanus canal, laid the rail tracks, built the bridges and tunnels and constituted many of the striking drivers in the Trolley Strike of 1895. Viewed with disdain by the Protestant elite, the Irish tended to live in shanties along Brooklyn's waterfront and were often set against workers of other ethnic groups to keep wages down.[39]

Primarily the Irish competed with Germans for work in the warehouses, factories, and docks. Almost one million Germans arrived in New York between 1840 and 1860, many of whom settled in Williamsburg, Bushwick, East New York, and New Lots. These new arrivals were also part of larger forces taking place across the globe, for many were dissidents driven out by political oppression in their homeland. Unlike the poorer wards of the Irish, the Germans created vibrant communities which sought to maintain their language and culture and proclivity for beer-making and festivities. Twenty-five German brewers would line the Brooklyn waterfront during the 1850s until Liebmann and Sons—in one of the earliest examples of corporate consolidation in Brooklyn—started buying many out to form the massive Rheingold operations.[40]

Rheingold's consolidation of Brooklyn breweries occurred at the start of what globalization scholars call the "take-off" decades. The influx of immigrants from across the globe, beginning in the 1840s, allowed Brooklyn's local industries to expand rapidly. At first, many of these operations were village-based and family run. But, owing to revolutions in transportation, technology, communications as well as organizational practices, these firms became replaced by larger corporations.

Aligned to industrial growth was development of the Brooklyn waterfront. By mid-century, the port of New York began handling over 60 percent of all of America's imports and exports. Soon docking and storage facilities in Manhattan were no longer adequate and entrepreneurs turned to Brooklyn for space to handle and store the overflow. From Wallabout Bay to the floodplains of South Brooklyn, the marshes and rolling hills along the eastern banks of the East River were filled in and leveled, and dock basins up and down the shoreline were built. Once a bucolic waterfront of bluffs, small public docks, and the occasional distillery, almost overnight the Brooklyn shoreline was entire entirely enclosed by commercial buildings. As Malka Simon writes, "by 1874, storehouses, grain elevators, piers, and wharves stretched in an almost unbroken line from the Wall Street ferry landing to Erie Basin."[41] Once fully accessible to all citizens, the banks of the East River were now off-limits. So many buildings and warehouses came to line the waterfront that Brooklynites were literally sealed in away from the water, and Brooklyn came to be known as "The Walled City." [42]

"It is a sad thing to lose this beautiful bluff," Walt Whitman wrote about one of his favorite haunts in Gowanus Bay, turned into landfill for use by developers. "They fill up the shores with it, preparatory to running out piers and wharves."[43] The trend of privatizing the waterfront would only continue in the coming yeas.

Figure 9: "The Walled City." Brooklyn in 1886. Frank Leslie's Monthly, Vol. 21. 1886. This image of the waterfront demonstrates the speed in which Brooklyn developed from a bucolic environment into a walled city.

The water brought countless people to Brooklyn's shores, including waves of slaves with the Dutch West India Company starting in 1626.[44] "Black people have always been connected with the water," says Stephen James, professor of African American Studies at New York City College of Technology (City Tech). "Let's remember, crossing the water is how we got here." Looking at Brooklyn's waterfront, one is confronted with a long, complex history of labor, exploitation, pollution, and struggles for environmental justice, as well as an evolving relationship between race, ideology, and power. James recalls his actual experience working on the waterfront. "Two years after I dropped out of high school, I needed a job to support my new family and signed up for a program that prepared members of underrepresented groups to take and pass tests for entry into the various construction unions. By the luck of the draw, I went into the Dockbuilders' Union." He worked as a dockbuilder from 1972 to 1977 creating temporary constructions, and also as a member of the "rubber crew," providing a sealant to the bottoms of concrete forms to protect them from the salty water. "Black people's connection with the water is deep and significant," he says. "During the Revolutionary War, blacks comprised one-third of the U.S. Navy. They made up a large percentage of the stevedores and longshoremen who led the union movement on the docks. In the time of slavery, the underground railroad utilized escape routes that depended, in large part, on the waterways of America."[45]

Figure 10: "Shopping carts by the docks in Red Hook." Photo by Caroline Shepard.

While Brooklyn in the 19th century was marked by growing industry, burgeoning international trade, and an influx of people from all over the world, just inland, its rural character was also fast disappearing. In *Of Cabbages and Kings: Agriculture and the Formation of Modern Brooklyn,* Marc Linder and Lawrence S. Zacharias write how the need for housing, coupled with speculators' lust to make profits in real estate, led Brooklyn farmers to sell their land. Up until 1880, Brooklyn farms were among the leading producers of fresh vegetables, potatoes, and milk products in the nation. Cabbages were their principal crop, and in the winter Brooklyn celery provided New Yorkers with their vitamin allotments. In the 1700s, Brooklyn farms had been a chief producer of grains, but as the West provided wheat and corn in abundance, they turned to more perishable farm products that needed to get to market quickly.[46] These local farms were vital to the economy, and literal health, of the city.

Figure 11: "A Community Garden in Clinton Hill Brooklyn Today."
Photo by Caroline Shepard.

Rail trains carrying vegetables from the south and suburban sprawl were to change the rural character of Brooklyn. Almost overnight, trolley trains edged out into the far reaches of the borough and the last farmers could no longer resist selling their lands for high prices to developers, who made even more enormous profits. This new tide of real estate development completely transformed the borough by 1890. As in the consolidation of Brooklyn into Greater New York in 1898, the forces behind these changes seemed inevitable. But an important question looms at the center of Linder and Zacharias's book. They ask if this process really was inevitable and necessary. As they write, "rarely have historians paid attention to what was lost, treating the landscape surrounding the core settlement as merely a city-waiting-to-happen."[47]

CONSOLIDATION

On May 14, 1898, *Scientific American* published a front page story about the battleships lying at anchor in Brooklyn's Navy Yard accompanied by a photo of Commodore George Dewey, "the hero of Manila Bay," and another of the ships themselves (the *New York*, the *Cincinnati*, the *Newport*, the *Iowa*, and the

Brooklyn). The article explained how this modern naval force was to be refitted in Brooklyn before heading out "for southern waters".[48] The southern waters were Santiago Harbor in Cuba, where the boats, on July 4th, would sink the Spanish fleet of Admiral Cervera. With this momentous victory, America emerged as a global empire with new colonies throughout the Caribbean and in the Philippines. The Spanish-American War had begun as a response to the infamous sinking of *The Maine*, one of many famed naval vessels built in the Brooklyn Navy Yard. *The Maine* had been launched in 1890 to enormous fanfare, in recognition of America's growing need to protect its international interests. No longer following a policy of neutrality, the United States by 1898 had fully realized its ambition to become a global power—and the forging of that power had happened in Brooklyn.[49]

Figure 12: From the collection of Mark Noonan: "The Maine lay in wait at the Brooklyn Navy Yard on the eve of the Spanish-American War."

The year 1898 also marked the consolidation of the City of Brooklyn into Greater New York. Despite Brooklynites' decades of resistance to ceding municipal independence, the forces against them seemed unstoppable. As Henry Loomis Nelson explained in *Harper's Weekly*, "Consolidation was inevitable. It represented a drift of the age which is irresistible. There was no reason for longer delay in bringing about what was sure to come, sooner or later ... The Greater New York cannot fail to command an enthusiasm and loyalty such as neither New York nor Brooklyn has ever known."[50] The need for this merger, according to Nelson, was that the "loose combination of the most heterogeneous elements of the population" needed guidance by the "native element."[51] This was especially urgent given the fact that 80 percent of the people in New York, and 70 percent of Brooklyn, were "either of foreign birth or foreign parentage."[52] The other stated reason for consolidation was the massive increase in the urban population, accompanied by an even more rapid increase in wealth, which offered "opportunities for the grossest corruption."[53] Consolidation, Nelson and others hoped, would bring about control and order by the leading citizens of both Brooklyn and New York, who prided themselves on reform.

In Brooklyn, the vote on the referendum had been close—very close: 64,774 for, 64,467 against. Emboldened by the tally, a League of Loyal Citizens was formed which enlisted the support of middle-class homeowners and local businessmen. The League warned of economic encroachment and development by Wall Street capitalists along the East River if the merger went ahead as planned. St. Clair McKelway, editor of the *Brooklyn Eagle*, urged his readers to stand firm and not "sell their rights or dodge their responsibilities for dirty money, no matter how high it be heaped."[54] These efforts to keep Brooklyn independent temporarily halted the merger plan until another vote by the New York State legislature cemented the deal. To some, the demise of Brooklyn as an independent world city had been foreordained, but the merger was in fact the result of an unusual alliance between Tammany boss Richard Croker and Republican boss Thomas C. Platt. Croker saw a chance for even more patronage jobs, while Platt sought to reform the huddled masses on both sides of the East River and to garner profits for his constituents in Long Island real estate development.[55]

Expansion at home and abroad were connected in another way in that an attitude of inevitability, which served to drown out the protests of a vocal minority, also accompanied the Spanish-American War. With the sinking of *The Maine*, yellow journalists—many under the employ of either William Randolph Hearst's *New York Journal* or Joseph Pulitzer's *New York World*—clamored for war with Spain, and, as some historians argue, manufactured one. For reporters and important political figures such as Theodore Roosevelt, the incursion into Cuba and the Philippines was viewed as a matter of Manifest Destiny, a natural expansion of American interests. And just as America was to be a protector of its new holdings, New York City, headquarters of this global empire, would be a protector of its own newly acquired lands.

Also favoring both the war and the consolidation of Greater New York were American sugar interests. By 1898, speculators had invested $350 million to buy up failed Cuban plantations and eagerly sought to make good on their investments. As historians Edward Burroughs and Mike Wallace write, "the Yankee invasion had a tremendous impact on Cuba's society as well as its economy: the elite was cut in, the rural middle classes were wiped out, and the peasantry reduced to seasonal wage-work. Protests were suppressed by the Marines."[56] Parallels can be drawn to the effects of consolidation on Brooklyn. The power of wealthy elites such as Henry Havemeyer, whose massive Domino Sugar operations were based in Williamsburg, grew exponentially while the power of the people diminished. The borough would be invaded with new tunnels and bridges, and real estate development, transforming neighborhoods for the good of investors—so it often seemed—more than the residents. Brooklyn, in other words, would no longer be sovereign of its own needs, but a servant to Father Knickerbocker, i.e. Manhattan.

The forces of consolidation had been long in the making. In 1883, the Brooklyn Bridge had been built, allowing tides of commuters to cross into Manhattan for work, and products and manufactures to more easily traverse the East River. The bridge had been an enormous boost to New York's commercial interests, but as Richard Haw writes, its construction had destroyed local businesses and transformed the "pleasant residential neighborhood" of Old Ferry into a slum "haunted by vagabonds and derelicts."[57] Adding insult to injury, the workers who had risked their lives to build the world's greatest engineering feat at the time were not even invited to participate in the opening ceremonies.

The distrust between labor, capital, and classes became even more pronounced in the 1890s. The most notable example of this, and a harbinger of what was in store for the new century, was the Brooklyn Trolley Strike of 1895. Demanding better wages, improved benefits, and safer working conditions, Brooklyn rail employees started organizing. And on one cold January morning, they refused to work the street cars. The participants included "five thousand motormen, conductors, car cleaners, switch-turners, of the largest systems of street-surface railroads, embracing nearly 50 different lines of cars."[58] The strikers also had the support of the working-class families in the Brooklyn neighborhoods where they lived. The federal government sent in thousands of scab replacement workers and called up Brooklyn's National Guard to keep the trolleys running. The result was a bloody showdown that lasted five weeks and left two civilians killed. When the strike was officially over, the picketers were allowed to interview to get their jobs back—but at reduced wages.

Figure 13: "The Strike in Brooklyn—Firing at the Mob." Harper's Weekly, Feb. 2, 1895. In this image we see the police shooting striking workers, a 19th-century example of mass resistance being met with violence.

***

At the northern end of Brooklyn Bridge Park is a ferry landing, marking the same route by which Dutch farmers in the 1600s brought their agricultural goods and livestock to market at Fort Amsterdam. To summon the ferryman, a horn that hung on a nearby tree was sounded. In 1817, Robert Fulton invented the steam engine, which would accelerate New York's transformation into the "Empire City." It would also lead to the creation of numerous ferry lines between Brooklyn and Manhattan, including the one that would take Walt Whitman to his editing posts in the morning and return him to his beloved home at night.

Whitman's poem "Crossing Brooklyn Ferry" describes Brooklyn in the 1860s and the poet's sense that the city was expanding even then. Just as "others" had taken the ferry before him, Whitman anticipated future generations of Brooklyn residents commuting to work and enjoying the beauty of the tidal waters sparkling in the morning sun or at the end of a long day of work. Whitman also describes the Brooklyn shore, where he sees "the fires from the foundry chimneys burning high and/glaringly into the night,/ Casting their flicker of black, contrasted/with wild red and yellow light,/and down the clefts of streets."[59] His eyes were most likely on the neighborhoods of Williamsburg and Greenpoint, two of the leading industrial districts in all of America at the time. Factories for glass, porcelain, publishing, petroleum refining, cast iron, and other goods and products were located here, providing jobs for some of the 266,000 residents of Brooklyn, America's third largest city at the time. According to Joshua Brown and David Ment, by the late nineteenth century there were "more than 10,000 Brooklyn factories, employing some 110,000 workers [who] produced goods valued at $269 million, fourth highest among American cities".[60]

Figure 14: "New Condominiums Blocking the View of the Brooklyn Bridge and East River." Photo by Mark Noonan.

Until 2010, warehouses continued to line the Brooklyn waterfront below the Brooklyn Heights Promenade where Brooklyn Bridge Park is now located. Sugar, coffee, flour, and tobacco were but a few of the bulky items stored and transferred here. Today, Brooklyn Bridge Park shows but the faintest outline of these once flourishing industries. In their stead, the park is devoted to Brooklyn's largest growing industries at the moment: leisure and tourism. The park also serves as the backyard for residents who live in the waterfront residences, those fortunate enough to afford a multi-million dollar apartment with a view of one of the most majestic cityscapes in the world. In place of the "walled city," housing affordable only to America's 1% has found its way along the waterfront just across Brooklyn Bridge Park. Also worth noting is that while Brooklyn Bridge Park itself thrives, parks and pools in the poorer inner neighborhoods disintegrate and close.

From Williamsburg to Red Hook, many Brooklynites tried to preserve the waterfront for regular people. Most often, these efforts failed. In 2015, a judge rejected a law suit brought by the Brooklyn Heights Association (BHA) and Save the View Now (STVN). These advocacy groups claimed that a number of condos along Brooklyn Bridge Park illegally blocked iconic views of the Brooklyn Bridge once visible from the Promenade. The area around Brooklyn Bridge Park is not the only place for concern. In the months after the 2008 opening of a new residential complex called the Breakers in Sheepshead Bay, long-term residents were shocked to find themselves denied access to a waterfront open to the public for as long as anyone could remember. "Everybody had expected this would be open," one resident grumbled. "It's a private property, developed by a private developer," countered Albert Wilk, a broker for the Breakers. "It's going to be gated, and accessed only by members. If the neighbors wanted access, then why didn't they participate in the costs of putting in the boardwalk and the dock?"[61] Community members yearning for access to public space and developers justifying exclusion—this is a pattern which takes place every day in Brooklyn, New York, and in communities around the world.

While writing this chapter, I (Mark Noonan) went down to Brooklyn Bridge Park and overheard a conversation between a teacher and some students who were disembarking a boat run by Harbor School. This public school is located on Governor's Island, which offers inner city students lessons on maritime history, sailing, swimming instruction, and marine biology. The students needed directions to the nearest subway stop to get back to their apartments in the inner borough. The teacher took her time explaining the complex route to the Borough Hall station, a half a mile up from the park. I wondered if the students would even find the station stop. It's certainly admirable and important to teach students lessons about New York's magnificent harbor, but the harbor, in its latest glittering incarnation, does seem to be getting farther and farther away from the majority of people who live in Brooklyn. Rents in nearby Boerum Hill, where I live, have risen by over 40% in the last two years alone. Many tenement style buildings have been torn down, replaced by multi-million dollar townhouses and, most recently, the Brooklyn Hilton. Brooklyn Bridge Park was never truly designed with the denizens of the inner borough in mind, and now the neighborhoods around it are no longer affordable to even middle-class professionals.

This latest tide of development is part of the long history of a borough that has been affected by global currents since the beginning. Brooklyn has evolved from a forest sanctuary for Native Americans, to a small village serving as the commercial hub to Dutch farms, to a bustling English port, then a major center of industry. Consolidation in 1898 would open up the floodgates of corporate capital and transform Brooklyn in ways that it no longer would be able to control. The process marked a merging of external forces, connecting Brooklyn history, colonialism's past, globalization's future and the world in countless ways. At the mercy of larger global forces, epitomized by containerization, the borough would enter a massive decline in the 1960s, from which it is only emerging now. Throughout these years, questions about who would live here and how residents would make sense of these forces would propel the literature born of Brooklyn's tides, the focus of chapter two.

Chapter two

Chants Undemocratic

> I hear America singing, the varied carols I hear;
> Those of mechanics—each one singing his, as it should be, blithe and strong;
> The carpenter singing his, as he measures his plank or beam,
> The mason singing his, as he makes ready for work, or leaves off work;
> The boatman singing what belongs to him in his boat—the deckhand singing on the
> steamboat deck;
> "I Hear America Singing," Walt Whitman[1]

Walt Whitman's tribute to workers in "I Hear America Singing" speaks to a time and place that has passed. Written in 1860, the same year as his commuter poem "Crossing Brooklyn Ferry," this work celebrates a city at work and the central role the East River played in job creation in particular. By this time, the Brooklyn Navy Yard, established in 1801, was heavily involved in ship-building operations. From 1860 to the end of the Civil War, fourteen large vessels were built and over 400 commercial vessels were outfitted for naval responsibility.[2] For much of the 19th century, shipyard jobs were highly prized. In addition to their comparatively short hours (eight hours a day versus the normal twelve for other manual occupations), they offered superior pay and regular breaks, as the pace of the work was, as in other craft industries of the time, determined by the workers themselves.

But by the depression of the 1870s, jobs were disappearing. When steam engine-driven boats replaced sailing vessels, the change affected the work environment in unanticipated ways. Dangerous and loud machines drowned out any singing that may have transpired. By the mid-twentieth century, the ships stopped coming altogether. Between containerization and the emergence of ports in California and New Jersey that could handle much greater volume, the Brooklyn docks were abandoned and the Brooklyn Naval Yard closed, robbing the city of some sixty thousand jobs.[3] In the years to follow, many of these workers found employment at Kennedy Airport, as New York became more and more connected to the world. The shift was significant. "Changes in the waterfront divorced the city from its past," writes labor historian Joshua Freeman.[4] Sailors stopped coming to Brooklyn to work, linger, or loiter, leaving the city without a presence dating back to its earliest settlements.

Figure 1: "A decaying Admiral's Row building on the Brooklyn Navy Yard." Photo by Caroline Shepard.

Probing this provocative history, this chapter looks at how the literature of the Brooklyn waterfront reflects changes in the relationship of Brooklynites to their watery environs and the work along the shore across eras. As we observe in Ernest Poole's *The Harbor* (1912), Betty Smith's *A Tree Grows in Brooklyn* (1943), Arthur Miller's *A View from the Bridge* (1955), Jonathan Lethem's *Motherless Brooklyn* (1999), Tony Kushner's *Intelligent Homosexual's Guide to Capitalism and Socialism with a Key to the Scriptures* (2011) and other works, global forces have continually changed the nature of work along the waterfront with a direct impact on the lives of the characters involved, real and imagined.

In *New York, Chicago, L.A.: America's Global Cities*, Janet L. Abu-Lughod deconstructs five major periods that urban historians use to divide transformative epochs for America's great cities. The first cycle, ranging from the founding of the colonies to around 1820, encompasses the period of "preindustrial" mercantilism, the age of colonialism, and decolonization. The second cycle, where this chapter begins, is demarcated by the opening of the Erie Canal in 1825 and the move toward mechanization and industrialization, ending with the depressed decade of the 1870s. The third cycle, from the 1870s through the 1920s, coincides with the emergence of large-scale monopolies and technological innovation, massive immigration, domestic migration, Fordism, and the application of steam power to factory production. The worldwide depression of 1929 begins the fourth cycle, marked by extreme busts and booms, growing commuter zones, and a regional realignment of employment—ending in the 1970s when factories close and blue-collar jobs leave concentrated urban areas, resulting in urban blight.[5] Our current cycle is marked by the globalization of production and the renewed mobility of labor, as well as the decline of good unionized jobs coinciding with, if not caused by, de-industrialization and the replacement of manufacturing jobs with lower-paying "service" jobs with few if any benefits. The literature of Brooklyn's waterfront reflects these cycles, the rising and receding tides of work in this global borough.[6]

Some Brooklyn writers quietly sat on park benches, as a young Richard Wright did in 1938 drafting *Native Son* near the Prison Ship Martyr's Monument in Fort Greene Park. There, he reflected on the difficulties of a new diaspora making its way from Southern to Northern cities such as Brooklyn.[7] To the east of Fort Greene, a young science fiction writer named Isaac Asimov also dreamed of other worlds.[8] Another writer, William Styron, recalled a young man who came to Flatbush to write after the second world war. In the first lines of *Sophie's Choice*, Styron writes: "In those days ... apartments were almost impossible to find in Manhattan, so I had to move to Brooklyn." His famed novel is a story about a Southern transplant, not unlike himself, who finds a home in "a place as strange as Brooklyn."[9] For many coming here, Brooklyn was another world inspiring creative responses in the form of stories, novels, and screenplays, many of which are now classics in the canon. Styron spent time in Brooklyn, living in a rooming house in Flatbush on Caton Ave.[10] Many writers have, including H.P. Lovecraft, W.H. Auden, Thomas Wolfe, Truman Capote, Norman Mailer, Edwidge Danticat, Colson Whitehead, Paul Auster, Joseph Heller, Martin Amis, Jennifer Egan, and others.[11]

Whitman, the borough's most prominent bard, saw it as the most radical city in America. It was a space for a wildly democratic experiment in urban living, with the movements of workers clashing, transforming, and remaking the city. He saw their songs as "chants democratic." Unfortunately, with the limits and compromises of workers under capitalism and an increasingly bureaucratized labor movement, "chants undemocratic" began to fill the air, as subsequent writers would record. Brooklyn writers also documented how workers fought back, advocating for a different kind of space, where they could live, thrive, and impact the city for the better.[12]

In Whitman's poetry of the waterfront, we hear of a time when work was not simply plentiful but a largely self-regulated affair that tended to enhance one's self esteem, ensured good physical health, promised economic fortitude, and encouraged fellowship with other laborers. Undeniably romanticized, Whitman's sentiments buttress a world recalled by the father of Bill, the protagonist of Ernest Poole's semi-autobiographical *The Harbor*, written in 1912. As a teen in the 1850s, Bill's father was lured into leaving the Midwest to come to New York to work as a time clerk in the East River shipyards. As Bill recounts, "He found a harbor that welcomed young men, where cabin boys rose to be captains, and clerks became owners of hundreds of ships. To work! To rise! To own yards like these, build ships like these [white-sailed clippers] and send them rushing on their courses out to all parts of the ocean world!"[13] The end of the Civil War, however, saw the port face retrenchment. With 40 per cent of America's ships lost or out of commission and little political will to protect the domestic shipping industry, British and German lines such as Cunard and N.G. Lloyd came to dominate the waterfront. Bill's father comes to be a part-owner of a warehouse. Unable to adapt, his operations remain idle. Eventually, he loses his business entirely. Though at first the era of big companies "had thrilled him," by the 1880s, he realized that the port had changed for good. It was no longer an era "of human adventures for young men but of financial adventures for mammoth corporations, great foreign shipping companies combining in agreements with the American railroads to freeze out all the little men and take to themselves the whole port of New York." As Bill shamefully admits, "My father was one of these little men."[14]

Poole's *bildungsroman* focuses on Bill, who initially despises his father's obsession with the port. Growing up in fashionable Brooklyn Heights, the young boy views the docks and warehouse—literally just below his family's townhouse—as a nether land of sweat and grime where "heathen dockers ... with the hairiest of faces ... labored often without shirts ... who ate dinner out of pails, took long drinks of a curious stuff all white on top," and, come evening, "flocked into their vile saloons."[15] Encouraged by his mother, Bill seeks the purer path as a high-minded artist. Upon graduation from college, he escapes from the port to Paris where he hopes to unearth richer material for the novels he will one day write. His quest is interrupted by the arrival of his college friend, Joe Kramer, who extols the upcoming proletariat revolution soon to spread across Europe. Joe entreats Bill to drop his dilettante ways and turn to political writing that might change the world. Recalling his loathing of the Brooklyn harbor, Bill rejects Kramer's plea before returning home with word of the death of his mother.

Back in Brooklyn Heights, the young author develops a new interest in the port. After he falls in love with the daughter of a wealthy man who has invested his entire fortune in a plan to turn the East River into a world port, Bill offers to use his pen in support of this idea. In a series of articles entitled "The First Port of the World," Bill promotes a vision of the port in which planning and guidance by "the men of brains" would ensure growth and American dominance. "My view of the harbor was different now," he explains. "I had seen it before as a vast machine molding the lives of all people around it. But now behind the machine itself, I felt the minds of its molders. I saw its ponderous masses of freight, its multitudes of people, all pushed and shifted this way and that by these invisible powers."[16] Just as his writing career takes off, Kramer re-enters Bill's life. He requests that his friend take a look at the port from another angle, the perspective of the worker—a challenge Bill accepts.

During his investigations, Bill comes to see the dangerous working conditions of longshoremen and dockers firsthand. He reports, "I saw a Polish docker knocked on the head by the end of a heavy chain that broke. I saw a little Italian caught by the foot in a rope net, swung yelling with terror into the air then dropped—his leg was broken. And toward the end of a long night's work, I saw a tired man slip and fall with a huge bag on his shoulders. The bag came down on top of him, and he lay there white and still. Later, I learned his spine had been broken, that he would be paralyzed for life."[17] Looking into what happened, Bill learns the shipping industry does little to prevent such accidents or help the injured; rather, it hides them from the public and tallies such mishaps as the cost of doing business. Looking at the day-to-day experience of the port, Bill engages a fight for social justice on behalf of workers.

Poole's novel follows the labor unrest that erupts during a strike in 1887, and then again in 1907. "The Big Strike" of 1887 began when the Old Dominion Steamship Line announced that it would be slashing wages by 20 per cent, a move that affected about 150 longshoremen affiliated with the Knights of Labor. A group of coal workers facing a wage cut joined the longshoremen and the Knights of Labor took control of the strike. The dispute soon escalated to a general strike on the New York-New Jersey waterfront involving 50,000 largely Irish workers. Once the coal workers reached an agreement with Reading Railroad for modestly higher wages, the Knights of Labor essentially abandoned their support for the waterfront strikers, who held out for a better deal that never transpired. The strike ended with Irish workers having been replaced by African Americans.[18]

The strike of 1907 began on May 1 and tied up the New York Harbor for six weeks. The workers' only demand was higher pay, which had stagnated as a result of the increased supply of immigrant labor. In an attempt to raise wages for all (to forty cents an hour, sixty for overtime), workers—across ethnic lines—went on strike. Exacerbating already existing tensions that would result in savage violence, shippers this time brought in thousands of strikebreakers, calculatingly playing one ethnic group against the other. Italian Americans, for example, replaced African American longshoremen on one line, while "Russian Jews replaced Italian Americans" on the Atlantic Avenue docks.[19] Despite the bloodshed and substantial business losses, the shippers maintained a policy of no concessions and workers eventually returned to the piers with unchanged pay rates.

Poole covers the latter strike in detail, placing particular emphasis on how the strikers initially strove to achieve solidarity across class and ethnic lines. The motto of the strike of 1907—"We are all Longshoremen"—is duly captured as Bill listens and records the strikers' actual words. For example, when one striking African American gets jeered because other African Americans from the South are being used as scabs, an Italian steps up to address the increasingly hostile crowd: "Fellow workers—I am an Italian man! You call me Guinney, Dago, Wop—you call another man Coon, Nigger—you call another man a Sheeny! Stop calling names—call men fellow workers! We are on strike—let us not fight each other...."[20] More illustration than evidence, Poole's quote speaks to an ethos of solidarity, perhaps imagined, sometimes realized. The novel closes with the start of World War I, reiterating a similar note of fraternity and promise. As Poole writes, "we shall stop this war of yours and in our minds we shall put away all hatred of our brother men. For us they will be workers all. With them we shall rise and rise again—until at last the world is free."[21]

As Poole's text also reveals, there was nothing simple about the black struggle for freedom during this period. W.E.B. Du Bois argued that the emptying of the plantations was tantamount to a general strike, the black struggle essentially a labor struggle. A dialectic between race and class pulsed through the labor and civil rights movements. Yet, over and over again, the labor movement betrayed people of color, as skilled trades, electric, and plumbing excluded black workers. Race cuts across struggles for social change, as does a tension between integrationist and separatist impulses. And far too often, black workers in Brooklyn were "underpaid and overworked." Du Bois argued black people needed their economic justice, not just political gains.[22]

The First World War curtailed much of the vitality of the U.S. labor movement. By 1912, the labor movement had coalesced, consisting of a mix of ethnicities struggling together for social change via careful organizing. Groups such as the Industrial Workers of the World (IWW) had come to consider union organizing a rightful extension of "socialism with working clothes on."[23] "An injury to one is an injury to all," was a slogan for the organization, which favored solidarity among all workers, immigrants, and people of color. After decades of bickering amongst themselves, workers across a wide spectrum saw the entire nation's social and economic system as violent and exploitive. Boasting over

100,000 workers, the IWW condemned the Great War as "a Boss' War."[24] Yet, much of this shifted with the passage of laws aimed at squashing dissent.

"Woe to the man or group of men that seeks to stand in our way in this day of high resolution," declared President Wilson, the day before signing the Espionage Act of 1917. It set fines of $10,000 and a prison term to those thought to be aiding the enemy or encouraging disloyalty in the armed forces. The subsequent Sedition Act imposed similar punishment for thoughts or words deemed "disloyal, profane, scurrilous or abusive."[25] These efforts and subsequent Sabotage and Selective Services Acts served to marginalize anarchists, Wobblies, and other labor agitators. The Red Scare framed radical trade union organizing as suspect. Federal troops moved in to break up Wobbly picket lines, charging those involved with slowing production of war supplies as criminals. Although massive May Day rallies and actions returned with the end of the war, the Red Scare crushed the aims of a once powerful labor movement and the working-class ideals it represented.[26]

The results of a debilitated labor movement led, in the 20s and 30s, to a port run by Irish and Italian gangs and a famously corrupt union, the latter the focus of both Budd Schulberg and Arthur Miller in their classic works of the 1950s. Crime and violence filled this void, with many of the challenges and limitations of the U.S. labor movement playing out along the waterfront. Here, longshoremen exploited thousands and thousands of their workers.[27] Six Italian "locals" controlled the work along a five-mile stretch from the Brooklyn Bridge to 20th Street, mostly performed by immigrants, who moved the cargo. In order to work the piers, workers were forced to participate in a kickback system, in which they paid a portion of their earnings for haircuts or grapes for wine making, whether they planned to make the wine or not. Sometimes half of their wages were spent on kickbacks in order to simply qualify for work. Union meetings rarely took place. Dockhands were forced to take loans from loan-sharks and support "gang cutting," in which fifteen men did the work of twenty, kicking back the ghost pay to the hiring boss. Such practices only increased the occupational risks faced by the workers.[28]

But work-related injuries were minimal compared with what befell workers such as Pietro Panto, who attempted to organize against the kickback system. "We are strong," he declared to members of his crew. "All we have to do is stand up." His campaign for union democracy, an end to the kickback system, and for regular shop meetings invited the mob's ire. "What the rank and file viewed as a reform movement," the mob viewed as a dangerous insurgency, accusing him of being a "Red." Panto disappeared shortly thereafter. Soon the ominous words "Dove Panto?" (where is Panto?) written in graffiti would be found on buildings and walls up and down the East River waterfront.[29]

These conflicts are evident in cinema from the 1940s and 50s. "You know what's wrong with our waterfront? It's the love of a lousy buck. It's making love of a buck—the cushy job—more important than the love of man." So declares Father Barry in Schulberg's script for the 1954 film *On the Waterfront*. The problem, for him, was greed. The solution was collective action. "Some people think the Crucifixion only took place in the Calvary.... They better wake up. Every time the Mob puts the pressure on a good man, tries to stop him from doing his duty as a citizen, it's a crucifixion. And anybody who sits around and lets it happen, keeps silent about something he knows has happened, shares the guilt of it just as much as the Roman soldier who pierced the flesh of our Lord to see if he was dead."[30]

Much of the literature of the era addresses similar concerns about the various pollutants in the urban environment. Consider Betty Smith's *A Tree Grows in Brooklyn*, published in 1943 but set in Williamsburg in the 1910s. Just a little way from her apartment, the novel's protagonist, Francie Nolan, walking with her brother and his friends, can actually smell the water from Newtown Creek. "God she stinks," comments one of the boys. "I bet that's the worst stink in the world," adds another. This was no exaggeration; a lack of regulation—with consequences to this day—had long allowed oil refineries and factories to discharge their disastrous by-products into this waterway. For Francie, however, the poisonous creek has an altogether different connotation. As Smith writes: "She was proud of that smell. It let her know that nearby was a waterway, which, dirty though it was, joined a river that flowed out to the sea. To her, the stupendous stench suggested far-sailing ships and adventure and she was pleased with the smell."[31] For Francie, water is a symbol of hope that promises the possibility of escape from the hard life she and her family endure; it connects her life with something much larger. For, while her mother scrubs floors to make up for the money her drunken husband fails to bring in, Francie and her brother collect paper, rags, discarded iron and copper fixtures as well as deposit bottles to help make ends meet. The Nolan family lives in the midst of some of the largest industrial firms in the nation, such as Pfizer Pharmaceuticals, Astral Oil, Brooklyn Flint Glass, the Havemeyer & Elder sugar refinery, and breweries such as Schaefer, Rheingold, and Schlitz—all using the docks to import raw materials and export their goods, while dumping their waste products in the East River. Francie feels like her family is at the bottom rung of the working-class ladder.

Smith's novel was written when work at the Brooklyn Naval Yard was at its height. World War II led to the yard becoming Brooklyn's biggest industrial facility, employing 70,000 men and women around the clock. New methods in efficiency and mass production made the facility the most productive in the country. The need for labor brought a good income to thousands of African-American families and allowed women to enter the workforce in unprecedented droves. America was back to work and with this came an unflagging support for the "American way." *A Tree Grows in Brooklyn* reflects this patriotism.

Despite the family's hardships, support of the capitalist system is unflinching. For example, walking along Bushwick Avenue, Francie's father notices his daughter in a reverie over a horse-drawn hansom. She dreams of becoming a cab driver herself, when her father, "carried away with his own personal dream of Democracy," boasts how "anybody can ride in a hansom cab provided they got money." Realizing that her father is not in fact *offering* to hail the cab, Francie asks, "What's free about it if you have to pay?" Nonplussed the father reiterates that they are free in the sense that *anyone* can ride them so long as they pay a fare. Sealing his argument, he "triumphantly" concludes that any other system would be Socialism, "and we don't want that over here."[32] Later in the novel, Francie draws a similar conclusion, working as a floral stemmer in her first job in a factory. On her first day, she is horrified thinking about how "one could work eight hours a day covering wires to earn money to buy food and to pay for a place to sleep so that you can keep living to come back to cover more wires. Some people are born and kept living just to come to this." They are caught, she ultimately surmises, "because they haven't got enough education."[33] The novel repeatedly stresses individual determination to advance and educate oneself as the key to success in America.

Such Pollyannism denies of course the darker side of the American system, so often hidden along the Brooklyn waterfront and within the very soil of Williamsburg itself. Even the much-heralded Brooklyn Navy Yard, it must be noted, achieved its success at the expense of human misery. "It was a hard place," one worker, Leo Skolnick, recalls. "I was concerned in new construction, and the closest thing to describe it was like Dante's *Inferno*, between the noise and the conditions and the fumes and the welding and everything. I don't think we built a big ship without losing people."[34] During the war boom, thousands of workers would die of asbestosis—cancer of the lung caused by exposure to asbestos particles due to unsafe condition at the yards. Skolnick calls attention to the importance of the period following the failed waterfront strike of 1919. After that, those who questioned labor practices or environmental and health issues were viewed as un-American.[35]

Figure 2: "Caribbean in Flatbush." Photo by Caroline Shepard.

Arthur Miller's *A View from the Bridge*, set in Red Hook in the 1950s, is another text underscoring Brooklyn's toxic working conditions. In it, we encounter a port in which the demand for jobs now far outweighs the supply. A system of bribes and corruption amongst shippers, captains, and union heads allows undocumented immigrants to enter the port, requiring them to pay off their "entry" fee by working on the docks. As long as they owe money, they attain loading jobs, but thereafter work is catch-as-catch-can.[36]

In Miller's well-known play, the Carbone family harbors two illegal immigrants from Italy, Rudolpho and Marco, but when Rudolpho falls in love with Eddie Carbone's niece, Catherine, all hell breaks loose. Eddie wants Catherine to get away from the waterfront, find a good job in the city, and marry up. He is initially upset that she takes a stenographer job across from the Navy Yard, but what really infuriates him is her interest in Rudolpho. Ultimately, Eddie pushes back against working-class mores and squeals to immigration officials about the whereabouts of Rudolpho and his brother, leading to a fight in which he is killed. Whereas the play is largely focused on the tragedy of a man who cannot accept changes outside of his control, it reflects a time when the waterfront presented a dangerous and unforgiving work environment that affected all those who lived there.[37]

Budd Schulberg's *Waterfront*, a novelized version of his screenplay *On the Waterfront*, focuses more exclusively on crime and immorality at the piers. In details much more elaborate than either his or Miller's plays, the format of the novel is used to capture, in Schulberg's words, "the knotted complexities of the world of the waterfront that loops around New York, a lawless frontier still almost unknown to the metropolitan citizenry."[38] This world of graft is a complicated hierarchy of forces headed by Mr. Big—Tom McGovern, head of the Longshoremen Union—who has in his pocket the shipping companies as well as the mayor's office and a stream of corrupt managers. Beneath him are union vice-presidents such as Johnny Friendly, in full control of local union activities, who in turn oversee a lot of henchman, private accountants, and the workers themselves, most of whom are in debt to loan-sharks also under union command. Into this world enters Terry Malloy, who is enlisted, unbeknownst to himself, to set up the murder of Joey Doyle, a labor activist. At first Terry accepts the role he is asked to play in order to maintain the status quo, but, like Bill in *The Harbor*, the more he learns of the human side of the waterfront, the more he sides with it.

In the film version, Terry is seen taking on Johnny Friendly and getting him locked up. But the novel is much darker and realistic. In a final confrontation with Terry, Johnny declares, "Listen, dead man. I'd lay you out right here ... But I can wait. Only I want to remind you one thing. Don't get brave all of a sudden because you figure I'm on my way out. Because I ain't. I'm still in. And I'll be in when you're eatin' worms for breakfast." Sure enough, Terry's body is found at the end of the novel "in a barrel of lime that had been tossed on one of the multi-acre junk heaps in the Jersey swamps. The coroner's report after the inquest attributed death to twenty-seven stab wounds, apparently inflicted by an ice pick."[39]

The crimes of the waterfront directed attention to it at a time when the port was about to enter one last retrenchment. With no space to grow, facing competition from new larger ports, and under pressure from containerization and the disappearance of local manufacturing, the waterfront saw its jobs disappear. In 1964, the once-massive Navy Yard closed for good. The effects of these changes were very real, and New York—Brooklyn especially—would enter a recession lasting into the 1990s.[40]

Without jobs, waterfront or otherwise, the streets of Brooklyn became riddled with a new wave of crime and illegal behavior, a world that forms the setting for Jonathan Lethem's *Motherless Brooklyn* (1999). Like Terry Malloy, who turns to the union as his surrogate family, the main characters in this novel are orphans. A working port, or water itself, seem to be nonexistent. Once claiming a harbor that offered sustenance, Brooklyn has become "motherless" and its residents must fend for themselves in the best manner they can.[41]

Figure 3: "The Navy Yard." Photo by Caroline Shepard.

As Caroline Hellman writes in her reading of the novel, "The concept of the late 19th century and early 20th-century waterfront jobs is replaced by work as masquerade—work as front for amorphous assignments and makeshift jobs shadowed by corruption that extends from Brooklyn to New Jersey to New England and beyond."[42] Gone is "Whitman's mast-hemm'd thronged locus of commerce and vitality ... In the 1970s, familiarity of the streets rather than the East River now constitutes home."[43] From Whitman to Lethem, the change in the meaning of work is dramatic. As Hellman shows, the physical labor of mechanics, carpenters, masons, boatmen, shoemakers, and wood-cutters has been replaced by nebulous, temporary work.

This uneasiness with place and work—in particular, the changing nature of the borough's occupations and loss of a working-class ethos—is a theme that again emerges in Tony Kushner's 2011 play, *The Intelligent Homosexual's Guide to Capitalism and Socialism with a Key to the Scriptures*. In it, Kushner offers a glimpse of a retired dockworker's life in the Bloomberg years, as real estate prices are booming and Brooklyn increasingly copes with gentrification. The play takes place in the living room of a brownstone on Clinton Street, in Carroll Gardens, during a long weekend in June of 2007. The family has converged to talk their father, former longshoreman and labor intellectual, Gus Marcantonio, out of committing suicide. Gus's plan is to sell his brownstone, collect a profit for his family, and depart from this world. The conflict recalls that of *Angels in America*, the work with which most Kushner fans are familiar. Instead of an unknown disease, however, commodification and speculative development serve as the unwanted antagonists knocking at the door. Gus compares the worth of his life to the return he could gain from selling his family brownstone, a sad but telling observation of a man reconciling existence in a world changing faster than he is capable of making sense of.[44]

Like most of Kushner's works, *The Intelligent Homosexual* is steeped in references to politics, culture, and local history. Gus's Clinton Street brownstone, for example, is just blocks from the early headquarters of the International Longshoremen's Association at 340 Court Street, between Union and Sackett Streets. When the play was staged at The Public Theater, a fence surrounded the then-vacant lot of the former association. The empty site represented the impasse between labor's past and globalization's future. Today, a condominium occupies the space. For four centuries, sailors and laborers found work and play along New York's waterfront. Until containerization, some 45,000 to 60,000 workers made a living there. Most of those workers lost their livelihood to automation, which replaced human hands with machines used to transport large boxes to and from ships.[45] And today, the headquarters for these workers is demolished.

Named by Kushner after a socialist who represented East Harlem in the House of Representatives in the 1950s, Gus Marcantonio was one of those workers. Throughout the play, Marcantonio reflects on the choices he made as a union organizer committed to revolutionary social change. For Marcantonio, the hallmark of his life's work was the Guaranteed Annual Income (GAI), from which some workers benefited, though many did not. The GAI, a contract measure negotiated by International Longshoremen's Association (ILA) president Teddy Cleason in the mid-1960s, was designed to address the welfare needs of ILA members facing social and economic dislocation. The contract helped the ILA remain a powerful force in labor and signified something important for workers: it helped them access a portion of the wealth they helped to create.[46]

Yet the win came at a high price, exposing a rift among classes of workers and a threat to the solidarity and integrity of the union. Those with seniority enjoyed the GAI, while those without seniority were dismissed. In *Identity and the Life Cycle*, Erik Erickson suggests that as we get older, most adults face a choice between generativity or despair: to live lives supporting others and growing, or recoiling into themselves, engaging in the lives of others or lamenting their choices and regretting the direction of their lives.[47] The latter is certainly the case for Marcantonio who grew to regret his union's choice to cut a deal for those with seniority while cutting loose later generations of workers. In 1967, New York would take further advantage of the pact, passing the Taylor Law, which prohibited public unions from striking. In a single stroke of the pen, the most important tactic of the labor movement ("direct action gets the goods") was negotiated away.[48]

At times, *The Intelligent Homosexual* reads like an extension of the Elia Kazan or Arthur Miller family dramas written during the height of McCarthyite anti-communism. Throughout the story, conflicts arise between family needs and historical forces. Gus's son Pill, a dour Reagan Democrat, is ready to scold his father at any turn, while Pill's sister, Empty, a revolutionary, remains quiet. What Gus does not seem to have is much actual support. Pill resembles Louis Ironson, the protagonist unable to cope with his lover's HIV diagnosis in *Angels in America*. Like Louis, he is a moral coward. In addition to leaving his lover in his time of need, Pill betrays his family by blowing thirty thousand dollars on his hustler.

Gus plans to kill himself so as to be free of modernity's oppression. His choice is a decision countless protagonists have considered throughout the years (Willy Loman in *Death of a Salesman* certainly comes to mind). Yet, with Kushner's brushstrokes, commodification and the spectacle are everywhere. They are in the relationship of Pill to his prostitute, in Gus's agonizing relationship with work and struggle for time. "I've always liked paying for sex," Pill confesses toward the end the play.[49] "Did it myself," he adds, with the caveat, "But I liked consuming, more than being consumed." Kushner's point is that everyone is entwined within the traffic of buying and selling, money and labor—all a part of an ever evolving reality exacerbated by capitalism. "Are we talking about Gus or the brownstone?" someone asks in the second act. "It's money, it's all it ever was, this house," Gus laments, reducing his longtime family home to a commodity. The bickering, shouting, pushing, the petty jealousies, the secrets, and the ever-present screaming start to sound like an old Archie Bunker episode. Yet Archie probably would not have asked, "Do I exist?," as Gus ponders in the first act.[50]

"I sincerely hope you do not kill yourself. You're not half bad," Empty pleads, in one of the few moments of warmth in the whole play. Yet her father appears unable or unwilling to hear her. Gus's sister sits at the family table for much of the story saying very little, except to occasionally drop a gem of sarcasm: "Think dialectically, death that leads to new life." And perhaps this is what the family, stuck in their roles, needs. "Marx, it leads you to despair. History against you— Reagan, containerization, globalization… Get back to work," Empty reminds her father in a conversation about the very nature of social and economic evolution in Brooklyn. In this family drama, Gus plays the beaten-down Willy Loman, while Empty plays the ever-suffering Sisyphus. Unlike Loman, however, Gus is not interested in "getting back to work."[51]

Figure 4: "Red Hook on the waterfront." Photo by Caroline Shepard.

As the play winds down, Gus muses about the notion of affinity and solidarity among workers, families, and communities. "If affinity is lost, you are lost. With no community, you are lost. You mean nothing," he confesses to his daughter, musing about the GAI once again. Kushner reveals that few of us always live up to our principles. "We had to negotiate with the ship company. Only senior workers got it. When we took it, we gave up the principle of the union itself. We became every man for himself.... The best thing for us is the worst thing we ever did...." Hence his despair. Without hope of a revolutionary transformation, Gus feels there is nothing left for him. "I surrender to despair.... The only real death for me is to live meaninglessly. It isn't my death that's the despair of my life. That is my freedom."[52]

As much as anything, *The Intelligent Homosexual* offers a glimpse into a conversation about living and thinking about the messy relationship between real estate, commodities, reification, work, and life in brownstone Brooklyn. Through this meditation on labor's past, the stories of strikes blur within the errors and aims of the Guaranteed Annual Income, union struggles with Red Baiting, messy endings, and the rubble beneath even the glossiest buildings arising among gentrifying neighborhoods.[53] Every building has a story.

***

Brooklyn texts, from Whitman to Kushner, speak to larger trends in the industrial history of the United States, not to mention other places in this shrinking world. The texts represent both the changing history of labor along the waterfront as well as changing ideologies in the face of globalization. It's worth considering what's happened to the space that these writers wrote about, and the questions they raise about Brooklyn that remain pertinent. What happens to a city of ships without ships, a Navy Yard without a Navy, a dock without dockworkers, a workforce without a collective backbone? Is there still room for agency amidst the wreckage, or are there too many ghosts?

To these questions the prognosis is mixed. Today in Brooklyn, interest in earning a living making and selling handicrafts and artisanal products has returned with a vengeance. In 2014, the Brooklyn Chamber of Commerce launched a "Brooklyn Made" certification program in recognition of the proliferation and growing prestige of locally-made items and products. After a decades-long slump in manufacturing, Brooklyn entrepreneurs, especially in food and fashion, have contributed and benefited from growing nationwide interest in local brands and sustainable food products.[54] Made by Hand also features Joel Bukiewicz, who benefited from the local foods movement in Brooklyn and elsewhere. Uninterested in working for corporate America, he rented a work studio alongside twenty other entrepreneurs. Recalling Whitman's poem "I Hear America Singing," he notes how "all these people would be doing stuff they were just pumped to do." Rather than aim for large profits, many have turned to handmade crafts for the human element modern industry has stripped away from manufacturing. As Bukiewicz explains, "where the commerce is really rich is in the community, the friendships you develop, the fact you get to do what you want to do, for the most part, not to be bossed around."[55] His handmade knives, each of which takes approximately 14 hours to make, are now in such demand that to get one requires a one-year wait.

The success of these operations ranging from a single person to hundreds of employees have both helped the economy and provided job satisfaction to people unhappy in former fields.

"Brooklyn is a global brand," notes New York State Comptroller Thomas DiNapoli. "Kings County's cachet has spurred an uptick in manufacturing jobs that we hope will continue and increase." Successful start-ups can be seen throughout the borough. Still, problems remain. Take Shamus Jones' Brooklyn Brine, for example. Jones wants to grow his pickle company, which is proving difficult if he hopes to stay in the borough. As he explains, "We're searching for a building to buy, to give us a stay of execution in a sea of condos and escalating real estate prices."[56]

In addition to the high price of rent, the reality is that, as Brooklyn booms, most of its new jobs are in the service industry, with low wages and few benefits. In Downtown Brooklyn along Adams Street are lots of new, mostly chain restaurants catering to hungry lunch-goers, including Shake Shack, Potbelly Sandwich Shop, and Country Chicken. Gone are many of the mom-and-pop operations that the authors of this book themselves used to frequent. One recently closed sandwich shop used to have pictures of the owner's daughters, who attended college thanks to the profits made from the business. The owners had immigrated from South Korea and were exceedingly proud of their achievement. The deli had a large following and also had pictures of clientele and the sandwiches created specifically for them. Today's food chains, in contrast, offer low-paying positions with little chance to eventually own. Meanwhile, in this same area, fourteen new luxury condos have gone up. The average price for a one-bedroom apartment is three million dollars.

While there is a return to hand-craft industries that Whitman celebrated in "I Hear America Singing," as well as high-end jobs in finance, real estate, and technology, the question remains where most workers in Brooklyn are going to live. According to the latest census, the median annual household income in Brooklyn is $44,850, whereas the average rent for a one bedroom apartment in the northwestern quadrant of Brooklyn is $2,800. Brooklyn also has 100 housing projects, home to more impoverished residents (58,699) than Manhattan's public housing (53,890). The average household income for these people is $22,994. Until the 1950s, Brooklyn was simultaneously a middle-class and working-class bedroom borough for Manhattan as well as a bustling port and manufacturing center.

"Walking underneath the trees, I began to wonder seriously if I had not made a grave mistake in coming to Brooklyn," Stingo, the protagonist in *Sophie's Choice*, confesses early in the story. "It really was not my element, after all. There was something subtly and inexplicitly wrong."[57] In the midst of enormous growth, Global Brooklyn once again seems to be less accessible as a place for the people. For residents concerned about rising prices, displacement, and blandification, a sense of foreboding is in the air. Like Stingo, they are beginning to feel differently about their once beloved borough. Before their eyes, Whitman's promise of a radical democracy is slowly slipping away.

Figure 5: "Under BQE memorial." Photo by Caroline Shepard.

Chapter three

Community, Migration, Displacement

"Our country's national crime is lynching. It is not the creature of an hour, the sudden outburst of uncontrolled fury, or the unspeakable brutality of an insane mob."[1]
Ida B. Wells (1900)

Figure 1: "Pushing mattresses in Brooklyn."
Photo by Caroline Shepard.

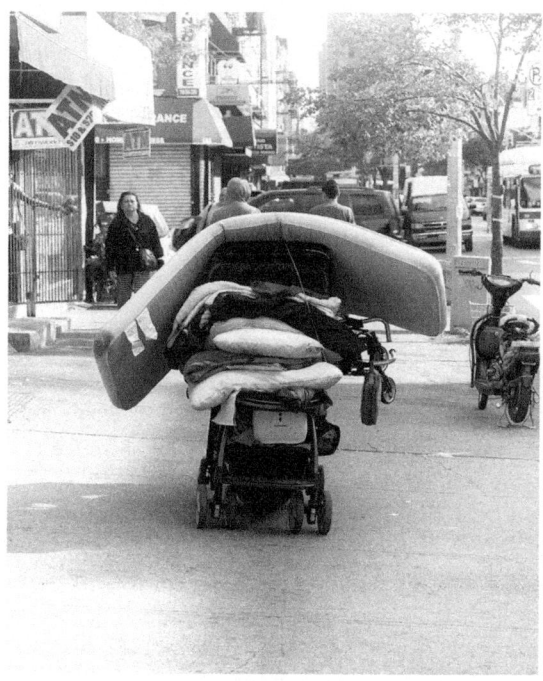

Even a cursory glimpse of the history of this global borough reveals a pattern of migration, community building, and displacement. This pattern repeats itself over and over again. Black people moved north with the collapse of the plantation system. The price of cotton went down, creating a glut in supply. The plantations shut down. Troublemakers were told, "You better go," and were pushed out. Facing a reign of terror, workers moved. Lynching increased with the decline in the economy. Businesses only pushed to stop the practice when they thought it might hurt outside investment in the region. Still, many blacks moved, settling in northern cities from the First World War into the 1930's, building communities. People being displaced, dispossessed by intimidation, high rents, and violence remains a familiar pattern.[2]

From the Caribbean and the South, "waves" of black migrants had poured into the city by the 1940s, notes T.J. English.[3] While many moved to Harlem, the foremost African-American community in the country, the migrants were too many for one neighborhood to absorb. Consequently, many black people began settling in other working-class neighborhoods throughout New York, nowhere more so than in Brooklyn. While the borough had been part of New York since 1898, it had long been home to migrants—Italians, Irish, Eastern European Jews, and many others—many considered a "different color of whiteness" upon their arrival.[4] Many of these working-class people, who had once been migrants fleeing oppression themselves, received the new neighbors with anything but open arms.[5] Adding to this all too familiar "mixture of fear, hostility, and outright racism" was the New York Police Department.[6] "By the early 1960's, the NYPD had evolved into a largely autonomous institution, whose officers and beat cops did things their own way. For generations, when it came to dealing with black people, that way generally involved brute force."[7] This was all part of a pattern of life in global Brooklyn.

Migration

For much of the Fall of 2014, the world waited for a grand jury to decide the fate of the police who had shot unarmed Michael Brown in Ferguson, Missouri. Many had started to see similarities between the way Brown and Staten Island's Eric Garner—who died after a police officer choked him for 15 seconds on July 17, 2014—were treated at the hands of police. Their fates would remind the world of the pain people of color have long endured in this country.

At New York City College of Technology in downtown Brooklyn, the students filled the first floor for a session on migration, community, and displacement. The first speaker, Marta Effinger-Crichlow, would speak about the turn-of-the-century civil rights activists Ida Bell Wells-Barnett. Professor Crichlow began her talk by reading Wells's words about the lynching of Thomas Moss at the hands of a mob. "There's nothing we can do about the lynching now, as we are out-numbered and without arms." A witness to the murder heard Moss beg for his life for the sake of his wife and unborn baby. "Tell my people to go west, there is no freedom here," he cried out to his attackers in his final moments. "Moss's words first appeared in the *Memphis Commercial* on March 10 1892 ...," Crichlow explained. "Upon learning of the murders, Wells, who later became the impetus of the anti-lynching crusade, continued to parallel Moss's final words with her own report of lynching... 'Go West people. There is no justice for us here.'"[8]

For Wells, the phrase "tell my people to go west" functioned as more than a literal call to go West. The slogan challenged all who had gone West, as well as those who stayed in Memphis; it challenged everyone, even those moving North, to fight the lynch mob. A black writer who was able to mobilize and navigate the country's public spaces, Wells was of a first generation of African Americans that could instigate such migrations. She showed that a black woman could move out, away from what had been home—she "raised the consciousness of a people and incited them to act."[9] Countless others heeded her call, followed her gesture of mobility, calling for a generation to move, both literally and metaphorically. Doing so, they demonstrated the possibility of searching and finding somewhere, living somewhere better, somewhere freer in the here and now.

COMMUNITY AND CONSTANT FLUX

Cities such as Chicago and New York, and by extension Brooklyn, became destinations for such movement.[10] These migrations, the hordes of people and ideas, have transformed urban space, profoundly impacting the spaces where people moved. "Social change has been a central factor in the sociological history of Brooklyn," note Rita Seiden Miller and Stephen Karp. The process has been continual as the space shifted from "Indian Settlement to Dutch Colony, from rural slave-owning town to large 19th-century ... independent city to ... borough. From Yankee domination ... to white, European immigration to contemporary expansion of Black and Hispanic residents, social change has been the one constant in Brooklyn's history."[11]

Many of the newcomers got involved with organizing, striving to make that place home. Take Billy Brown, an 86-year-old African American woman with short hair and animated eyes. "This was yours," she explained, describing what she had learned about her neighborhood. "This was my plot where I belong so I want to make it the nicest part of my life and the nicest part of my entity to live here. It was just like a castle, like a castle that belonged to you." She continued: "Just wherever you went, that was your home. If you were a part of it, you lived there. It's small neighborhoods, that's what it was, small neighborhoods. ... You could organize wherever you went, you could organize."[12]

A love for community was intricately connected with this story. Having heeded the calling to go find a new space to call home, many of these migrants got started making a space for themselves. In Brooklyn, people built spaces of their own from Brownsville to Greenpoint, East New York to Cobble Hill. They celebrated victories, brought up kids, helped make this new space home, defended their homes from evictions, and struggled with neighborhood threats.[13]

Flux was constant, even as people moved to and from; the world was changing. "Stories of gentrification are by definition stories of change," notes Kalefa Sanneh, "and yet scholars have had a surprisingly hard time figuring out who gets displaced, and how."[14] Multiple forces were involved in this story. Throughout the 1950's, highways divided neighborhoods where immigrants had settled in.[15] This was the case with Williamsburg/Greenpoint, in North Brooklyn, where an elevated highway cut the neighborhood in two, displacing Italian-American residents and businesses, just as they were grappling with the influx of some 900 families, many African American, who had moved into the new housing projects during the decade. And then on September 11, 1972, a wrecking ball tore down still more homes, forcing their inhabitants, many elders, to leave because of eminent domain, only to watch their homes demolished to make way for a box manufacturing plant. The remaining residents fought back against the tide, transforming their small enclave into a well-organized neighborhood. Many were becoming activists, getting involved, connecting issues, successfully pushing back against a new incinerator plant in the next decade, while creating strange new alliances between residents of the once homogenous neighborhood.[16] Still the threats to the neighborhood, to neighborhoods all over the city, were many.

Displacement

No sphere of life is constant, certainly not housing, where residents have long been forced to cope with the whims of the market, landlords, and bank policies. Housing activist James Tracy has long argued that urban activists should frame their battles against high rents, for housing and stability, around the concept of displacement. "Don't call it gentrification," he advises. A cofounder of the San Francisco Community Land Trust as well as a poet, Tracy holds that "displacement" is a better word for the process of people being pushed out of their homes to make way for more appealing tenants. "I prefer to use the word 'displacement' because it drives home the end result of gentrification: someone loses their home and their community. You can't play fast and loose with the word! On one end of political thought, there is this underlying assumption that higher-income people improve a low-income community just by arriving there. It plays into this mythos deeply embedded in our psyche that rich people will somehow randomly meet their neighbors and help them up the economic ladder."[17]

Organizing to slow the process has been the experience of decades for Tracy. He saw it when he worked as a delivery man driving the streets of San Francisco, noting how landlords were making donations of the left-behind belongings of former tenants who had been displaced. Even then, Tracy saw a storm brewing. "Throughout my life, I've seen moments like this through the battles for home and public space," he writes. "They are always fleeting, as are the tenuous alliances that bloom and wilt again. Neoliberalism has literally stolen the city from those who most contribute to its vibrancy. While things will never be (and maybe never should) be the same, resistance—not only capital—shapes urbanism."[18]

At City Tech's session on migration, community, and displacement, Tracy drew a picture of his life as a housing activist and the struggles he's fought over affordable housing, the right to a home and public space, connecting his experience with generations of others. "There has always been a dance between electoral politics and direct action," notes Tracy. "Direct action was central in the fights for the right to expand suffrage to women and later Blacks. [The] squatters of Homes not Jails embody a spirit of past social movements, such as the Unemployed Workers of the 1930's, which is rooted in the everyday needs of community members. They build direct democracy with crowbars as their ballots and vacant housing as their ballot boxes... confronting evictions and joblessness on the neighborhood level."[19] Members of Occupy built on this ethos of tenants who banded together to protect each other from eviction and foreclosure. As Tracy notes, "Housing activism tends to do best against the backdrop of larger social movements."[20]

Cities around the world have been forced to cope with the ravages of massive displacement, with waves of movements rising to respond movements. "If the goal of an anti-displacement movement is to stop displacement," Tracy argues, "then the movement has failed by any stretch of the imagination." These movements have had mixed results. After all, cities such as Brooklyn and San Francisco are increasingly becoming exclusive, class-bound spaces. "What remains of working-class and artistic life there is on the ropes. Thankfully, the knockout cannot be called in this round." The work of organizers has kept the battle going, allowing some of the soul of the city to "remain intact."[21]

A conversation about housing and displacement inevitably involves questions of what kinds of urban space are available under capitalism. "The very notion of a commons, of resources provided outside of the market, is tied to society's perception of race, class, and gender. Specifically, commons (and reforms) are created at the intersection of the aspirations of social movements to expand popular power and desires of elites to contain popular protests," argues Tracy. The commons expands as public spaces. "[T]o defend public housing means simultaneously fighting for the human right to housing, while refusing to embrace politics that flatten out the historical bigotries and exclusions."[22]

Here, Tracy suggests housing battles, particularly struggles over public housing, involve efforts to cope with social controls. "Federal housing policy has been used to control and contain Black Americans, often to accelerate profit accumulation of urban development regimes. At times, this is meticulously planned; at other times, it is a product of opportunism. In either situation, the conditions that Black people live in are generally a good indicator of what is in store for the general population. In reality, what happened to public housing residents—particularly Black residents—was the canary in the housing-crisis coal mine."[23] Affluent or desirable families were offered housing opportunities "if they cashed in on Section 8 vouchers, risking future housing assistance." Many were later "sold risky loan products, such as adjustable rate and interest-only mortgages." They bought homes. By 2008, many "fell victim to foreclosure as housing payments skyrocketed. Yet again, corporate—and government—housing policies colluded to displace Black people, and to provide a template by which other communities were displaced."[24] From here many found themselves without homes or in the fastest-growing public housing in the U.S., the jail system. Some fought back against these forces.

An Eviction Defense

One of the most pernicious dynamics of capitalist globalization is the commodification of what feels like everything, including space where people live. Here, developers hope to extract maximum profits from space. Those who can pay a premium move in. Those unable to contend with increasing rents face eviction, dispossession, and displacement. "Through dispossession, primitive accumulation strips many people of their outward signs of humanity as well as their ability to provide for themselves," writes Michael Perelman, referring to Marx's highly ambiguous term from eighth part of the first volume of *Capital*, in which he argued that the process was a precondition of capitalism.[25] "In many ways, primitive accumulation displays considerable continuity," elaborates Perelman.[26] "The confiscation of land continues unabated ... but on a far more extensive scale than ever before ... The victims of this practice are frequently indigenous people..."[27] Perelman sees the process as ongoing. "[A]dvanced capitalist interests behave in much the way as Marx's traditional primitive accumulationists at least from the perspective of the people victimized by the process ... the grasping spirit of an emerging capitalist economy on the make is perfectly consistent with both classical primitive accumulation and modern capitalist practices."[28]

Building on Marx and Perelman, social welfare scholar William Sites describes a modern, continually coercive, form of primitive accumulation as "primitive globalization." "[T]hrough capital surplus-value is made and from surplus-value more capital," Marx famously writes in volume one of *Capital*.[29] "The whole movement, therefore, seems to turn in a vicious circle, out of which we can only get by supposing a primitive accumulation...." [30] Framing his understanding of primitive accumulation as a "set of social forces" Sites suggests it takes shape through ongoing "forced separations from traditional ways of life," that punish "beggars and vagrants", the displacement of bodies from the land where they work and neighborhoods where they dwell.[31]

"[P]rimitive accumulation remains a key concept for understanding capitalism—and not just the particular phase of capitalism associated with the transition from feudalism, but capitalism proper," concludes Michael Perelman.[32] "To this end, we must carry the history of primitive accumulation through the epoch of classical political economy by connecting this concept with Marx's notion of the social division of labor."

Revolutions are born when people fight this process. For Marx, "those moments when great masses of men are suddenly and forcibly torn from their means of subsistence, and hurled as free and 'unattached' proletarians on the labor-market"—these are moments which ignite social movements. "The expropriation of the agricultural producer, of the peasant, from the soil, is the basis of the whole process."[33] A response to the patterns of displacement, and eviction was part of what ignited the Occupy movement in New York City in the fall of 2011.[34]

Concerned with the human cost of development booms followed by foreclosures in Brooklyn and around the nation, a group calling itself Organizing for the Occupation (O4O) agitated for a movement against foreclosures in Brooklyn. O4O's first action would take place on August 19th, 2011. It aimed to save an elder woman named Mary Lee Ward from being evicted from her longtime apartment in in Bedford-Stuyvesant.

Word about Friday's eviction defense action was all over Facebook: "Stop the Eviction of Mary Lee Ward!" An "Eviction Blockade" was to take place at "Ms. Ward's Home in Bed-Stuy." The Facebook invite provided background on the scene:

Mary Lee Ward, an 82-year-old grandmother and resident of the Bed-Stuy community for 44 years faces eviction from her home due to the deceptive practices of bankers and speculators. Predatory lenders like the now defunct Delta Funding, Inc. and real estate speculators like 768 Dean Inc. are targeting and destroying diverse communities of color like Bed-Stuy... stripping them of their equity, wealth and homes! We, the members of Organizing for Occupation (O4O), a citywide network of concerned NYC residents active in the struggle to make housing a human right, can no longer sit back and watch the destruction of our communities! Stand in solidarity with Ms. Ward this Friday morning, August 19, 2011! Stop the eviction of Ms. Ward from her home! EVICT THE SCHEMING BANKERS AND SPECULATOR FROM OUR COMMUNITIES!

Figure 2: "Flyer for anti-foreclosure action in support of Ms. Ward. The action largely anticipated the actions of the Occupy Wall Street Movement to take place a month later."

Stop the eviction of Ms. Ward!!
Tell the marshal: NO foreclosures in Bed-Stuy!

Friday, August 19, 2011 at 9am
320 Tompkins Avenue
G to Bedford-Nostrand or A/C to Kingston-Throop

Ms. **Mary Lee Ward**, an 82-year-old grandmother, African American woman and Bed-Stuy resident for the past 44 years is facing eviction from her home due to the deceptive practices of banks and speculators!!

Predatory lenders like the now defunct **Delta Funding** and real estate speculators like "**768 Dean Inc**" are destroying Bed-Stuy, intentionally stripping communities of color of their equity, wealth, and homes!

We, the members of **Organizing for Occupation** (O4O), a citywide network of concerned NYC residents active in the struggle to **make housing a human right**, can no longer sit back and watch the destruction of our communities!

Stand in solidarity with Ms. Ward!
Stop the Eviction of Ms Ward from her home!

Evict the Scheming Bankers and Speculators from our Communities!

Organizing for Occupation
www.o4onyc.org
212-213-3920

One of the writers of this book, Benjamin Shepard, took part in this resistance effort. Riding his bicycle toward Ms. Ward's home, he heard the roars of the crowd, cheering after countless cars and trucks honked in solidarity, followed by more cheers in a reciprocal display of neighborhood support. "Housing is a human right; fight, fight, fight!" the crowd chanted. Members of Picture the Homeless were there, many locked inside Ms. Ward's home, ready to physically resist the marshals. Activists from neighborhood organizing efforts around the city, as well as global justice circles, were there in support. TV cameras, politicians, undercover police, and participants in the Doe Fund, a program for the homeless, down the block were there. "They are not going to kick out that grandmother," one man commented as he walked by. Looking down from the second-floor window of Ms. Ward's apartment was Seth Tobocman. Tobocman is the author of *War in the Neighborhood*, a graphic novel about squatter battles of the 1980's and 1990's, when residents fought displacement from Lower Manhattan's East Village. Then and now, the message was the same: housing is a human right. Black and white signs hung from Ms. Ward's apartment: "Evict Speculators = Not Grandmothers" and "Predatory lending = Racism and kleptocracy."

"Hey, my people. We have a story. Tell the whole wide world this is people territory," people began to chant, clapping along, waiting for the marshals to come make an attempt to take Ms. Ward's home. "Defend the block." And that they did. More and more people filled both sides of Tompkins Street. "They are not going to come today," people started to conjecture, standing at the action. "Too many camera crews." Evictions don't tend to take place when everyone knows about the plans; too many cameras. Those involved in such unsavory activities work in the shadows.

"Is Ms. Ward in her house? Yes she is, yes she is!" the crowd chanted.

"Will Ms. Ward keep her house? Yes she will, yes she will!"

By 9 AM, people were coming in and out of the apartment, where film crews sat along with the activists ready to fight the eviction. And out came a lawyer, who notified the crowd that local politicians were working with the "landlord" to work out a deal so Ms. Ward would not be displaced from her longtime home, at least not for now. As the morning went on, it started to look like the marshals would not come, that the eviction blockade had worked, and Ms. Ward would remain at 320 Tompkins, for the moment.[35]

The combination of the mobilization of social networks, legal pressure, direct action, as well as neighborhood leadership, all helped provide a show of strength for the neighborhood. Longtime squatter Frank Morales, who was locked down in the second floor of Ms. Ward's home upstairs, suggested the action was intended to help everyone rethink the situation. To slow the eviction process, activists defended her home, "with our bodies," he explained: "We're in a situation now in this country where because we've allowed the banks to steal peoples' homes, that a lot of people are facing evictions... And the only way to prevent people from being pushed out of their homes is to physically block the evictions. And so what we need to encourage is for people to come out to their neighbor's places and lock arms and fill the house up with people... And face down the marshals and other people who are coming to kick them out. It's immoral, unjust, and illegitimate because [of] the whole process, the banks are ripping people off, stealing people's houses, everybody knows this."

In Ms. Ward's case, she had a predatory loan she tried to cancel. "But they were not willing to abide by that," Morales continued. "It's like trying to cancel a subscription, some bullshit magazine that you don't want. They keep sending it to you. Subsequently, they were trying to take her house, saying in order for her to get her house back she had to pay like $350,000. She owed like $14,000 on a house. She'd been in there like 44 years. The whole thing is self-evidently obscene and criminal. But still in all, there's a lot of criminality that goes on. But unless people take action, put their bodies on the line, we're not asking people to risk their lives. They are probably not even going to get a trespass ticket. Because what happened with Ms. Ward is that the marshal just canceled. He didn't come. Even the local police who know Ms. Ward said 'we're not going to support this guy.' So basically, we just iced him."

The whole campaign to help Ms. Ward stay grew as a community narrative, a story that we could all participate in. "Well, that's part of organizing," Morales concluded. "To get people to occupy a new space in their brain so that they don't see that 'I lost in court and that's the end of the road.' No, that's not the end of the road."

Ward's is only one story among many. Having observed a campaign against foreclosures extending from Brooklyn to Barcelona, reporters around the world started covering this campaign. "Hopefully, with all the help I've been getting, I will finally get my house back," said Ward. "Home is home. You should be in your home. I've been here since 1969. I hope by winning my case, I can help all those other people who lost their homes."[36]

MOVEMENTS AGAINST DISPLACEMENT AND A REOCCURRING WOUND

Figure 3: "We are all Trayvon. The whole damned system is guilty! Anti-Police Brutality Sticker in Brooklyn." Photo by Benjamin Shepard.

After the event on community, migration, and displacement at City Tech, a few of the organizers went out. We talked about how the grievances of the past keep coming up, repeating themselves anew. "Every image of the past that is not recognized by the present as one of its own concerns threatens to disappear irretrievably," states Walter Benjamin.[37] It was not a new conversation. The topic on everyone's minds was what was happening around the police, and the burgeoning Black Lives Matter Movement. Ferguson had struck a nerve, a raw wound. Every current generation must reengage and complete the unfinished business of the past Benjamin reminds us.

Over and over again, new groups fight for a place to call home, find community and disconnection. These patterns of displacement are indicators of stagnant mobility, as challenges around race and class merge. It is one thing to think of police abuses in terms of race. But with fewer and fewer jobs and more and more scarcity and economic redundancy, violence seems poised to increase. At least it was that night, with the news we were about to learn.

We went home around 11:30.

Across Brooklyn, a man, Akai Gurley, was walking down the stairs of his apartment complex. Local activist Stan Williams, from his perspective, explained what happened next:

At 11:15 pm, Officer Peter Liang fatally shot Akai Gurley, an unarmed Black man who was leaving his girlfriend's apartment in the Pink Houses in East New York. The cop said he was nervous, so he drew his weapon and shot the first person he saw. The NYPD says it was an "accidental discharge." There is nothing accidental about it. This is the deadly consequence of the ever so increasing militarization of the police, from New York City, to Ferguson, and beyond. We condemn the De Blasio administration for supporting this militarization by appointing Commissioner Bratton. We condemn City Council for requesting more of these militarized police to patrol NYCHA housing, leading to an unending slew of abuse and harassment by the hands of the police. We condemn Bill Bratton for administering the repressive policing practices which have resulted in the murders of Eric Garner and Akai Gurley. Tomorrow, in the spirit of Ramarley Graham, Shantel Davis, Kimani Gray, Eric Garner, Mike Brown & countless other victims of the police in NYC and beyond, the Black Autonomy Federation-North East Branch, our allies in the Fire Bratton Coalition, and members within the community will march from the Pink Houses to P.S.A. 2 (560 Sutter Avenue). In the weeks that follow, we will organize disruptions and direct actions that halt business as usual. In the months that follow, we will use the memory of our fallen and channel it into developing our own organizations for self defense & community mediation...[38]

Throughout the fall of 2014, grand juries had been hearing evidence in the police murders of Michael Brown in Ferguson and Eric Garner in Staten Island. Activists all over New York and the country had been planning rallies for the day that each of these grand juries announced their decision, calling for justice for Michael Brown and Eric Garner. And now there was a new name to add to the list: Akai Gurley.

Figure 4: "Justice for Akai Gurley."

FLATBUSH EQUALITY

On November 21, 2014, three days before the grand jury decision in Ferguson, Brooklyn social worker Imani Henry and I (Ben Shepard) sat down to talk about his work with Flatbush Equality, a Brooklyn anti-displacement group.

"Ferguson is about to blow," said Henry, looking at his phone as we ate Chinese food. And he was right. Three days later, things would erupt.[39] He's lived on or around Flatbush Avenue, the main artery of Brooklyn, for almost two decades. With family from the Caribbean spread out across the world, he was drawn here. "New York is a hub for immigrant communities. It's a place where you can get your start," he said. So after finishing college in Boston, Henry came to Brooklyn. "It's my adoptive home."

Like Victoria Earle Matthews, the first black social worker in Brooklyn, Henry has taken on community organizing as a central part of his practice. "For black social workers, that was what you did historically. You live in the community where you provided services. You do organizing," he explained. While Flatbush Equality provides services, the emphasis is on organizing programs such as Cop Watch, "helping people get plugged into trainings, organizing against landlords." The mission is simple: "Equality for Flatbush is a people of color led campaign fighting for better living conditions for East Flatbush & Flatbush residents." The group is involved with three core campaigns around issues of affordable housing, anti-police brutality work, and anti-gentrification, which it sees as a strategic alignment of missing pieces, with countless other campaigns growing under this rubric. "I could suffer under it or fight to do something about it," said Henry. "Last night we did an intake with a Polish man, someone being evicted. We mobilized, wrote representatives about not increasing police and rents."

"We do anti-police repression work," said Henry, referring to the case of Kyam Livingston, a young women caught up in a family dispute and then arrested in July 2013.[40] "She goes to Central Booking, sick, and she died, writhing in her cell." Henry recalls countless names and incidents, "Kimani Gray, Livingston and Davis... who was shot and killed after school. We show support, that's part of our work."

"Our main campaign is Before It's Gone // Take It Back. People can call us. That's where social work comes in. Know your rights. Landlords write illegal eviction notes, an elder thrown out, others pushed out ... we found someone housing. We've gathered supportive housing applications, documents. That's where we're doing it." For Henry, the group is part of a gentrification resistance movement. "We have lawyers fighting prime mortgage rate scams. Instead of losing it, we're documenting it, focusing on ways to both save and access affordable housing."

"We've been here," said Henry. "We're not a colony to find and explore." Brooklyn is not some kind of "new frontier" to be discovered, argues Henry, who suggests landlords and developers are taking so much of what once made Brooklyn accessible to everyone. Destroying people's homes. He quotes the landlord. "'You didn't pay your rent,' says the landlord. 'I gave it to the super.' 'That's not proof,' he says. For six years, people in Homewood Gardens fought this."

Long-term tenants at Homewood Gardens (651-667 Brooklyn Ave., 652-668 Brooklyn Ave., and 416-444 Hawthorne St.) contacted the state's Tenant Protection Unit (TPU) to help them with the landlord who they said was victimizing them by failing to cash rent checks, failing to provide services including heat and hot water, pressuring tenants to vacate their apartments, subjecting tenants to frivolous housing court proceedings, and doubling and tripling the rent soon after purchasing the property.[41]

Finally, Govenor Andrew Cuomo's office and TPU got involved in the case alleging the landlord was violating the rights of tenants in Flatbush and Crown

Heights. According to Cuomo's office, the subpoena demanded documents from Homewood Gardens and seven other properties with a total of 181 units, owned and managed by Yeshaya Wasserman. Wasserman has allegedly engaged in a pattern of abusive behavior and flagrant violations of rent laws. [42]

An audit of agency records showed that the landlord often registered rents with the agency as exactly $2,500, regardless of the amount previously registered. Doing so allowed the landlord to claim that the rent had reached the deregulation threshold established by state law. Agency records show that the landlord may have also unlawfully deregulated apartments while receiving a J-51 tax abatement, which mandates that apartments remain rent-regulated.

Aga Trojniak from the Flatbush Tenants Coalition, which worked with the TPU on the investigation, said, "For tenants who have been suffering and struggling with harassment, knowing Governor Cuomo's agency is investigating provides immeasurable relief. But the relief is not just for the tenants of one bad landlord—it extends to other tenants who may similarly be tormented by an abusive landlord. Tenants and advocates now have somewhere to turn." Edward Josephson, director of litigation at South Brooklyn Legal Services further asserted: "Landlords cannot engage in corrupt practices which threaten and endanger tenants. Harassment by landlords that violates the law will not be tolerated."[43]

Yet, it takes organizers drawing attention to these problems. "We're talking about gentrification in an intersectional way—race, class, and age. There are people talking like gentrification is going to return Brooklyn to its former splendor," noted Henry in an interview with Camille Lawhead.[44] "Well I want to be clear that even when the [residents] were white, they were still middle class and working class communities. What these people [developers] are talking about is making it for rich folk. And that's different. And that's why we have a stake in it. Again, even now, white people have lived here for a long time but the white people who stayed couldn't afford to go.... They're one of us, we're fighting for them too, and they're fighting with us."

While the patterns of displacement are a global phenomena, Henry does not see anything inevitable about gentrification. His group works with elders facing harassment by their landlords and young people just getting out of college, getting everyone organized. "I ask kids, 'Do you want to live with your parents or with ten roommates.'" Henry sees landlords charging three or four thousand a month for studio apartments as part of the problem, or developers asking people if they can buy them out of their homes.

"These were rougher neighborhoods when I was a kid, and I obviously benefit from some of the neat stuff that's popped up in Northwest Brooklyn over the last decade," noted Camille Lawhead.[45] "But I also don't want a Starbucks and a Chase on every corner. I like pumpkin beer and kale smoothies, but when I think of what's been lost, these changes don't feel natural and exciting. They feel like decay and defeat, one neighborhood of color at a time, and I can't stand the irreverent applause that accompanies it."[46]

"I think a lot of the writing is on the wall," Henry lamented. "I have two Masters degrees and have had no pay increase in seven years. That's a piece of it. How do you retain an apartment in New York? If you are an adult and you need three roommates to pay rent, then you are with us." He recalled the story of just such a case. "Their landlord kicked 'em out of their apartment in Bed-Stuy. 'That's wonderful you want to live communally, now get the fuck out.'"

Henry recalled placing flyers along Flatbush and how a man with a suit looked at one and said he just got a $600 rent increase. "Where's that coming from? the man asked. No one gets a pay increase. The landlord just told him that his rent was going up $600 a month. Good luck with that. Gentrification is the deliberate pricing out by landlords, banks, and government to push people out to make room for more profitable families, catering to the money," argued Henry. He refers to the Sycamore Bar at 1118 Cortelyou as a case in point. "Now they charge $15 for a glass of wine. People are watching the writing on the wall. How long before we're pushed out?" Reflecting on his life in the borough, he added: "I started off in Park Slope, then Prospect-Lefferts, then farther and farther out, at the corner of Flatbush or within a block of it for over twelve years."

Yet, instead of mourn, Henry suggests those coming to Brooklyn get organized, know their rights, connect with tenant associations, and fight for affordable housing. In addition to Flatbush Equality, groups such as Crown Heights Tenant Union, and Flatbush Tenants' Coalition are actively fighting back against the displacement steamroller.[47]

From Migration to Home

A central theme of discussions about displacement is a question about home. Chapter four of Marta Effinger-Crichlow's *Staging Migrations* is titled, "I Want to Go Home." What does going home mean? Rhodessa Jones, who works with women in jail, asks those at her workshops to think about how to be free. She gets women to think about what leads them to this place, to think about the shame of poverty, drug abuse, of sexual abuse. How do you find home? Do you expect someone to find it for you? How do you find ways to construct a home for yourself? Thinking about home, how do you create a home? How does someone defend a home or create a space where they can stay?[48]

Part of the process involves rethinking situations, reimagining what communities in cities can look like, and how we can all fight for fairer conditions, as those in the Occupy movement did with eviction defense. We lead with a vision that housing is a human right and it should be affordable. James Tracy confesses that he's fairly pessimistic about capitalism's capacity to fix things. Re-

regulate things and that would take care of a lot, he suggests. There are countless vacant buildings that could be repaired and occupied. Also alarming, more and more building owners throughout Brooklyn are leaving project-based Section 8 designation and rent stabilization to pursue new opportunities in a changing market. We need a new green deal to fix these buildings and fight to keep low and, even middle-income, communities intact. None of that is outside the possible.[49]

If we live in the great stories of our culture, how do we take control of the story and shape it? Ida B. Wells opened a narrative, which invited generations to participate. "Go there because there is no justice here," she declared. So, a group of people moved West to start homesteading. There's another story out there. But she also suggested staying home and organizing so that those in power stop ignoring you. "Look toward the West, understand the injustices," she advised. There are many. Much of it is buried deep within the soil, the collective memory, within the history of cities, in the water, and infrastructure of the city.

Figure 5: "Stop police from murdering people. Mural in Bushwick, Brooklyn." Photo by Benjamin Shepard.

Chapter four
Toxicity

Figure 1: "View of the Gowanus and downtown Brooklyn." Photo by Benjamin Shepard.

There is a brownfield on Smith Street and Ninth Street in Carroll Gardens, alongside the Gowanus Canal. An active shipping and industrial zone since the mid-1860s, this polluted waterway of oil, chemicals and other remnants from the area's industrial past meanders between streets in three neighborhoods: Carroll Gardens, Park Slope, and Boerum Hill. The Gowanus water boasts a noxious sludge composed of gas, polycyclic aromatic hydrocarbons (PAHs), polychlorinated biphenyls (PCBs), and other chemicals from asphalt and gas plants, as well as decades of dumping by those suspected to be involved in organized crime. Its surface sediment has been found to contain e. coli bacteria and cholera.[1]

The neighborhood has suffered from sewage overflow from the canal for as long as anyone can remember. Here, despite the rapidly gentrifying nature of the space, commanding glossy new condominiums and Manhattan-like costs for rent, pollutants remain just below the dirt. Toxicity has long been part of life in this global borough. It extends from the sewage beneath the surface to the pollutants in the cultural environment, including red-lining, speculative gentrification, noxious racial politics, and foreclosures. These are all part of the tides of industrial development. Toxic dynamics inform the story of this global borough.

Water

For much of the nineteenth and early-twentieth centuries, Brooklyn was an industrial base for manufacturing, shipyards, gas plants, chemical works, lead smelting, rail and trolley powerhouses, and oil. Today, this past is hard to see. Yet, as Robin Michals, a photographer and CUNY professor, reminds us, "[t]his history has left as a legacy contaminated ground."[2] New York State's Department of Environmental Conservation identifies fifty brownfields in Brooklyn currently subject to remediation. According to the Environmental Protection Agency, a brownfield is land that presents a potential financial liability because of its possible contamination. Brownfields cannot be identified by sight. The dangers are invisible. Michals explains: "Many people who live and work near brownfields do not know about the toxicity of these sites. In addition, there are many sites that have not yet been identified as toxic. Brownfields can be a nexus of the past and the future if new technologies are used to clean and redevelop these sites, or they can become a nightmare haunting the future with disease and genetic damage."[3] Today, Brooklyn is transforming. Yet much of that which was below the surface remains, lingering in the sometimes toxic physical and mental environment.

Chapter four: Toxicity 97

Figures 2 and 3: "Images of the polluted waters in the Gowanus Canal and, below, a sign for a fuel company long gone, whose legacy remains deep in the now-polluted waterway. Today, glass condominiums sit here." Photos by Benjamin Shepard.

These changes are highlighted in images of the history of the waterfront, displayed along a fence at Smith and Fifth Street. One of the signs calls attention to the large number of oysters that once flourished in the brackish waters of the Gowanus marshes. Midden shell piles, some 100 feet deep and thousands of years old, attest to the enjoyment of the local bivalves first by Native Americans, then by the Dutch, then the English, and, until around 1920, New Yorkers. So plentiful were oysters across Long Island and Staten Island, many were sent by rail or ship ending up on the dinner plates of Midwesterners and Europeans. Colonial residents spoke of oysters growing to be as big as the plates themselves. High in protein, oysters fed New York's poor and were also found on the plates of the city's elite. A combination of overharvesting and pollution, however, caused "the oyster capital of the world" to be no more. By the early 20th century, contaminants thoroughly wiped out the industry and today the only oysters found in Red Hook are at the hipster hang-outs Fort Defiance and Brooklyn Crab, whose daily catch comes from cleaner waters in New England and Nova Scotia (though Blue Point oysters from Long Island have been making a comeback as well).[4]

Figure 4: "Scrap metal works on Smith Street offer details of tides past and future." Photo by Benjamin Shepard.

Another sign along the fence speaks to the importance of tidal economies in Dutch times. It explains how the Brooklyn shoreline—before being flattened, filled in, and paved over—was an efficient tidal wetland ecosystem. The Dutch built one of the country's first gristmills, harnessing tidal energy to grind grain into flour. Experts at dredging ponds to increase the water supply, they continued to build tidal mills across Breukelen, as it was then rendered. The salt marshes that remained, alongside the flourishing oyster beds, played a critical role in filtering the water flowing in and out of Brooklyn's inlets and keeping land intact.

By the 1800s, industrialization had reached Brooklyn. Throughout the century, city planners filled in the marshlands, built shipping docks and basins, and transformed Gowanus Creek into the Gowanus Canal, to be used for transportation, sewage conveyance, and shipping. The transformation of the Gowanus from an ecologically balanced tidal marshland into an industrial artery was, for a time, great for business but a disaster for the environment. Along the banks of the canal were some of America's most toxic industries, including tanneries, slaughterhouses, cement makers, flour mills, and a dye works that "brightened its waters with the various colors of each day's production."[5]

A particularly noxious process that contributed to the contamination of the area was gasification. From the mid-nineteenth century into the 1920s, barges of coal would come down from the Erie Canal, and the coal was transformed into fuel for lighting, heating, and cooking. Brooklyn's gasification plants were entirely unregulated, and the by-products of the gas have remained in South Brooklyn's soil and waterways to this day. And just how polluted did the Gowanus Canal become? In a recent study of the presence of toxins, oysters were left in the canal to see if they would spawn. According to Mark Kurlansky, author of *The Big Oyster: History on the Half Shell*, "They not only died within two weeks but their shells were partially eaten away by acidic compounds in the water."[6]

REDLINING AND LAND USE

But the pollutants in the physical environment were just a part of the toxicity. So were the politics of the neighborhood.[7] Over the years, Brooklyn has become a site in a class war between those who live, work, and play in public and those who seek to control, curtail, and privatize this space. As Kushner describes in *The Intelligent Homosexual's Guide to Capitalism and Socialism with a Key to the Scriptures*, somewhere between the fiscal crisis of the 1970s and the Bloomberg years, value moved from labor produced with one's hands to land uses and real estate practices such as speculative gentrification, red-lining, and subsequent foreclosures.

Figures 5 and 6: "An afternoon in Bushwick" and "Bedford–Stuyvesant Elevated line." Photos by Caroline Shepard.

Looking at the ongoing tides of people coming into Brooklyn neighborhoods such as Fort Greene, displacing others, Kelly Andersen, in her documentary film *My Brooklyn*, wondered: "What was Brooklyn becoming, who was it for, who was calling the shots?"[8] During the Bloomberg years, neighborhood after neighborhood in Brooklyn—20 per cent of New York—was rezoned for real estate-friendly purposes, and subsequently lined with hotels, office buildings, and residential towers.[9] From Williamsburg to Downtown, Brooklyn neighborhoods were making room for 30-to-40 story towers, catering to a very specific clientele.

"What Brooklyn faced after World War II," Craig Wilder, who appears in *My Brooklyn*, states, "was what all American cities faced." People needed mortgages to get housing. Banks divided Brooklyn into some 66 neighborhoods and graded them. Those with five per cent or more of African Americans got "D's". For this they received real estate quarantines. These neighborhoods, including Wilder's Bedford-Stuyvesant, were marked with red lines, restricting access to mortgages. Banks would not loan money in these zip codes. Capital dried up. Unlike the pollutants underground, the effects of "white flight" and red-lining were not hard to see, but ignored nonetheless. While 95 per cent of Bedford-Stuyvesant was white after World War II, by 1970 many had left and the property values declined. Brooklyn in the meantime had become home to the largest black community in the United States. Red-lined neighborhoods endured dwindling public services. Fire stations were closed in these neighborhoods. These spaces seemed to be targeted for destruction.

Still, many numbers of residents fought back. "Improve Don't Move" became a slogan. In Downtown Brooklyn, they created block associations and established new, locally-owned businesses. And the neighborhood came back to life. Rezoning changed all this. By 2004, many of the businesses which helped the neighborhood revitalize were forced out as waves of new luxury condos replaced them.[10] The battle over what Brooklyn would be become was at the center of a concentrated struggle, decades in the making.

East River School[11]

Fighting back the tides of globalization comes in many forms. Thus far, we have considered the efforts of local residents to organize: to engage in peaceful protests, to stage street actions, to go on labor strikes, to form associations and legal advocacy groups, to battle for alternative spaces and communities. Resistance also comes in the form of art and literature.

Is there an East River School of art and literature? Certainly well-known is the Hudson River School of artists whose leading practitioners—Thomas Cole, Asher B. Durand, and Albert Bierstadt—made famed use of the majestic scenery of Hudson River valley. These landscape painters, in turn, were kindred spirits with American writers such as Washington Irving, William Cullen Bryant, and William Curtis, who turned to Nature to evoke deeply felt religious and moral sentiments and to register nationalistic pride in the sublimity of the Hudson Valley. But along Manhattan's eastern shore, often from the vantage point of Brooklyn, another distinctive school of art and writing—the East River School—arose and continues to flourish. East River School writers and artists appear in many varied guises, but what connects them is a shared understanding of an environment seeped in history, saturated by toxic elements, and shaped by powerful tidal forces.

Figure 7: "Rubble and seaweed along the East River." Photo by Benjamin Shepard.

Reclaiming the borough from its toxic elements, in particular, has long been the prerogative of artists, writers, and filmmakers of the East River School. In 1949, Arthur Miller used the setting of Brooklyn during the postwar tide of expansion for his greatest play, *Death of a Salesman*. In it, we learn of a misfit named Willy Loman whose work no longer has personal meaning, whose sons also look for access to the American Dream but cannot seem to find it in the occupations available to them. Forces beyond the family's comprehension have made them feel powerless, as older work patterns and traditions have been supplanted by modern values based on profit and individual needs. Loman's changing Brooklyn neighborhood, based on where Miller himself grew up in Midwood during the Depression, helps to emphasize the play's theme of alienation in a relentlessly expanding and increasingly toxic world. In an early scene, for example, we hear a conversation between Willy and his wife, Linda.

Willy: The street is lined with cars. There's not a breath of fresh air in the neighborhood. The grass don't grow any more, you can't raise a carrot in the backyard. They should've had a law against apartment houses. Remember those two beautiful elm trees out there? When I and Biff hung the swing between them?
Linda: Yeah, like being a million miles from the city.
Willy: They should've arrested the builder for cutting those down. They massacred the neighborhood.[12]

The massacring of Brooklyn's neighborhoods is also the central theme of Hubert Selby's powerful body of dystopian work. His landmark collection of interrelated stories, *Last Exit to Brooklyn* (1964), tells of a borough that, for the underclasses, has become akin to living in Dante's *Inferno*.[13] Each tale is prefaced with a proverb from the Bible, which serves to underscore the irony of the debauched and brutal lives of the characters. Unseen forces have taken away their jobs, forced them to live under inhumane conditions in housing projects, and created an urban landscape of extreme violence and degradation from which there is indeed "no exit." The opening tale, "Another Day, Another Dollar," recounts how a vicious group of gangsters, led by Freddy, prey on three drunken soldiers heading back to their Brooklyn army base. The gang chases the soldiers and catches one as he's about to climb over a fence. As Selby writes, "They formed a circle and kicked. He tried to roll over on his stomach and cover his face with his arms, but as he got to his side he was kicked in the groin and stomped on the ear and he screamed, cried, started pleading then just cried as a foot cracked his mouth."[14] Robbing the soldier and leaving him to bleed just outside his barracks is just another day and another dollar for the young resident thugs.

"Landsend," set in a Red Hook housing project, also tells of a "typical" day in the lives of several of its residents. In stark, naturalistic language, Selby renders scenes of domestic abuse, degradation, and, again, extreme violence. Particularly frightening is Selby's rendition of the children in such a debased environment. In one scene, he writes of two young gangs about to engage in a fight:

A group of kids, about 5 and 6 years old, stood on the steps of the entrance to one of the buildings. Another group stood huddled about a hundred feet away. The two groups eyed each other, spitting, cursing, staring. Some of the kids on the steps wanted to fight the mothafuckas now and killem, the others wanted to wait for Jimmy. Jimmy was the biggest guy they had. When he come we/ll get the bastards. He run fasteran any ofem. Sheeit man, we/ll catchem all and killem. Yeah man, we/ll burn the mothafuckas alive.[15]

Stuck in a world absent of positive role models and recurrent danger, these children, it's all too clear, live in a dark present that promises equally bleak futures, reflected in dialogue that reveals their limitations.

Even more disturbing is the gang rape of the prostitute Tralala, the title character of Selby's most famous piece. After a night of heavy drinking the 15-year-old is violated by waves of men even after she passes out. Because of subject matter such as this, *Last Exit* was subject to an obscenity trial in England in 1966, resulting in a guilty verdict and a fine for the publisher. In an interview in 1988, the Brooklyn-born Selby defended his work by arguing that the reality of life in Brooklyn at the time was what was obscene. "The events that take place are the way people are. These are not literary characters; these are real people. I knew these people. How can anybody look inside themselves and be surprised at the hatred and violence in the world? It's inside all of us."[16] In depicting such brutal scenes, Selby sought to expose the toxic environment Brooklyn had become for many of its poorer and forgotten residents. He would do so again in his 1978 work *Requiem for a Dream*, focusing on the heroin epidemic plaguing Coney Island at the time of the novel's publication. With the shipyards closed and New York gone bankrupt, the 1960's and 1970's saw Brooklyn at its nadir.[17]

Unfortunately, many of these same toxic elements continue to plague large portions of the borough today. Following in the footsteps of Selby, contemporary artists and writers have also called attention to Brooklyn's neighborhoods devastated by neglect and underfunding. In 1991, Matty Rich produced the film *Straight Out of Brooklyn*, based on a screenplay he had written at age 17. The film is based on his family's experiences living in a Red Hook housing project. It follows the fate of a young man named Dennis who is tired of living in a household with an alcoholic and abusive father and stuck in a cycle of seemingly permanent poverty. With two friends, Dennis robs a local drug dealer at gunpoint but does not shoot. Realizing they have been recognized, his friends leave the money with Dennis, who decides to confide to his family that he now has the means to escape the projects. Just like his girlfriend who drops Dennis for his dangerous act, his father too lashes out at him, as well as his mother, who ends up dying in the hospital. The film ends with the death of his father, killed by a gang member seeking retaliation.

Chapter four: Toxicity   105

Figure 8, 9 and 10: "Scenes of the Domino Sugar Factory, Prospect Heights, and Red Hook, Brooklyn." Photos by Caroline Shepard.

Less successful but addressing similar issues is Spike Lee's *Red Hook Summer*. What's particularly disturbing about Lee's work is its revelation that in the years between Rich's film and his (1991 and 2012), so little has changed for those living in the Red Hook projects. As both Rich and Lee convey, the residents are locked in containers that seal both time and hopes, even as the rest of Brooklyn expands and develops.

For high-income residents, in contrast, Red Hook is a transforming neighborhood, home to beautiful waterfront views and trendy restaurants. In the midst of its extraordinary disparity of wealth and poverty, positive strides are being made, however, for those feeling the downside of globalization and urban neglect. The Red Hook Community Court, for example, is famous for just treatment of those moving through the system, challenging the revolving door of the criminal justice system which typically moves people through a cycle of prison, parole, re-arrest and reentry. The Court is part of the Red Hook Community Justice Center, a multi-disciplinary community court, which provides social services and prevention services designed to reduce the revolving door which plagues much of the criminal justice system today. The genesis of the court was the killing of Patrick Daly in 1992. Daley was the principal of P.S. 15. He was killed in the crossfire of a drug-related shooting while going to a local home to check up on a student who failed to attend school that morning.

A waterfront neighborhood that had been the center of commerce for some three hundred years, by the 1980s, Red Hook was in deep disrepair. Commerce on the waterfront had been lost to containerization in the 1950s and '60s, with most of the dock jobs disappearing from the port community tucked between Buttermilk Channel, the Gowanus Canal, and Downtown Brooklyn, facing the Statue of Liberty. Many residents moved away; others turned to the black-market economy to survive. By the 1980s, crack overwhelmed the neighborhood, which by then included the Red Hook Houses, the largest housing project in Brooklyn, with some 5,000 residents. A July 1988 article on crack in *Life Magazine* described the neighborhood as one of the "worst" to live in in America. The Red Hook Community Justice Center was an effort to get to the root of the problems which were perpetuating ills such as the drug violence which killed principal Daly.[18]

Shawn Carter is perhaps the most prominent artist to emerge out of Brooklyn's most impoverished sections. His autobiography, *Decoded*, and large body of work call attention to the tribulations of growing up in a world in which many urban youths feel they have to look out for themselves to survive. Carter named himself Jay-Z after the subway stops near the Marcy Projects in Bed-Stuy where he grew up. Once the site of an old Dutch windmill, the Marcy Projects, in the words of Denis Hamill, consisted of "27 dirty, six-story municipal brick buildings across 28 scary Brooklyn acres of crack, guns and gangbangers that a kid named Shawn Corey Carter, a.k.a. Jay-Z, plowed into one of the most successful musical harvests in the history of New York."[19]

In *Decoded*, Jay-Z writes of the extreme segregation existing in Brooklyn's poorest neighborhoods to this day. "There are no white people in Marcy Projects," he writes. "Bed-Stuy today has become somewhat gentrified, but the projects are like gentrification firewalls. When I was growing up there, it was strictly Blacks and Puerto Ricans, maybe some Dominicans, rough Arabs who ran the twenty-four-hour bodegas, pockets of Hasidim who kept to themselves, and the Chinese dudes who stayed behind bullet-proof glass at the corner take-out joint."[20] Jay-Z also laments the absence of positive role models for young males. His own sole salvation was in words. As he explains in an interview, "I loved to read. My mother always told me that nothing in life is any good unless it comes hard to you. But when I first started writing, it just flowed out ... I realized it came easy because I read a lot. That's the message I want to send to these kids—all kids."[21]

The themes he would often stress in his lyrics were based directly on his experiences growing up in, and literally just surviving, his toxic environment. In "Where I'm From," he writes:

I'm from where the hammer's rung, News cameras never come...
Where the plans was to get funds and skate off the set...
Faced with immeasurable odds still I get straight bets...
Cough up a lung, where I'm from, Marcy son, Ain't nothing nice
Mentally been many places but I'm Brooklyn's own.[22]

Turning toxicity into majestic rhyme and rhythm, Carter propelled himself to the top of the charts.

The toxic history of the borough was also the subject of a poignant work of sculpture called "A Subtlety, or the Marvelous Sugar Baby" by Kara Walker. Recognizing the impact of Brooklyn's important role in the global sugar market, Walker subtitled her piece "An Homage to the Unpaid and Overworked Artisans who have Refined our Sweet Tastes from the Cane Fields to the Kitchens of the New World on the Occasion of the Demolition of the Domino Sugar Refining Plant." The sphinx-like sculpture of Aunt Jemima was massive, 75-and-a-half feet long and 35-and-a-half feet high, and made entirely of bleached sugar, donated by Domino. In the spring of 2014, Walker displayed her work in Domino's soon to be demolished factory.[23]

The sculpture offered important connotations on many levels. Foremost, it called attention to the black (often enslaved) bodies that, for over 300 years, grew, picked, and packed sugarcane. By the 1890s, 50 per cent of the world's sugarcane came to Domino's Williamsburg refining plant that bleached the brown raw sugar white and distributed packets to merchants across the world. As Walker's work reminded us, by the time sugar was poured into America's coffee cups, this history itself had been bleached. It also recalled the history of labor along the Brooklyn waterfront and the rise of corporate control in the global marketplace. Built in 1882, the Domino Sugar Factory had its own share of labor troubles. As Hilton Als writes, "as recently as 2000, it was the site of a long labor strike, in which two hundred and fifty workers protested wages and labor conditions for twenty months."[24] A temporary installation in a factory building to be replaced by million-dollar condominiums, Walker's work served as a reminder of how the wheels of global commerce continually spin, leaving the sweetest prizes for the wealthy, while the underclasses continue to struggle for livable wages and affordable housing.

Paying attention to the actual toxicity in the ground and waterways of Brooklyn is the work of photographer Robin Michals. Her 2009 exhibition, "Toxi City: Brooklyn's Brownfields," captured the legacy of the borough's industrial past in the form of pollutants that affect residents on a daily basis. It featured 30 photographs of sites in Coney Island, DUMBO, East New York, East Williamsburg, Gowanus, Greenpoint, Red Hook, Sunset Park and Williamsburg where toxins left by industrial use have saturated the soils and groundwater. "The alphabet soup of DNAPLs, NAPLs, BTEXs, PAHs, SVOCs, VOCs, TCE, PCE, and PCBs that have been left behind at these sites can never be entirely removed; their dangers can only be better managed," Michals says. "As we careen towards the greater impacts of climate change, brownfields remind us of the damage we are willing to inflict on the environment for the benefits of industrialism."[25] Her simultaneously beautiful and haunting photos ask viewers to pay attention to how Brooklyn's past has lingering import for the present, though the evidence of toxicity is sometimes scarcely visible.

Chapter four: Toxicity 109

Figures 11 and 12: "Brooklyn Navy Yard, 2016" and "East River, Williamsburg, 2015" by Robin Michals. "This part of the Brooklyn waterfront is certain to look very different by the time your book is published," observed Michals in early 2017. In her photography, Robin Michals calls attention to Brooklyn's industrial past amidst uneven development and gentrification.

Another artwork that speaks to Brooklyn's toxic industrial history is a large mural along a wall leading to a bridge that goes across the Gowanus Canal. Entitled "Terra Incognita," the work depicts a beaver surrounded by an industrial landscape. Staring wistfully at an image of New York City, the animal—once so abundant up and down the banks of the Hudson and East Rivers—seems not to recognize his home anymore. The presence of the mural itself in a neighborhood that seems to be flourishing despite the toxic canal below calls attention to another important residue that Brooklyn's industrial past has left behind: texture, feel, a sense of otherness, authentic space.

Figure 13: "Terra Incognita, Union Street in the Gowanus."
Photo by Mark Noonan.

In *The Accidental Playground, Brooklyn Waterfront Narratives of the Undesigned and Unplanned* (2013), Dan Campo speaks of the importance of preserving New York's vernacular landscape, its underutilized spaces, rotting piers, abandoned buildings, and forlorn waterways. While many of these spaces have disappeared in Brooklyn's latest stage of hyper-development, the need for such "other places" has not. In symbolic terms, Manhattan has represented the global—the white-collar metropolis of towering and glistening buildings—whereas Brooklyn has been, alternately, the working-class enclave, the suburban bedroom, and more recently, an oasis for art and alternative lifestyles. Many of its current residents were originally lured to Brooklyn for its subaltern vitality, its playfulness, its greater authenticity—and relatively cheap rents.[26] In 2010, Brooklyn sociologist Sharon Zukin examined how the soul of New York was being threatened as the city redeveloped on the foundation of a commodifiable, gentrified culture.[27] Today this octopus has stretched its tentacles across Brooklyn, spreading a loathesome ink of blandification from which no hipster haven, artist commune, cobblestone street, local bookstore, community garden, nor neighborhood bodega is safe.

The brick nineteenth-century warehouses that still linger and loom along Brooklyn's waterfront, the tugboats and barges that still ply the East River, the gothic arches and suspension coils that still ballast the Brooklyn Bridge, the waterway itself with epic views of Manhattan, are also a significant part of what makes Brooklyn Brooklyn. In *Industrial Sublime: Modernism and the Transformation of New York's Rivers* (2013), the editors call attention to the rise of a new style of landscape painting that responded to New York's growth, from 1900-1940, as a "global industrial power." Artists including Robert Henri, John Sloan, Georgia O'Keefe, and George Ault came to the water's edge to celebrate the smoke, bridges and industry of the modern age. "Looking to their forebears for the romantic elements of the sublime, the artists of a spanking new 20th century combined romance and Modernism's obsession with structure and form, and so created an exciting visual vocabulary—the industrial sublime."[28]

Brooklyn's changing industrial landscape, spirit of authenticity, and working-class vitality have been celebrated by its own magnificent school of writers and artists. So entranced by the sublime grandeur of Brooklyn's waterfront, Hart Crane rented an apartment at 110 Columbia Heights from 1924-1929, the same apartment where Washington Roebling, the designer of the Brooklyn Bridge, lived while recuperating from compression sickness. Looking out his window, pen in hand, Crane composed, "The Bridge," the world's greatest homage to a feat of engineering and the waterway it crossed. For him the bridge represented a miracle of labor, a symbol of humankind's highest aspirations, and a fusion of time and space:

O harp and altar, of the fury fused,
(How could mere toil align thy choiring strings!)
Terrific threshold of the prophet's pledge,
Prayer of pariah, and the lover's cry,[29]

The industrial waterfront, in turn, was a place of deep emotions and associations, both fluid and contradictory, a reflection of the dynamic pulse of human life along its banks.

A tugboat, wheezing wreaths of steam,
Lunged past, with one galvanic blare
    Stove up the River.
I counted the echoes assembling,
    One after one,
Searching, thumbing the midnight,
    On the piers.

The blackness somewhere gouged glass
    On a sky.
And this thy harbor, O my City, I have
    Driven under,
Tosses from the coil of ticking towers...
    Tomorrow,
And to be... Here by the River that is East.[30]

Other writers of the East River School, such as Ernest Poole (*The Harbor*), Thomas Wolfe (*Of Time and the River*), and W.H. Auden ("New Year's Poem"), were also transformed by their association with the Brooklyn waterfront and the lessons it intuitively taught them.

Often overlooked as a distinctively Brooklyn writer, but perhaps the borough's most profound chronicler and philosopher, was Norman Mailer. His first novel *The Naked and the Dead* (1948), was begun in Brooklyn Heights at 102 Pierrepont Street, in an apartment right above the head of Arthur Miller, who lived below the Mailer family with his wife, Mary Grace Slattery. Mailer's second novel, *Barbary Shore* (1951), is set in the same rooming house (at 20 Remsen Street) where he finished editing *The Naked and the Dead*. To begin his next novel, *The Deer Park* (1955), Mailer returned to yet another writer's studio along the Brooklyn waterfront. In the spring of 1952, he rented space in Ovington Studios, a seven-story building of artist studios, located at 252 Fulton Street. He would use this studio until 1962 when the building was torn down, under Robert Moses' "slum clearance" program that replaced charming buildings such as this one, and another four blocks of older moderate-income houses, for a high-rise luxury housing project. Fortunately for Mailer, he had become successful enough at the time to buy an elegant residence on 142 Columbia Heights overlooking the East River. This apartment, as Mailer quipped, allowed the author "to keep an eye on Manhattan," but its proximity to the waterfront also inspired many of the themes in his work, as it had for Crane, Wolfe, and Whitman before him.[31]

Although it never received the critical appreciation he had hoped for, Mailer's *Ancient Evenings* (1983) is a clear product of living near the East River as well as the rewriting of a Brooklyn boy of humble origins, who, test after test, emerges as an immortal figure, the pharaoh of American writers.[32] Artist Mathew Barney's recent five-and-a-half hour film, *River of Fundament*, is loosely based on the novel and serves to elaborate how Brooklyn's rich yet toxic environment is the ultimate testing grown for art and manhood. While the narrative is chaotic, and often difficult to follow, what's truly extraordinary about the film is its spectacle of the industrial waterfront. Barney's own studio is based in Long Island City, Queens, along the border of Brooklyn's Greenpoint and Newtown Creek. Barney's film is simultaneously a hymn to the beauty of

New York's industrialized landscape and a reminder of the "crude thoughts" and "fierce forces" in Mailer's Brooklyn background that helped transform him into the artist he became.[33]

Figure 14: "Hot Gowanus"—José Parlá ("As Parlá's painting seems to suggest, Brooklyn has become a global commodity, a space increasingly denuded of history and authenticity").

A recent work by another Brooklyn artist, José Parlá, brings this point home. His "Hot Gowanus" is composed of layers of paint, gestural drawing, and the written word that evokes the history of a specific urban neighborhood currently undergoing transformation once again. On one hand, its layers celebrate the history of Red Hook. The neighborhood is an extraordinary time capsule, richly textured and nuanced. The colors, in turn, reflect the oily and putrid waters of the Gowanus Canal. As Parlá seems to assert, there is a kind of beauty in the toxicity of the legendary waterway. The bright orange lettering giving the piece its title, however, implies that the neighborhood is in danger of losing its character.³⁴ By virtue of its very hotness, Red Hook, like so much of Brooklyn, has become a global commodity, a brand rather than a lived place, a space denuded of history and authenticity. Once the grimy space of work, then a bohemian enclave, Brooklyn is in danger of becoming "no space," in which blandification and high real estate prices have extinguished the remaining vestiges of a vibrant and livable community of and for the people. Parlá, whose works are on permanent display at Barclays Center and the Brooklyn Academy of Music, reminds us of what makes Brooklyn so truly monumental and worthy of preservation: its diverse populations, creative pulse, and rich cultural heritage.

***

In 1900, the art critic Sadakichi Hartman in "A Plea for the Picturesque of New York" boldly announced:

I know that a large majority will object to my arguments; those who do not feel that there is an imposing grandeur in the Brooklyn Bridge ... who do not feel the poetry of our waterfronts, the semi-opaque water reflecting the gray sky ... Such men claim that there is nothing pictorial and picturesque in New York and our modern life, and continue their homage to imitation. The truth is they lack the inspiration of the true artists.³⁵

Hartman in turn offers a long list of subjects worthy of great art from "the platform of the elevated railroad train" to a "roof garden restaurant" to "the crowded sidewalks" to "the fulton fish market." Hartman also repeatedly seeks to call attention to the goldmine maritime scenes offered. As he writes, "the traffic in the North and East rivers and the harbor offers abundant material ... the canal-boat at Coenties Slip; the huge storage houses of Gowanus Bay."³⁶ Hartman's early acknowledgement of the artistic possibilities of the docks and factories dotting New York City's two rivers led in time to the famed Ash Can School. While John Sloan, William Glackens, and Everett Shinn worked on their canvases, the East River Schoolers worked on theirs—and many continue to do so. Once considered a space of refuse and toxicity, Brooklyn and its waterfront has been transformed by its own distinctive array of writers, painters, and photographers as a space of possibility and beauty worth preserving, despite the toxic residue still lingering beneath the surface.³⁷

Chapter four: Toxicity 115

Figure 15: "A quiet view of the Gowanus." Photo by Benjamin Shepard.

Figure: 16: "*A scene from the Gowanus.*" *Photo by Caroline Shepard.*

Chapter five

Fighting Police Brutality in Global Brooklyn:

From Ferguson to NYC

Figure 1: "Eric Garner Grand jury response protest. December 2014."
© *Erik Mc Gregor.*

> "The world is wrong; you can't put the past behind you. It's buried in you. It's turned your flesh into its own cupboard. Not everything to be remembered is useful but it all comes from the world to be stored in you."
> Claudia Rankine, (2015) *Citizen*[1]

Just as the residue of pollutants from the past lurks below the ground in brownfields, memories of toxic social relations—of people being bought and sold, neglected and abused—it lingers, shaping the ways we experience the present moment. As Claudia Rankine notes, events from decades, even centuries, past inform our experiences of the current moment. Gunshots in an alleyway can remind us of earlier wrongs, as they did in 2014 when protests erupted from Ferguson, Missouri to Brooklyn.[2]

New York City, including its borough of Brooklyn, has long been viewed as a global city, like London or Tokyo.[3] Characteristics of such spaces include rapid flows of goods and services, capital, people and customs, as well as patterns of financial speculation, environmental decline, gentrification, foreclosures, aggressive policing, and dislocation.[4] Brooklyn residents have long contended with these dynamics and the uneven development they yield.[5] Yet, rather than cave, Brooklyn's residents have challenged patterns of hyper-control of public space and, by extension, the unintended consequences of aggressive "zero tolerance" policing.[6] This chapter, and subsequent ones, borrow from a participating observation perspective and consider the ways local actors inform these questions, drawing from first-hand reports of a wave of street actions around police accountability over the last decade.[7] Through their efforts, we trace the stories of a group of activists struggling to create their own model of a Global Brooklyn. This is a story of a different vision of urban life. Rather than a neoliberal city with high poverty and low crime due to "stop and frisk" policing, this is a vision of a just, sustainable city, built around networks of friendship and community. Throughout their efforts, these activists hope to rid the city of militarized policing, while addressing long-standing questions of social and economic inequality seen first in the streets and public spaces of the city.

BROKEN WINDOWS

Over the years, Brooklyn has become the site of a class war between those who live, work, and play in public and those who seek to control, curtail, and privatize this space. Shortly after Rudolph Giuliani's election as mayor in 1993, his police chief William Bratton released a blueprint for policing focused on reclaiming New York's public spaces from the presence of the poor, and other social outsiders.[8] This involved a "broken windows" style of policing, which included zero tolerance for the smallest of infractions. Histories of police brutality in New York City dedicate considerable attention to this aggressive policing approach.[9] Police have increasingly targeted specific communities, such as youth of color.[10] Critics noted that the underside of "quality of life" policing was increased police brutality and social control.[11] Such policing was thought to be necessary to support the neoliberal economic model of a global city, reducing crime and controlling the public.[12] But as a consequence, social outsiders and the poor were forced to contend with a violent, often deadly, police force. Abner Louima was sodomized with a police broomstick; Randolph Evans and Kimani Gray were shot unarmed.[13] From the Pink Houses of East New York to the immigrant communities of Sunset Park, police brutality has long been part of life in Global Brooklyn, but awareness of these incidents is on the rise.[14] This chapter considers some of the recent means of resistance to this increasingly global form of social control and brutality, as regular people have fashioned efforts to shape a different kind of interaction between police and the specter of difference in public space.[15]

BUSHWICK, 2007

In 2007, a group of thirty-two African American and Latino young people in Bushwick were arrested while going to attend the funeral of a friend.[16] Initially, Police Commissioner Ray Kelly claimed the teens were blocking traffic and damaging property. He said they were committing "unlawful assembly" as they walked from a park to the subway station to attend the funeral of an alleged gang member. The Brooklyn district attorney, Charles Hynes, claimed "they were not just walking on one car; they were trampling on all sorts of cars. It was almost as if they were inviting their arrest."[17] But no evidence supported the police claim that the students were blocking traffic or jumping on cars. "Witnesses who saw the kids, including one man who used his cell phone to take photos of some of them who were handcuffed on the sidewalk, said they had been orderly, quiet and well behaved," wrote *New York Times* journalist Bob Herbert.[18] Greer Martin, a witness to the arrests outside her front window, spoke on the record. "[S]he felt the police officers had abused their power," noted Herbert. "I was shocked beyond shock," she said. "My windows were open, and it didn't look like the kids had done anything wrong."[19]

In the wake of the event, organizers with Make the Road by Walking, a nonprofit membership-led organization located in the Bushwick neighborhood, started mobilizing. The group is dedicated to promoting economic justice, equity and opportunity for all New Yorkers through community organizing, electoral politics, leadership development, education and legal and support services. Make the Road helped students in Bushwick get organized. The students formed a group called Student Coalition Against Racial Profiling (SCARP), which was able to get the charges thrown out for its members and procure a legal settlement, with several thousand dollars being paid to minors who were held by police for a day and a half.[20] Supported by local leaders and elected representatives, the group fought back, organizing press conferences, rallies, and media awareness. At one event, the youth actually dismantled a police barricade that officers had erected to surround them, reminding the police that they were the ones shooting people and spreading misinformation, not the youth. The pattern is not uncommon.[21]

The prolonged detention for minor infractions that the teens suffered is a byproduct of the policing which has become part of life in Global Brooklyn. It is also one of the battlefronts. While SCARP and Make the Road by Walking have fought for a right to the city,[22] their experiences suggest that structural violence continues to be a common experience for social outsiders. Michael Scolnick, a lawyer for those arrested in Bushwick, said, "What I have been told by my clients is that their being stopped on the street merely for being on the street is about as common an occurrence in their lives as me getting up in the morning and brushing my teeth, and that's pretty outrageous."[23]

These arrests reflect a larger pattern of hyper-regulation of public space and pre-emptive action against any behavior deemed deviant by the NYPD or the business interests it supports.[24] This involves no tolerance for the smallest of infractions, flexible deployment, and the ongoing generation of new rules and regulations micro-managing public space.[25] "[A]uthorities responded by criminalizing whole communities of impoverished and marginalized populations," noted David Harvey in his recent history of neoliberalism.[26] Patterns of stops and frisks, racial profiling, and aggressive policing were thought necessary to support a better business climate for economic growth.[27] In response, many communities sought to reshape this dynamic.

By 2014, the accumulation of deaths of unarmed black men across the U.S.—of Michael Brown, Eric Garner, Akai Gurley, Kimani Gray, Trayvon Martin, and so many more—sparked a great reckoning.[28] Two generations removed from the great migration of some six million black Southerners fleeing Jim Crow, many of those who had watched their descendants suffer similar forms of violence in the North, started to ask how the migration has gone, with waves of protests serving as a referendum.[29] One hundred and fifty years after the emancipation of Blacks from slavery, and fifty years after Jim Crow officially ended, the assessment was less than positive. A view from the streets of New York City, connecting marches from Union Square to Times Square, sit-ins on the Brooklyn Bridge, die-ins, and cavalcades of bodies blocking streets highlights some of the feeling. The following are reflections from the waves of protest from the Black Lives Matter movement, which gripped Brooklyn, New York, and the globe from the Fall of 2014 into 2015.

October 2014: "Hands Up! Don't Shoot," Black Lives Matter, and the Ferguson Verdict in NYC

For much of the fall of 2014, the world waited for a grand jury to decide the fate of the police who had shot unarmed Michael Brown in Ferguson, Missouri. Many had started to see similarities between the way Brown and Eric Garner, who died after a police officer choked him for 15 seconds on July 17, 2014, were treated at the hands of police. By Monday, October 24, 2014 we started hearing that maybe just maybe this really was the day we were going to get the grand jury verdict for Darren Wilson, who fatally shot unarmed Michael Brown earlier in the year.

Chapter five: Fighting Police Brutality in Global Brooklyn: From Ferguson to NYC

For weeks, the activists Ben Shepard worked with in Public Space Party, a Brooklyn-based direct action group, had been planning the Bike Bloc for Justice for Michael Brown and Eric Garner at Union Square. "On the day that each of these grand juries announces their decision, whatever those decisions are, we will take to the streets all across the country," declared the invitation for the event. The Public Space Party was supposed to have a meeting and prop making session. But instead, the Bike Bloc would meet at Tompkins Square Park and then ride to Union Square Park. Police helicopters flew overhead.

Arriving at Union Square, people were chanting and Imani Henry was giving an interview. "This is a global struggle," declared Henry, who would organize marches for the next few weeks for the movement.

Figure 2: "We Are Not Targets."
Photo by Benjamin Shepard.

Figure 3: "Broken barricades after the grand jury verdict was announced." Photo by Benjamin Shepard.

Chants filled the space:

"Turn Up! Turn Down! Do the Right Thing for Michael Brown."
"Old Jim Crow, New Jim Crow! the Whole Damned System has got to go."
"No justice! No Peace! Fuck the Police!"

We were standing in protest pens on the north end of Union Square. The south end of the park was filled with Christmas shopping. Someone mentioned the song, "Fuck the Police" by NWA. That was the music we all listened to when the Los Angeles police who beat Rodney King in 1992 were facing charges, 22 years prior. They were found not guilty, despite beating him in plain sight—plunging L.A. into days of violence. The feeling of that acquittal still stung, a coast away, two decades later. Many had similar feelings as they stood there.

The chants continued:

"Michael Brown didn't have to die; we know the reason why!"
"They say Jim Crow, we say hell no!"
"Turn it up, turn it down! We do this for Michael Brown!"
"Being Black is not a crime!"
"Ferguson to NYC, we don't need no police brutality!"

Chapter five: Fighting Police Brutality in Global Brooklyn: From Ferguson to NYC

Standing waiting, my friend Stan had heard leaks that there would be no indictment. Not even a slap on the wrist. "Let them burn Ferguson," another man suggested. The helicopters flew overhead.

We spent hours in the park talking, as the hour of the indictment announcement was pushed back from 6 p.m. to 9 p.m. I wondered about the lynchings Ida B. Wells described.[30] It was hard not to think this was part of that pattern; the pain resonated from a similar place out of the past. It never quite recedes. Yet, sometimes amnesia takes hold, before the next incident stirs up another round of emotions and subsequent street actions.

"At least the papers cover it," explained Stanley Aronowitz, during our class on the Dialectics of Race and Class at the Commons on Atlantic Avenue.

Standing at the northeast end of Union Square, it all felt familiar.

"I'd like to see some direct action," said one young woman. "Not just people saying they are going to shut it down, who don't shut it down." And direct action she would see, with waves of street blockades, marches over bridges and across traffic on highways, over the next few weeks. Little did she or anyone else know that the Black Lives Matter movement would expand to inherit the direct action tradition of the Black civil rights movement of the 1960s when activists struggled to dismantle the Jim Crow system.[31] Yet, there was still a lot of dismantling to do. None of us were surprised when we finally got the news.

It was surreal to stand in the silent park and to watch the space as everyone listened to their phones.

"No indictment," people began to shout around 9:20 pm.

"Take to the streets," others rejoined.

Together, everyone pushed through the barricades surrounding us and marched west. Go west, Ida advised.[32] So we walked west, through the streets, breaking police line after police line, in scuffle after scuffle with the police. Some were screaming, "NYPD, KKK, how many kids have you killed today?" Others put their hands over their heads, chanting "Hands Up! Don't Shoot!" just as Brown had before he was killed by some accounts. "Black lives matter!" others shouted. We were people from all over the city, person after person walking, grief stricken, heartbroken, angry, shocked, numbed, remembering, feeling lonely, disappointed, let down, slapped, helpless.

"Hands up, don't shoot!"

Police scooters zoomed to push us off the street as we walked west to Sixth Avenue and then up to 42nd Street.

"Whose streets? Our streets!"

The protests would last for days.

The first night, members of Public Space Party rode from Union Square to Times Square, some all the way up to 125th Street, many crossing and blocking the Triborough Bridge along the way. The next day, more actions were planned.

One of the signs that really stuck out the first night of the Ferguson protests declared: "Justice for Blank. Left it blank. Will probably need it next year." When we first heard about Michael Brown's death, that's what many thought about—Amadou Diallo, Patrick Dorismond, Oscar Grant, Trayvon Martin, Rodney King, the list of young Black men killed by the police goes on and on and on.

The next day, the long-planned post-verdict rally would take place. Throughout the social policy class that I teach at City Tech, we talked about the "New Jim Crow" and the historic racial and economic inequalities at the root of the protests. We talked about the ways the Great Society programs helped reduce poverty in this country from 22 per cent in 1959 to 12 per cent a decade later. In subsequent years, panics over race and crime followed, as the War on Poverty, shifted to the War on the Drugs, a war on the poor, as police targeted communities of color and created a pattern of mass incarceration, fueling the New Jim Crow.[33] My students wondered why police don't do more to try to de-escalate and prevent confrontations. Others asked why they are not trained to handle things differently. Some talked about the ways that laws, such as Stand Your Ground, are written, and possible approaches to frame things in more productive ways.

"We used to be a great society," one student reflected. "But boy, we are blowing that. We have to have ways to handle difference."

For the Ferguson Verdict March, activists organized a cell-phone messaging loop, announcing the movements of the shifting amoeba of the protest, so people joining in could get information about where the street actions were moving. The loop started getting cell-phone messages that the march from Union Square had made its way to Houston Street. Some had already taken over the Lincoln Tunnel, messages declared.

"Where are you ?" I wrote.

"On Houston Street," Keegan responded on the cell loop. "Where on Houston Street?" "All of Houston Street." Arriving on Houston Street, a huge crowd was marching. The Rude Mechanical Orchestra was playing.

My friend Tibby, a veteran of decades of activism, was standing there smiling.

"I can't march anymore," she said, beaming. "This is so wonderful."

"How long have you been marching?"

"I've been marching 50 years," she beamed. "And I feel like I have been replaced. This is so wonderful."

Activists from all over New York were on the streets, friends from Occupy to Right of Way and Public Space Party, from the Trayvon Martin Organizing Committee to people we'd met at the protests the night before. "Get up, get down, there's a revolution in this town!" people screamed.

Barbara texted, noting the Bike Bloc was on the FDR Drive. They had taken the FDR. No one had done that since Critical Mass 2004, the month before the Republican National Convention. And the city litigated against the ride afterwards. But here we were—making up our own Critical Mass.

As we walked east, a group of police seemed to try to block the entrance. Waves of people swarmed around them, between them, and we made our way to the FDR, a riverside highway where we'd walk all the way to the United Nations. There, we ran into more friends. A woman was screaming that the whole country should take notice. Things had to change. One step up, two steps back was the way things had been going, but we were pushing forward.

"I've lost my screaming partner," she screamed looking around.

"You've got about 10,000 of them with you here," others responded.

"Can you believe this?" Keegan gushed, looking around. He had been pulled over twice by the police the night before and was still marching. "Have you ever seen anything like this?"

"No," we replied, staring at people running down the FDR.

People were parking their cars on the other side, honking in solidarity.

"Indict the system," read one sign.

I walked with my bike. At one point a few of us jumped off to ride away, jumping back on in a couple of blocks because it was too exciting. A young man helped me pull my bike back onto the FDR and kept on marching all the way to the UN. People were blocking the Brooklyn Bridge and Williamsburg Bridge, with others moving to and from Manhattan and Brooklyn all night. The streets were full of energy and promise and hope for a different kind of change. There was a lot to be angry about. But there was also a lot to celebrate as we marched together. So many lovely people together, walking, screaming, and being alive, moving like a wave over the highway, maybe crossing to a new place for this country and a new step in the civil rights movement. Martin Luther King Jr. was killed after he spoke out about the need for economic justice for striking workers in Memphis. Echoing W. E. B. Du Bois, he suggested there was a different story which begins when race and economic justice overlap with education and action to create a different world for black people. "The cost of liberty is less than the price of repression," he declared.[34] These protests represent a rightful extension of this narrative.

STRANGE FRUIT HANGING

The subsequent months would build on waves and waves of protests. Many of the students in my community organizing classes connected what was happening in the streets with their own experiences in their Brooklyn neighborhoods. When a local high school student, Kimani Gray, was killed by the New York Police Department two years prior, we had talked about what this meant.[35] Several students said that they had known him, and that this practice of aggressive policing which killed him was far too common in their communities. Connecting their own personal histories with larger policy debates, several students became involved in research on stop-and-frisk policing, focusing their semester's work on the ways the city could change this policy. Within a year, lawsuits would put an end to the policy, and a new mayor was elected who denounced this practice. Their participation, dialogue, and organizing around the issue was part of the groundswell which put this issue on the agenda for the next mayoral election, affecting the evolution of policy. The Black Lives Matter protests would test this resolve.

The waves of street actions went on for months. Sometimes we heard police helicopters zooming overhead before a protest as we sat in class, sirens blaring, or witnessed arrests on the Brooklyn Bridge just outside. Sometimes we joined in. When the grand jury decision delivered its decision about Eric Garner, who was killed when an NYPD officer put him a chokehold as he was being arrested,[36] several students started talking about the chilling protest song "Strange Fruit," made famous by Billie Holiday. The words were still eerie and resonant.

Southern trees bear a strange fruit
Blood on the leaves and blood at the root
Black bodies swingin' in the Southern breeze
Strange fruit hangin' from the poplar trees

Today, they lay in the street, their murderers let off, one student noted, after we heard about the news that the police officer who illegally choked Garner to death was not charged with a crime. "Killed by cops or killed by a lynch mob—it doesn't feel that different," she added "A lynching is lynching." There we were in class. Two more student groups had to present their organizing projects. One presented on hunger, inequality, and the assaults on the supplemental nutrition program; the other group on police brutality. The latter group noted that Garner was selling cigarettes when the police approached him. They seemed to be punishing him for making an extra buck to feed his kids, for being poor.

That night people all over the city pushed back. Two decades after the LA Riots, resistance stretched from South Central to Times Square, part of an ever-expanding story of global movements against austerity. Those early December evenings of 2014, we met all over the city. Some sat in on the Brooklyn Bridge, others shut down the Lincoln Tunnel and Grand Central Terminal. Marching for hours through glorious protests, I thought about Eric Garner's last moments. To see this large but seemingly gentle man beg for room to breathe before taking his last breath—this was hard to fathom. Day after day, we marched to strike back at the system which killed Eric Garner and Michael Brown, taking black lives with impunity. Watching the video of Garner's death and the failure of the emergency service to deliver CPR, it was hard not to see this case as modern barbarity, the state monopoly of force to discipline colored people, laborers, deviant bodies, those making subsistence to survive. If they push back or assert themselves, they are shot, assaulted, forced to the ground, or pushed out of this life, as Eric was. Despairing, but pushing into the street, many found a new connection among those screaming out for something better, rejecting the notion that we are separate, that history is static or predetermined. There, we'd find care for each other among the bodies marching to take their place in this struggle.

Later that week, December 5th, Police lined up on Tillary Street outside the college, across from the Brooklyn Bridge entrance. But waves of bodies filled the bridge, claiming space as we had during Occupy, when hundreds were arrested crossing the bridge in October of 2011.

Figure 4: "Protests clogged the Brooklyn Bridge after the Garner Grand Jury response."

One policeman explained to a woman standing by me that as long as the protestors were not breaking anything or dangerous, they had no problem with it. "It's a good thing," he stated as we stood on the walkway of the Brooklyn Bridge.

All fall long, the city had been allowing street activists more room on the street in order to avoid lawsuits that the city was still paying for arrests dating back to the Republican National Convention of 2004. "De Blasio gives a lot of rope," noted Seth Tobocman, who'd seen the Koch, Dinkins, Giuliani and Bloomberg administrations through their increasingly aggressive approaches to policing dissent. By the end of the evening, tolerance for protest had worn thin. Many police began to pepper-spray those in the streets.

In Manhattan, there were bodies of protestors as far as the eye could see.

"One, we are the people," cried the crowd.

"Two, a little bit louder".

"Three, we want justice for Eric Garner."

We made our way through the streets, people talking, screaming, finding solidarity. We marched north, west on Canal Street, south down Broadway past Zuccotti Park where so many of this generation of activists met in our call to challenge the ravages of income inequality. The Black Lives Matter movement would very much continue the work Occupy had been doing.[37] We marched down to the Staten Island Ferry, turned west, and then up the West Side Highway, where more activists clogged the streets. The city has to change. It just had to.

"It was a wild and wonderful night, but the police got very brutal toward the end," related my friend Stacy Lanyon, who witnessed the police using pepper spray on peaceful protesters. Late in the evening, a sound cannon went off, splintering the crowd with its boom of decibels. Designed to disperse masses, their warnings could be heard all over the city.

Yet the street actions continued. Somehow, the city was changing—or more people were talking, getting to know each other. Change begins with these kinds of conversations, from the bottom, one step forward in the cavalcade of history.

Decolonize NYC

Figure 5: "Decolonize." Photo by Benjamin Shepard.

In the fall of 2014, I was taking a class at the Commons, a movement building space on Atlantic Avenue near downtown Brooklyn, called the "Dialectic of Race and Class." The conversation from the streets extended into the classroom. Many of us reveled in the deep concern we saw for community as the Black Lives Matter movement expanded.[38]

Some in the class suggested we need more analysis. I followed that the cohorts of friends, bottom-up networks that supported each other, just as Ella Baker organized in SNCC, were doing just fine.

"Which leaders use dialectical thinking?" wondered Jim Fouratt, a veteran of decades of organizing, from Gay Liberation Front to Occupy. "How can we learn from mistakes, piecing together our struggles into an arc of change? Who controls the streets?" What we needed was a way of thinking about history in action, about public space. This was a big moment of change. Everyone seemed to feel it, crying out for this moment, beyond post-modernism, reembracing what we could do. History was repeating itself but we needed to see it in dialectic terms. The streets offered a space to think about race and class, work and wages and the discipline of labor that killed Eric Garner.

After class, I rode to Washington Square Park for the Millions March on December 13, a march to demand justice: "For Mike Brown, For Eric Garner.

For Akai Gurley. We March Together, As One. #BLACKLIVESMATTER FERGUSON IS NEW YORK." Our feeder march from Brooklyn exhorted: "Racial Justice requires Racial Solidarity."

Throughout the afternoon, we continued this grand conversation about change, talking about where the movement had come from, where we were going, and how we could support the movement's expansion. Some cried or lay down. Others screamed as we connected in the streets.

Figure 6: "Black Lives Matter." Photo by Benjamin Shepard.

Chapter five: Fighting Police Brutality in Global Brooklyn: From Ferguson to NYC   131

Figures 7 and 8: "March to the Pink Houses." Photos by Benjamin Shepard.

The march went on for hours. At around 6 pm, I rode home. Others kept on marching. The cheers became darker as people made their way over the bridge, toward Brooklyn. The Reverend Donna Schaper, the Senior Pastor at Judson Memorial Church, worried about the dehumanization in the name-calling she saw, as the sun set. The cell-phone loop sent messages all night, finally pulling my neighbors and me out for a late-night march. Greg, Molly and I rode down through Brooklyn to the Pink Houses, following the police lights and helicopters deep into East New York.

"It's like the Bataan Death March," said my friend Joe, sounding punchy. He had been marching for some nine hours with the Rude Mechanical Orchestra. Police were everywhere. The music filled the night.

At the 75th Precinct, near where Akai Gurley was killed, we staged a die-in and a speak-out.

"Look at them, they are not listening to us," noted one man, sitting by me during the die-in. "They are joking over there."

Frustrated, the activists started taunting the police.

"You see that minority representation there. Only one Black cop," noted another man.

"You better make sure they don't shoot you."

"We need police to be from our neighborhoods so they are not afraid of us," added another. Others on hand argued that the city needed fewer cops regardless of where they came from.

Chapter five: Fighting Police Brutality in Global Brooklyn: From Ferguson to NYC   133

Figure 9-12: "Fury and heartbreak." Photos by Benjamin Shepard.

Chapter five: Fighting Police Brutality in Global Brooklyn: From Ferguson to NYC

The police joked with each other about what a bad neighborhood this was, warning white protestors to get home safely. One of the activists, a young woman, listened with disbelief and sadness, shaking her head.

Others sang a sad lament: "We are not gonna leave till we are free."

"I still hear my brother crying, 'I can't breathe.' Now I'm in the struggle singing. I can't leave." The march continued to the Pink Houses where Akai Gurley was killed.

"We have to get it right this time," another man seemed to say to himself as we walked.

"Thank you for coming," an elderly woman cheered us on as we made our way back home. "You've been wonderful." The contrast between the police warning and her greeting was striking and telling.

By that point in the movement, protesters had been corralled and arrested, run over and subjected to sound cannons of deafening noise. When we breathe, we breathe together. Over the months to come, the conversation continued, between activists, neighborhood members, even protesters and police. Hopefully, the police would hear us just as we would hear them. During Occupy, the rock star Lou Reed lamented the behavior of the cops, but added: "I want to be friends with them." Black Lives Matter brought generations of bodies into the streets, ideas clashing and melding. As we met, read and acted up, waves of mass protests over the deaths of Michael Brown, Eric Garner, and many others pulled us into an age-old conversation.

With roots in the Black Power movement, the milieu that inspired James Baldwin, that Occupy supported, Black Lives Matter expanded a dialogue. The Black Panthers were formed to hold the police accountable. Along the way, members read Marx and fashioned a program. Black Lives Matter built on this trajectory, crafted among kinship networks, as well as strangers supporting ever expanding pickets, rallies, and tweets about a dirty secret of institutional racism and income inequality. Their actions exposed them for the whole world to see; those involved essentially screaming "don't kill me" with each subsequent action.

"Today ... the face of the Black Lives Matter movement is largely queer and female," contends Keeanga-Yamahtta Taylor in *From #BlackLivesMatter to Black Liberation*.[39] Her words echo LA Kauffman's thinking.[40] "This resurgence of disruptive direct action in people-of-color-led movements didn't start in Ferguson," wrote Kauffman in 2014, citing precedents including the Republican Convention protests in Philadelphia in 2000, the massive immigrant rights marches of 2006 and the summer 2013 acquittal of George Zimmerman for the killing of Trayvon Martin in Florida.[41] "But it's the tenacious young black organizers on the frontlines... many of them women, who clearly deserve the most credit for the scale and character of this nationwide upsurge. Their risk-taking in the face of the tear gas, rubber bullets, and military gear of the police there—and their strategic use of social media to broadcast their message and methods—have transformed grassroots protest in the United States. In both Ferguson and New York, the protests have been decentralized, with different groups and organizers taking the lead at different points."⁴² Much of Keeanga-Yamahtta Taylor's work offers a response to MLK's "A Testament of Hope" from 1969; she reminds us that movements are bundles of stories: "I am not sad that black Americans are rebelling; this was not only inevitable but eminently desirable. Without this magnificent ferment among Negroes, the old evasions and procrastinations would have continued indefinitely...." wrote King. "They have left the valley of despair; they have found strength in struggle; and whether they live or die, they shall never crawl nor retreat again. Joined by white allies, they will shake the prison walls until they fall." King's words resonate across cohorts, connecting all of us. "America must change."⁴³

On January 19, 2015, we gathered to "Reclaim MLK Day." We met at 110th Street and Lennox Avenue. Whitman's vision of democracy as a city of friends takes shape through such moments on the streets. Marching, we talked about why we were there.

Figure 13: "#DREAM4JUSTICE NYC March." Photo by Benjamin Shepard.

Chapter five: Fighting Police Brutality in Global Brooklyn: From Ferguson to NYC

A young woman told us about the police locking up her mother when she called them for help from a developer encroaching on their family plot in her home in Oklahoma. Tears began to flow down her face as she recalled the humiliation of watching her family endure their treatment at the hands of the police. She recalled another occasion when the police confiscated her driver's license, locked her up, and told her it was suspended, asking for cash to get it back. "I kept asking them, 'Are you Christian? Cause this is wrong. I tell my students to believe in the system. But what you are doing is discouraging me from telling them that.'" The next day, the DMV noted her license was in good order. The police had been lying. Below her tears was a story, a wound so many still endure.

A generation after the end of Jim Crow, we are still left with police and real estate agents, hospitals and schools, which do not treat everyone equally. But we are pushing forward, to do more with this democracy, collectively.

And so we talked and walked as more and more people joined the march. Maybe we don't need as many cops, noted sociologist Alex Vitale as we walked. Or perhaps they should be unarmed, wondered his colleague, Brooklyn sociologist Greg Smithsimon.[44]

Black Lives Matter is a movement about a love between people, even toward the police, who you often see engaged during the rallies.[45] It is a movement about people caring, looking out for each other, and even a little dancing. Walking, an elderly woman started to dance to Stevie Wonder's "Happy Birthday," his tribute to King. And several of us started dancing with her. The action came alive. "Happy birthday to you!" everyone sang to MLK, shaking their hips.

Within a few weeks, we would hear that the officers who had shot unarmed Akai Gurley in the stairway of his home in Brooklyn had been indicted.[46] Perhaps, just perhaps, the world was beginning to hear the pleas for justice?

Figure 14: "DREAM4JUSTICE NYC March January 19, 2015" © *Erik Mc Gregor.*

Chapter six

The World City and the Space of Neighborhoods:

The Battle of Brooklyn

Figure 1: "Scene of Smith Street in Carroll Gardens." Photo by Ben Shepard.

Like all cities, New York is changing.[1] Everyone seems to agree.[2] Yet, as cities change, observers have to come wonder if there is still a place for local actors, or have they been relegated to the position of passive spectators to larger social forces?[3] Is there a different path and a space for local agency in global cities? It's a good time to ask these questions, especially as Brooklyn undergoes a vast transformation.[4] Between globalization, hyper-development and accompanying homogenization, the city's neighborhoods are being remade in front of our eyes.[5]

"Brooklyn is booming," wrote Kenneth Brown in the business glossy real estate advertisement *Brooklyn Tomorrow*.[6] "In a decade, it will be vastly different, packed with more parks, waterfront destinations, glittering residential towers with Manhattan-style views." The "facelift of Coney Island" and the Atlantic

Yards Project "will change the heart of Brooklyn."[7] A decade later, an article in the Travel Section of the *New York Times* would boast:

Brooklyn is a bona fide cultural capital, with world-class art, performances, street fairs, and museums. And the depth and quality of its food and drink options are impressive and rewarding. Best of all: Despite increases in cost of living and tasting menus that can run over $300... deals can be found...[8]

The article highlights two dynamics—apartment costs that dwarf those in parts of Manhattan and secret nooks still open for discovery.[9] In recent years, Brooklyn has become a sort of "global brand."[10] Yet, to what end? Centuries after the 1776 Battle of Brooklyn, the landscape of Brooklyn is being remapped once again as a struggle over what it will become.[11]

Global cities are spaces "which successfully compete for major city status in at least one of several important functions of integrating the transnational capitalist economy."[12] Brooklyn has long maintained characteristics of a world city, including: culture, financial institutions, universities, commerce, health services, immigration, and the return of a major sports franchise the Brooklyn Nets, followed by another, the New York Islanders.[13] It has increasingly become a place where people come to eat and congregate.[14] Today, its waterways are being cleaned up; park spaces expanded; its skies filled with the cranes, the streets congested with construction crews.[15] Its post-industrial waterfront, long dormant as a work space, has become a space of play and leisure.[16] Of course, the downside of Brooklyn's development also includes many of the negative characteristics of a rapid economic growth. These include: patterns of displacement of the poor, foreclosures, ecological damage, pollution, police brutality, and a general squeeze on public space.[17] While its neighborhoods are pulsing with arts and music, as well as an immigration and cultural mix, much of the feel of Brooklyn is threatened with being washed away.

As a global city, Brooklyn must contend with powerful tides related to de-industrialization, gentrification, and transformation.[18] Carroll Gardens is undergoing a building boom which inspired the neighborhood to rezone itself, restricting heights for construction. Sunset Park is rapidly turning into a pulsing Chinatown, a "Little Mexico" on Fifth Ave. And East New York was recently rezoned in what many described as a boon to developers.[19] Neighborhoods including Fort Greene, DUMBO, Williamsburg, and Carroll Gardens are blossoming as young professionals and artists settle into them. Yet questions remain about the pace of this development. Who stands to benefit and who stands to be pushed out? One thing is for sure, as Brooklyn is being remade, traditions and touchstones of historic Brooklyn are in danger of being buried, obscured from sight and memory. While urban spaces are thought to magnify democratic possibilities,[20] their development tends to expand social inequalities.²¹ The contradictions with such development are many. The borough has a vast cultural history.²² But, this cultural capital does little to mitigate patterns of migration, community development, displacement, and cultural erasure which tend to accompany the process as the third and fourth chapters of this book highlight. This is essentially the story of capitalism, over and over again.²³ The evictions and environmental disrepair that follow uneven urban development are all too familiar in global spaces such as this.²⁴ Nonetheless, regular people throughout Brooklyn have long resisted elements of the homogenization steamroller.²⁵ While Manhattan is a model of congestion and hyper density,²⁶ they hope for a different model of urbanism, built around an ecologically friendly, livable scale friendly to people and the environment.

The Battle of Brooklyn is a struggle to grapple with the social, cultural, and ecological costs; it suggests there could be a different route for a global city. But, what do these changes mean for regular people? How can one make sense of so many lurching changes or develop alternative models for a cosmopolitan city?

This new Battle of Brooklyn is an effort to help keep what is distinct and rich about Brooklyn, its streets, distinct neighborhoods, and people. While certainly some of the renaissance taking place in Brooklyn is a good thing, growth is paradoxical. Today, the battle is a struggle against the sea of identical details, stadiums, out-of-place buildings, and displacement. What is the future of Brooklyn's neighborhoods once they have been rezoned? And can there be a new model of sustainable development for a world city? This chapter highlights the ways Brooklyn residents, groups, and neighborhoods are experiencing urban development and the strategies activists have employed to address the issues of dispossession and homogenization of urban space. It considers alternative models of urban development in which the character of streets is not blandified, and community space is supported rather than squeezed out. Throughout this chapter, we also consider models of non-polluting transportation and bike infrastructure as examples of human-scale urban living, supporting an image of a more livable city. This model begins with an image of open public space.

REZONING AND THE BATTLE OVER THE WATERFRONT

I (Ben Shepard) will never forget seeing the Hungry March Band, a Brechtian anarchist street band, perform on the decaying Williamsburg waterfront in the late 1990s and 2000. The band would meet at a space off Kent Avenue, in the long-closed Brooklyn Eastern District Terminal. Since 1985, it has been a majestic open space looking over the East River, with decaying piers, a place in between Brooklyn's industrial past and uncertain future with music, poetry, and daydreams created among the piers.²⁷ The vernacular uses of the waterfront are many. And over time the state of New York came to recognize these uses, purchasing the two-block area and making it into East River State Park in 2001.[28] In other cases, the city or developers closed off access to the waterfront.[29] With industrial use gone, allowing new residents to pour in as historic buildings were gutted by the day, the National Trust for Historic Preservation declared the waterfront an endangered site. The waterfront would become the center of a culture war over what the borough would become. Throughout this struggle, many hoped the waterfront could serve as alternative, neighborhood-based model of a global city, rather than an impersonal image of displacement, oversized buildings, condominiums, and privatized waterfronts.

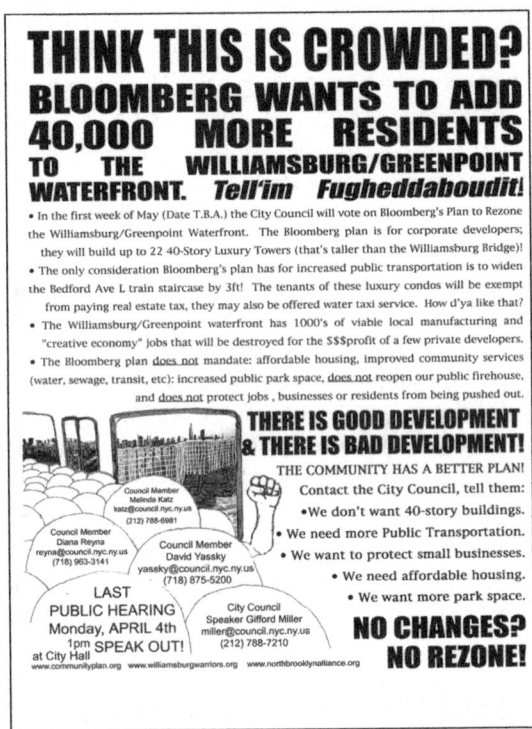

Figure 2: "Flyer for battle over Williamsburg rezoning."

In 2005, it would become subject to a fierce battle pitting community interest against a Bloomberg plan to rezone the area. For me, much of the battle began when I received a few emails from my friend Beka Economopoulos.[30] "Dear Friends," she began. "One of the most aggressive rezonings in NYC's history has been proposed for Williamsburg/Greenpoint by Bloomberg and his greedy land-grabber friends. And it's happening under our noses." This was a pattern taking place all over the city. "Development's happening. What will it look like? Who's gonna win? It's an epic battle." Laying out the players, Economopoulos wrote: "Team Bloomberg has a plan that will add a wall of 40-story luxury condos along the waterfront, will privatize access to the river, won't add park space, won't increase L service, won't keep rents affordable or safeguard local businesses ..." The city plan would be "Gentrification on Steroids." It would allow for development of 22 40-story luxury condominiums along the waterfront, offer no affordable housing units, privatize the waterfront access and increase the population of Williamsburg/Greenpoint without addressing the resultant infrastructural needs, including transportation and education needs.[31]

"Team Community" put together an alternative plan to "develop and defend" their community. The community members looked to "a section of the city charter called 197a, which allows communities to propose their own plans for development." And so they did, initiating an assessment of community needs into a task force to examine: 1) affordable housing, 2) economic development, 3) height and bulk, and 4) parks and open space.[32] "Unfortunately, the 197a are recommendations: they are not legally binding," noted Economopoulos. In response, the City Planning Commission drafted their own developer-driven rezoning plan, addressing few of the community needs emphasized in the 197A plan.

In December 2004, the Community Board One voted against the city plan, in a raucous meeting attended by some 1,500 local residents. In January 2005, the borough president, Marty Markowitz, condemned the Bloomberg plan. By March and April, the City Planning Commission would hold a public hearing on the plan, followed by a vote by the City Council.

"Things to Bear in Mind. This is a citywide struggle," Economopoulos' email concluded, "What's happening here is happening in all 5 boroughs. If we run a kick-ass campaign, we can amplify the voices and the work of resisters throughout the city."

On February 28, a wide coalition—from neighborhood organizing, arts, global justice, and anti-war activists crammed into the Not An Alternative Space on Havemeyer Street to lay out a plan. The Williamsburg Warriors, dressed like characters from the 1979 cult film *The Warriors,* as well as members of the Church of Stop Shopping, were there. So were many people who had gotten to know each other organizing against the Republican National Convention the previous summer. At the meeting, the organizers outlined a plan of action for a "Creative Industries" coalition, beginning with a timeline of actions as well as means to mobilize people from around Williamsburg. The message was simple: "Save the neighborhood: stop Bloomberg's Williamsburg/Greenpoint rezoning plan! Say no to 40-foot high-rises on the waterfront! Vote no on rezoning."

Over the next two months, the Creative Industries coalition would get the word out with public information sessions, a press conference at City Hall, and a colorful waterfront festival in Williamsburg with supporters dressed as flowers, carrying shovels emblazoned with the word "Community Plan."[33] The artist Fly made a sign declaring, "WE DON'T WANT NO STINKIN TOWERS!"

WE WANT SPACE TO PLANT OUR FLOWERS!!!" Bike Riders with cardboard horse heads organized a Paul Revere Ride to notify the community about the changes coming. And the papers started taking notice.[34] "[T]his is happening all over New York," wrote Elana Levin (2005)"[T]he things that make our neighborhoods unique, and New York-y are being killed by the landgrabbing billionaires for Bloomberg...."[35]

When supporters of the community plan held a press conference condemning the mayor's rezoning plan in 2005, the mayor passed by on his way to City Hall. Activists chanted "Community Plan! Community Plan!" Hearing their chant, the mayor leaned over in a guffaw, in a provocative gesture which seemed to ridicule the idea of community input into the process, as we stood on the City Hall steps. A few days later, the group, once again dressed as flowers with their shovels, sang "Won't You Help Us Gifford" to the tune of the 1981 hit "Don't You Want Me" in front of Council Speaker Gifford Miller's office, holding a mock battle between those dressed as towers and as flowers. In the match, the towers were vanquished by the flowers. The same could not be said of the real-life battle. By May, the City Council would vote in support of the developer-backed rezoning.[36]

While the community plan was opposed by the mayor, it garnered support from some of the most thoughtful observers of cities. "What the intelligently worked-out plan devised by the community itself does *not* do is worth noticing," wrote the 88-year-old Jane Jacobs, the iconic organizer who had successfully beaten back Robert Moses' bid to put a highway through Greenwich village four decades prior. "The community's plan does not violate the existing scale of the community, nor does it insult the visual and economic advantages of neighborhoods that are precisely of the kind that demonstrably attract artists and other craftsmen, initiating spontaneous and self-organizing renewal," she stated. "I will make two predictions with utter confidence. If you follow the community's plan you will harvest a success. If you follow the proposal before you today, you will maybe enrich a few heedless and ignorant developers, but at the cost of an ugly and intractable mistake."[37] The *New York Times* would sit on Jacobs' letter until after the council vote in favor of rezoning. Nonetheless, Jacobs' statement remains prophetic. Today, semi-completed forty-story condos stand, mostly completed along the waterfront, an homage to short-sighted planning.

After the vote, I remember walking into a party only to see a resigned crowd of the activists involved, complaining to my friend Savitri D about the loss. She grabbed me by the shoulders and declared emphatically, "This is happening all over the world."

The struggle over Brooklyn rezoning would not end in Williamsburg. It was one of over 100 rezoning measures seen over the last decade in New York. Each involved core questions about what Brooklyn would become as it contends with globalization. Would Brooklyn's transformation be driven by residents or

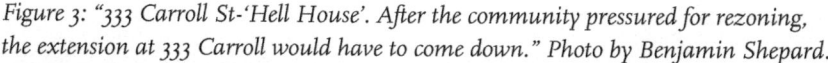

developers?[38] Community residents would fight back, as the struggle against out-of-scale buildings began extending all over the borough.[39] So activists pushed back. The only guarantee was they would lose if they failed to try. It was not a new battle.[40] Many residents across the borough hoped they could avoid ugly glass towers and out-of-place buldings.[41]

Figure 3: "333 Carroll St-'Hell House'. After the community pressured for rezoning, the extension at 333 Carroll would have to come down." Photo by Benjamin Shepard.

RALLYING TO PRESERVE AND PROTECT CARROLL GARDENS

In the summer of 2007, I noticed a 40-foot-high shell on top of a 19th-century building at 333 Carroll Street, looming over all the historic brownstones of Carroll Gardens. Not long after, I learned the neighborhood would be losing the Second Street entrance of the F train on Smith Street to make way for a project by Robert Scarano, a notorious architect famous for violating building codes in some 25 other projects around the city.[42] He planned to develop another out-of-scale building at 360 Smith Street.

Many wondered about the site where the project was slated to stand. "What's in the dirt at 360 Smith Street?" neighborhood residents asked. And what about the delicate ecology between Brooklyn streets, blue skies, tree-lined sidewalks, with towering condos obscuring views? Instead of over-development propelling inequality and unsustainable hyper consumption,[43] the residents of Carroll Gardens wanted the space to remain open to views of blue skies rather than out-of-character buildings and shadows.[44] The negative impacts of such excess consumption are many.[45] Over time, this conversation found expression outside the F station at Second Street, where the Scarano building was planned.[46]

Figures 4 and 5: "Street graffiti at President Street Subway stop 2008. 'The neighborhood is dying'—read one caption." Photos by Benjamin Shepard.

As graffiti and flyers started to appear, the space became the epicenter for a debate about zoning and downsizing. "What's going on here?" one read, announcing a community meeting. "Safe?" someone else painted, alluding to the project. "Is it safe?" "What's getting built here?" "Calling all Brooklynites? I am losing the blue sky?" another painting charged over an image of a superhero perched atop the buildings of Carroll Gardens. "The Carroll Gardens neighborhood is dying! 360 Smith Street" another warned. Others called for the signing of a petition to put an end to the "Frenzy of development."

By the fall of 2007, neighborhood residents had collected some 3,000 signatures calling for a building moratorium in the neighborhood, restricting the height of buildings so they remained in proportion with the neighborhood. Neighborhood activists also held meetings, strategy sessions and demonstrations. "RALLY TO PRESERVE AND PROTECT CARROLL GARDENS, SOUTH BROOKLYN, NEW YORK," read a flyer for an action on January 29th, 2008. "To support a resolution calling upon the Department of City Planning to immediately commence a downsizing study of Carroll Gardens to protect our neighborhood and Department of Buildings to implement the appropriate procedure to preserve the character of Carroll Gardens." Over the next few months, neighborhood groups worked with the City Council to help pass the hundredth rezoning amendment of Michael Bloomberg's term, a zoning text amendment restricting the height of new construction to 50 feet, or 70 on streets which already have higher buildings—this time with full support of the community.[47] The bill wasn't everything, and it did not stop the 360 Smith Street project or other out-of-scale buildings projected for the neighborhood, but it was an example of an historic district speaking up for itself in the face of developers dead set on building higher buildings, with more units, wherever they could.[48]

WALMART OUT OF EAST NEW YORK

One of the primary limitations of corporate globalization is the sense that all cities must contend with an ever-expanding sameness. While the landscapes along US roads once included mom-and-pop businesses, today they are filled with McDonald's signs and big-box stores, such as Walmart, which decrease wages and community economic power.[49] Over half the people in America live within five miles of a Walmart store.[50] Global trade seems to demand this encroachment into the physical surroundings of cities and towns.[51] Still, do all global cities need to look the same, with a Starbucks on every corner?[52] For years now, New York has resisted Walmart's attempts to bring a store to New York. Anti-consumerist activists, such as the Church of Stop Shopping, as well as neighborhood groups such as New York Communities for Change, argue the city already feels enough like a shopping zone without another retail big box store.[53] Walmart is not necessary for Brooklyn neighborhoods. These groups worry the city's rich vistas are being lost in a sea of identical details. While an infusion of corporate capital and uneven development is seen as part of life in global cities,[54] others have to come to ask if there is a different way of shaping urban saces.[55]

Figure 6: "Flyer for the successful campaign to beat back Walmart."

"New York is not a shopping mall, it's not a shopping mall!" cried East Village activists with Reverend Billy and the Church of Stop Shopping in 1999, shortly before the World Trade Organization protests in Seattle. Over a decade later, the call remains the same, yet the epicenter of the struggle is no longer the East Village. Instead, it is taking place throughout Brooklyn, where Walmart had set its sights on a space in East New York.

On February 7, 2011, opponents of Walmart held a rally in City Hall Park. Members of Times Up!, a bicycle-oriented environmental group, rode down to City Hall from the Lower East SIde on bikes with cardboard horse heads, again invoking Paul Revere's calls, screaming: "The big boxes are coming! Walmart is coming!" By the time we got to City Hall, we were joined by Rev. Billy and his Choir, the Retail, Wholesale and Department Store Union and the United Food and Commercial Workers International, community groups, such as New York Communities for Change, members of the Working Families Party, Jobs for Justice, and others in the Walmart Free NYC Coalition. As we waited to get through security to enter the plaza in front of City Hall, members of Families United for Racial and Economic Equality (FUREE), a Brooklyn-based organizing group, chanted : "Up with the People, yea yea, down with Walmart, down down!" and "NYC is Walmart-free! NYC is Walmart-free!" and "New York is not a shopping mall!" Those on the city hall steps chanted, reminding everyone that Walmart is a job killer. "For every two jobs, three jobs lost!"[56]

Figure 7: "The author and other advocates locked out of City Hall during the City Council hearing on Walmart." Photo by Brennan Cavanaugh.

By the time we got to the entrance, the security informed us we would not be allowed inside. I told them I was concerned that the restrictions protests at City Hall are unevenly enforced, noting that the police and fire departments were allowed to bring as many as they want into city hall park for rallies. I also alluded to the First Amendment and Congress not passing "law[s] abridging... the right of the people peaceably to assemble and petition the government for a redress of grievances."[57] That was when they said they might have to arrest me. The conflict between civil liberties and security has become commonplace in New York. Still, speakers from City Hall, including then Public Advocate, Bill de Blasio, denounced Walmart as a job-killing entity unwelcome in East New York or anywhere in the five boroughs.[58]

This was just the beginning of a campaign. Over the next few weeks, opponents of Walmart would zap board meetings of supporters of the plan and even organize a "flash mob" in a shopping mall owned by Related, the company that was planning to lease Walmart the space.[59] After finishing the flash mob, a man started talking to me as we rode down Lexington on our bicycles.

"The era of materialism is ending. The people of Japan are learning that," he declared referring to the events after the reactor meltdown in Fukushima.[60] "They are just glad to be alive. The same is coming here. I love you." And he rode off. There are other ways to create urban space.

In March, cyclists with Times Up! rode down to the location for the proposed site in East New York, deep in Brooklyn. There we met members of Jobs for Justice, New York Communities for Change (formerly NY ACORN) and Rev. Billy and the Church of of Earthalujah in a vast field behind a shopping mall which already included several big-box stores. With a baby-carriage strewn aside, an old pair of discarded sneakers, and a few assorted empty beer cans in between sand dunes, the undeveloped sandlot resembled a wasteland.

"Here we are," began Billy, "in [a] lovely field of shore dunes and ravines in East New York. The place has an uncertain future. It is slated for development and over the years communities gathered to make a plan."[61] Those involved hoped to create a place a place with small businesses, places for kids, adults, spaces to walk, and even playgrounds. "Now the billionaire mayor and his friends are arranging for an addition." Arguing that shoppers were leaving New York to shop in Walmart outside the city and the business created jobs, the Mayor supported Walmart coming to New York. The Reverend preached about what it would take to beat back the Wal Mart. It would start with making the community plan a reality. "Make that playground. Make a contest—make music, make films here in this field. Find the old-timers who grew up here." Recognize the vernacular uses of the space. "There are neighborhood children, of course, that use it as a secret place of adventure. So the stories come back."[62] The Reverend concluded: "Imagine what we can do."

Big-box stores are part of an evolution of capitalism which reproduces social inequalities. "[T]he production of a particular kind of nature and space under historical capitalism is essential to the uneven development of a landscape that integrates poverty with wealth, industrial urbanization with agricultural diminishment," writes Edward Said.[63] David Harvey elaborates: "The unequal development of the global economy, with its burgeoning extremes of wealth and poverty, its astonishing pace of urbanization and environmental deregulation, has accelerated, rather than diminished."[64] Certainly these features are part of what takes shape in each neighborhood Walmart enters, devastating local economies, killing local businesses, and making Walmart shareholders richer.

They are also part of the local and global Battle of Brooklyn. The struggle would take any number of dynamics. Some struggles, such as the battle against

Walmart, involved residents fighting corporations and cultural erasure; in other cases, they fought to create effective alternatives to global problems, such as congestion and global warming. It would be another year and a half of street actions, flash-mobs, and public hearings before Walmart declared defeat, canceling all plans to locate a store in East New York.[65] After the speak out ended in East New York, some of us departed by bike for Prospect Park where we planned another event in defense of the beleaguered Prospect Park West bike lane later that afternoon.[66]

SUPPORTING BIKES OVER CARS IN PROSPECT PARK

"How One New York Bike Lane Could Affect the Future of Cycling Worldwide": that was the title of an article in London's Guardian newspaper the day before a March 2011 Brooklyn Community Board 6 meeting addressing the contentious topic of a two-way protected bike lane off of Frederick Law Olmsted's iconic Prospect Park.[67] Over the last decade, urban cycling has become the subject of a protracted urban battle involving debates over land use, civil liberties, sustainable development, and urban living itself.[68] Nowhere has this battle taken on the same intensity as in Brooklyn. This case study considers the battle over bike lanes and competing visions of urban space.

The subtext of the battle involved a tension over the ways a city copes with the vexing interconnection between globalization and global warming. "Globalization is fueling global warming," argues author Les Leopold.[69] And while cities cannot depend on large-scale agreements, such as the those coming out of Copenhagen or Paris at the COP 21, what they can do is build an infrastructure that supports non-polluting transportation—part of the solution for a sustainable future and the common preservation of cities.

I (Ben Shepard) have always loved cycling. After years of taking the subway from Brooklyn to the Bronx for my daily commute, in 2007 I started working on Jay Street in Downtown Brooklyn, a 10-minute bike ride from my home in Carroll Gardens. I was ecstatic to read the city plans to lay out an extensive network of some 200 miles of bike lanes through the five boroughs of New York, including one down the street—Smith Street—between my house to work. But as the bike lanes were laid out, many drivers ignored them, treating the spaces as double-parking zones, places to text, or chat on the phone. Police on Dekalb Avenue even placed a garbage dumpster in the bike lane in front of the 88th Precinct.[70] A Hunter College study would confirm the point, noting there is a 60% chance of encountering a car parked in a bike lane.[71]

Figure 8: "Flyer by opponents of the Prospect Park Bike Lane."

> **PROSPECT PARK WEST ALERT !!!**
> **ACCIDENTS ARE GOING TO HAPPEN !!!**
>
> Dear Neighbors:
> **"A Two-Way Bicycle lane is going into effect as of June 2010 along the entire length of Prospect Park West.**
> **"This will eliminate the B-69 Bus Route and reduce Traffic along PPW to 2 Lanes.**
> "By reducing Traffic to 2 Lanes on Prospect Park West – Traffic will be hazardous to pedestrians and pets.
> "This will adversely affect Ambulances, Fire, Emergency Vehicles and All Local Services.
> "There has been No Public Notification to the Residents of Park Slope. We already have a working Bicycle Path in Prospect Park that could accommodate 2 Directions!
> **PLEASE VOICE YOUR OPPOSITION BY E-MAILING AND CONTACTING THE FOLLOWING:**
> Mayor Bloomberg: WWW.NYC.GOV/MAYOR
> Contact NY 1 News: DESK@NY1NEWS.COM
> Marty Markowitz: askmarty@brooklynbp.nyc.gov
> 718-802-3700
> Community Board 6: INFO@BROOKLYNCB6.ORG
> 718-643-3027
> Janette Sadik-Khan D.O.T. Commissioner:
> www.nyc.gov : go to contact DOT & by letter – DOT Commissioner, 55 Water Street, NY, NY 10041
> Brad Lander Councilman: Lander@council.nyc.gov
> 718-499-1090
> Jim Brennan Assemblyman: 718-788-7221
> BRENNANJ@ASSEMBLY.STATE.NY.US

Over time, my friends and I would organize to help educate the public about the bike lanes—which many loved, some ignored, and a vocal minority of Brooklynites seemed to detest. We would organize bike rides in which we "ticketed" cars parked in lanes, joking with those drivers about why they parked in the bike lanes. We would write up press releases for each ride, inviting journalists to come witness the cars illegally parked in the bike lanes. As the rides continued from 2005 to 2008, the intensity of the debate over the lanes only increased, with each new lane. When the city established a bike lane on Kent Avenue, local residents, most vocally from the Hasidic Community, complained they would lose their parking spaces; that immodest women rode through the neighborhood; that the lane created unsafe conditions. They said they would block access to the lanes.[72] When my friends and I heard about this, we planned to be there to defend the lanes. On most rides, we were able to get our message out through our actions and a simple press release. Yet, this ride felt different. We were facing a group of politically connected residents who seemed to resent being linked to a network of 200 miles of bike lanes connecting the borough with bikers, ideas, and styles of dress with which these residents felt uncomfortable.[73] Whether they liked it or not, they were still part of a global city, contending with global problems, such as climate change and congestion. Bike lanes were a simple way to reduce car use and by extension carbon emissions. They were also part of the five boroughs of New York, which are as socially and economically connected to the world as they are to the U.S.[74]

Speaking with journalists before the ride, I realized the global dimensions of the story were not finding traction in the local press. While most of the reports on the ride were quite positive,[75] few of the papers considered the larger global perspective on the story, seemingly rejecting Brooklyn's position as a vital ingredient of a global city,[76] even belittling the need for alternatives to automobiles.[77] The point of the action was to get the city and the borough to consider the larger picture. Williamsburg was part of this city that had seen a 36% increase in biking in the time the papers were debating the Bedford Bike Lanes. Biking was on the rise city-wide. The upsurge in cycling seemed to represent a vision of a sustainable city built around non-polluting transportation.[78] A global city requires a global view of its problems and possibilities. The Kent Avenue bike lane was part of the solution, increasing health and reducing carbon emissions. Most of us recognized there was enough room for schools, commerce, and bike lanes.[79]

Over the next few years, the debate would only intensify as supporters of bike lanes as a solution for a global city would be forced to contend with a new form of Green NIMBYism, in which opponents supported the calls for a greener city—just not in their own backyard.[80] The Department of Transportation continued to implement its plan for the bike paths. In December 2009, Mayor Bloomberg would travel to Copenhagen for the UN Conference on Climate Change 2009. There he hoped to certify his *bona fides* as an innovator of green urbanism. Little did many know, the mayor had also offered a green light to the Department of Transportation to remove the Williamsburg Bedford Bike Lane in exchange for political support. The lane was removed in early December. Several members of Times Up! were already scheduled to attend the climate conference in Copenhagen. A supporter of the group went as far as to boast to the *New York Post* that they would confront the mayor in Copenhagen. The paper ran with that bit. "The city's decision to strip away 14 blocks of bike lanes in Brooklyn is turning into an international crisis," Jeremy Olshen began his report in the *Post*. "When Mayor Bloomberg arrives at the climate-change meetings in Copenhagen Monday he'll be confronted by a group of activists from the borough, demanding to know how an environmentalist can take an anti-cycling stance."

"How can he fly all the way there to talk about being a green mayor when at home he is yanking bike lanes off the streets?" asked Baruch Herzfeld, an unofficial spokesman for the groups of riders who repainted sections of the Bedford Avenue bike lane in protest at the removal."[81] Brooklyn transportation policy was becoming an international story, a media controversy for a global city.

The heat would only increase in 2010 when the city laid out a bike bath along Prospect Park West. I immediately loved the lane, especially when I saw kids who had been in cars, riding their bikes to our daughters' school in September. The Community Board unanimously supported the bike lane.[82] Others felt otherwise. These included Norman Steisel, a deputy mayor from the Dinkins administration, and former transportation commissioner Iris Weinshall, as well as her husband Chuck Schumer, the US senator, who formed a group called Neighbors for Better Bike Lanes, and filed a lawsuit calling for the city to remove the bike lane.[83] While the neighborhood had asked for the lane as a way to make Prospect Park West safer by reducing speeds cars could drive, Neighbors for Better Bike Lanes resented the lane, using ties with the city government to undermine support for it.[84] Over time, evaluations and surveys suggested the lane had achieved its goals.[85] Still, opponents resented the changes. And they were given top billing at City Council hearings and community board meetings about the bike lanes. Along the way, they helped trigger a backlash.[86]

In response, advocates would make the case for bike lanes, applauding efforts to expand the network of bike lanes throughout New York City, noting that bicycles are part of the future of a transportation network for a global city. The practice makes people happy, reduces car congestion, and offers a clear transportation alternative to the Metropolitan Transportation Authority increased fares and compromised service, helping cool a planet suffering from far too many carbon emissions. In short it represents the future of cities.[87]

Yet, the practice is anything but safe. Riding a bike through the city, cyclists are doored, ticketed, and hit by cars. It does not have to be this way. As the New York Department of Health report "Bicyclist Fatalities and Serious Injuries in New York City:1996-2005" lays out, the experience is often contentious. The study notes that cyclist fatalities remain a steady problem. For example: "Between 1996 and 2003, a total of 3,462 NYC bicyclists were seriously injured in crashes with motor vehicles. The annual number of serious bicyclist injuries decreased by 46% during the 8-year period of the report. Between 1996 and 2005, 225 bicyclists died in crashes. Bicyclist deaths remained steady."[88] Since the 2004 Republican National Convention, cycling has been the subject of an inordinate amount of scrutiny and harassment. Cyclists have been violently pulled off their bikes by police and arrested, had their bikes confiscated—all at enormous taxpayer expense.

On May 30, 2008, the Reverend Al Sharpton made this same point before a Critical Mass Ride, organized in honor of Sean Bell, an unarmed New York City resident shot by the NYPD.[89] "We're going to work together to have a Critical Mass in this city where we can ride in justice... so when you ride tonight, we come to stand with you because we must stand together, whether you are white, whether you are black, whether you are Latino or Asian, whether you are fat, skinny, gay, straight: we are all Sean Bell, we are all Critical Mass, we are all here together."[90]

Figure 9: "Supporters of the Prospect Park Bike Lane, including the daughters of this writer." Photo by anonymous.

Cyclists litigated. And the city was found to be guilty of violating cyclists' basic rights. In the Fall of 2010, the city agreed to pay cyclists arrested on Critical Mass rides $965,000.00. Instead of apologizing, the city set its target on cyclists.

Still, the backlash against cycling gained steam.[91] At community board meetings, former deputy mayor Normal Steisel paced up and down with his hands in his suspenders as opponents spoke, only to declare that he promised to litigate. In November 2010, the City Council's Transportation Committee held a hearing on NYC Bike Policy. After hours of one-sided testimony, Brooklyn Borough President Marty Markowitz waltzed in to testify against the Prospect Park West bike lane, without having to wait in line. There he proceeded to sing "My Favorite Things" to the crowd of cycling supporters, who by this time, had been sitting there for three hours, mocking those with concerns about pedestrian or cyclist safety. As he was grandstanding, people who lived around the park and supported the project were forced to stand outside in the cold, waiting for their turn to speak, long after the politicians had left.

On Thursday December 16, 2010 at 9:30 am, the bike clowns, who had staged the pie fight at Prospect Park West, came to Brooklyn Borough Hall dressed in holiday costumes. I carried a sign declaring, "Marty if our of Touch with Brooklyn." And his staff members asked us to leave. So we sang holiday songs, such as "Bikes to the World" to the tune of "Joy to the World," and presented Borough President Markowitz with his holiday gift of a donated bicycle painted gold. The gesture was our response to Markowitz's own clownish behavior at the hearing. In contrast to Markowitz's anti-bike stance, the "Love Your Lanes" clowns' songs featured positive messages about bicycling.

"Markowitz used his time last week to sing a song, rather than give any real facts to explain his opposition to the Prospect Park West Bike Lane," said Barbara Ross of Time's Up! "Meanwhile, a packed house of New Yorkers in favor of more protected bike lanes waited for hours in below-freezing weather for their turn to testify. Many didn't."

"If Marty wants to clown around, we can too," said Ross. "His stance is not shared by most New Yorkers. Marty does his constituents no favors by lacking both knowledge and a desire to be educated on the challenges faced by pedestrians and cyclists alike."

"Don't be a schlemiel Marty, love your bike lanes!" "Come on, get on your bike and ride with us!" I invited, while holding a sign declaring: "Marty is out of Touch with Brooklyn."

While the bike backlash ebbed for most of 2011, by summertime a New York State court dismissed litigation to stop the Prospect Park bike lane. Many of the supporters of the bike lane rejoiced; City Council member Brad Lander, a bike lane supporter, aired a sigh of relief. "I'm glad to put this behind us," he said. "I don't think any of us—on either side of the debate—thought we would be spending so much time debating one mile of green paint."[92] The local papers even called for opponents to call off their appeal and recognize support for the lane.[93] Yet, opponents dragged the case through various appeals for the next five years, before they finally dropped their case. "What saved the bike lane were four things," noted Ben Fried. " the lawsuit's lack of basic merit; the refusal of Council Member Brad Lander, DOT Commissioner Janette Sadik-Khan, and Mayor Bloomberg to cave; the advocates who fought back; and the large number of people who used and appreciated the new design, which worked really well. If, at any point, the city had actually removed the PPW bike lane, the protest would have been enormous."[94] With ridership increasing, it looked like the battle of the bike lanes was waning. Still, other struggles over land use and public space remained.[95]

CONEY ISLAND, THE FALL AND RISE, OR DEMISE OF LOCAL BUSINESSES

Figure 10 and 11: "The old Coney Island." Photos by Brennan Cavanaugh.

Figure 12: "Coney Island subway stairs." Photo by Caroline Shepard.

"Coney Island is discovered one day before Manhattan—in 1609, by Hudson—a clitoral appendage at the mouth of New York's natural harbor," writes Rem Koolhaas in *Delirious New York*. Over time, a collective mythology formed around the space. "In a laughing mirror-image of the seriousness with which the rest of the world is obsessed with Progress, Coney Island attacks the problem of Pleasure, often with the same technological means," Koolhaas continues. This beach came to be seen as queer space, open to everyone. The rich had the Hamptons; the fun people had Coney Island. When the Brooklyn Bridge was erected in 1883, masses of Manhattanites made their way there. "On Summer Sundays, Coney Island's beach becomes the most densely occupied place in the world." With tides of bodies making their way to the shore, the space would have to adapt. "To survive as a resort—a place offering contrast—Coney Island is forced to mutate: it must turn itself into the total opposite of Nature, it has no choice but to counteract the artificiality of the new metropolis with its own Super-Natural," Koolhaas elaborates.[96] Gradually over time, it developed a distinct oddball character as an amusement park, beach, and freak show, with a board over walk of characters, bearded ladies and muscle men, who looked as if they just stepped off a Fellini film set. Some dressed like Mermaids or Polar Bears; others plunged into the cold water every New Years. The space was in constant flux, always shifting, altering, changing, until a long period of decline after

New York's fiscal crisis. Throughout the 2000's, it experienced a resurgence and popularity. Like many neighborhoods in New York, the city rezoned Coney Island in 2009 making plans to do away with older businesses, for a glossier, sanitized version of this quirky space on the Southern tip of Brooklyn.⁹⁷

Figures 13, 14 and 15: "Day, night and a baseball game at Coney Island." Photos by Benjamin Shepard.

Over the next few years, many of the old haunts disappeared.

"It doesn't feel like Coney Island," one of my daughter's friends lamented walking on the boardwalk in 2011. It was the end of summer; my two daughters and I were out for an end of summer ritual—taking in rides and a baseball game at Coney Island. But the iconic kids' rides of Astroland were nowhere to be seen.[98] So we walked and tried to make sense of the mix of the old and new. While Astroland was gone, new rides at its replacement Luna Park were still inviting. They felt like they could be anywhere. Polished and plastic, many did not have the same zany, never never feeling of the older amusements, such as Shoot the Freak, the popular entertainment on the boardwalk which offered participants a chance to shoot paint balls at a man who ran away in a vacant lot down below. Yet, the new rides and arcades were still fun. Over time, we adjusted to find new favorites. The Coney Island of Woody Guthrie and Lawrence Ferlinghetti constantly intermingles with the rezoned entertainment space being created there.[99] After the rides, we stopped by Paul's Daughter, at 1001 Riegelmann Boardwalk, on the way to the Cyclones baseball game. Paul's Daughter, a 41-year-old mom-and-pop restaurant, was one of eight historic businesses told by the city that their leases would not be renewed. Locals dubbed them the Coney Island Eight.[100] Paul's Daughter was being evicted, replaced by corporate chain Sodexo. "Shoot the Freak" was illegally bulldozed. Ruby's Bar was to be replaced by a sports bar. "We don't want the clientele who come to your business," the owners of Paul's Daughter were told after they received "To Whom It May Concern" letters from the city, giving them a month to depart after decades on the boardwalk. The Coney Island Eight litigated, staged protests, and won the right to another summer, which was ending in 2011.[101]

"It's the last hurrah," Al, one of the owners of Paul's Daughter, told me, giving my daughters, who went to school with Paul's granddaughter, free lollipops.

"Are any of you going to stay?"

"No, it's over." Walking over to the Cyclones game, we enjoyed a sunset on the still-pulsing boardwalk.

"New York has always been a wastrel with its cultural treasures," noted writer Kevin Baker witnessing the remapping of Coney Island. "Again and again, we have let unique places vanish, victims of a passing market force or individual whim: the great jazz clubs and jitterbug palaces of Harlem, the Cotton Club ... Ebbets Field."[102] Rather than destroy its history, the city would be well advised to revisit the planning process, inviting ideas for what the space could be. "The dozens of small businesses that stuck it out through Coney Island's worst years and did so much to preserve its honky-tonk flavor should be encouraged to stay."[103] By 2011, it started to look like the city might be learning this lesson. While few actual New Yorkers go to Times Square after its rezoning and purge, the same fate would not befall Coney Island. Rather it bustled with people from all walks of life all summer long.

And they were willing to fight for their own quirky boardwalk. That fall, we'd attend events and rallies in Coney Island, hosted by the Coney Island Eight.[104] Some jazz musicians organized a New Orleans style "Jazz Funeral for Coney Island" with the Jumbalaya Jazz band, featuring a horse, carriage and symbolic coffin. The jazz funeral and second line parade figuratively said good-bye to the old Coney Island, expressing hopes for the rebirth, for the dead to be reborn, before turning into a second line of dancing bodies and musicians celebrating the saints of old and new. Over time, the community events, the BBQs, the parties supporting the Coney Island Eight started to bear results. Crowd after crowd rallied; Savitri D held a hunger strike to try to stop the redevelopment plan.[105] By the fall of 2011, the city would bow to pressure from supporters, giving new leases to Paul's Daughter and other businesses on the boardwalk.[106] The Coney Island Eight prevailed when community pressure made clear the people in Brooklyn wanted them to remain.[107]

Brooklyn of old constantly mingles with Brooklyn of new. Amidst the funeral and rebirth of the old Coney Island and the Russian immigrant mix on Brighton Beach, just down the boardwalk from Coney Island, one can see the ingredients of alternative models for urban development.[108] Certainly, displacement remains. As a vital hub of a global city, Brooklyn has a great deal to learn from other cities. And today, neighborhoods such as Boerum Hill have borrowed from models of other cities such as Berlin where restrictive zoning helps the city retain its unique feel and history.[109] They did this by organizing. While this is hardly a populist solution to beat back inequality, it is one strategy among many to preserve the character of a neighborhood. It is one of many alternative approaches, including the innovative bike lane on Prospect Park West supporting non-polluting transportation, the Zoning Text Amendment in Carroll Gardens, and the fight against Walmart—which bore fruit during this period.

New York works best when it is organized by everybody, Jane Jacobs used to say, emphasizing a bottom-up model of community planning.[110] While certainly not comprehensive, the cases here highlight the work of a small cohort of organizers. They suggest there are ways to create a different kind of global city if citizens organize and engage; there are ways to battle zoning laws (sometimes even using alternative zoning), big-box stores, and city hall through community mobilization, legal advocacy, social networking, research, and a little direct action. This use of a clear goal and organizing through mobilizing, direct action, mobilization, clear communication, and legal strategies point to a winning strategy. Of course, the first case study against the Williamsburg rezoning suggests that the merging of real estate with financial capital creates a formal adversary; especially in a city where land is viewed as a commodity to maximize by the inch.[111] Over and over again, the city is viewed as a growth machine, rather than as a space for convivial social relations. Yet, there are ways to contain it.

In 2011, the Carroll Gardens Zoning Text Amendment forced a skeleton of a building, the 'Hell House' on Carroll Street that stood half developed for nearly a decade, to come down, because it was oversized, and out of character with the rest of the brownstones in the area. When a neighborhood forces big buildings to shrink to a livable scale consistent with neighborhood aesthetics and skylines, that is an effective victory.[112]

Nonetheless, the patterns of displacement continue among those neighborhoods coping with both climate chaos and speculative gentrification. For example, in August of 2011, I found out that some of the prime organizers who had fought the Williamsburg rezoning had been priced out of their own neighborhood, displaced like too many others. "We saw potential beyond a home/office, and when the 2004 Republican National Convention was announced, Not An Alternative was formed, and we started to use the storefront as our headquarters," read a dispatch from Not An Alternative in my mailbox later that week. "Our first major effort involved a series of projects aimed at challenging the 2005 rezoning and gentrification of North Brooklyn. But the neighborhood has changed dramatically since then, and we've had front row seats. The block built up, the foot traffic grew, and so did the rent. The latest hike is the last straw: a 240% rent increase, from $2,500 to $6,000. And so we find ourselves displaced, like countless other spaces, businesses, and residents around here over the years...."[113]

"At our space we were dedicated to how we can leverage our role as hipsters to do something about [gentrification]," said Beka Economopoulos, of Not An Alternative. "But we fell victim to the very narrative that we aimed to intercept."[114]

Some spaces would remain; others would be pushed out as the Brooklyn Wars raged over what the borough would become. "Brooklyn wouldn't look the same today if the city wasn't rezoning everything in sight," argues *Village Voice* writer Neil deMause. He continues:

...but it also would be far different if the housing market weren't governed as it is by a weird amalgam of bare-knuckles market speculation, tax-incentive plans like 421-a, and the tattered remnants of mid-20th-century rent regulations and public housing programs—or, for that matter, if the *New York Times* real estate section were a normal journalistic enterprise instead of operating as a kind of fifth column for the development industry... The Brooklyn wars, then, look like residents and shopkeepers and city planners and moneyed investors all tussling over whether areas like the Fulton Mall or the Sunset Park waterfront will keep serving the people they have in recent decades, or whether they'll be remade to fit, and draw, a more upscale clientele; and they look like the shifting allegiances among residents, amusement park operators, developers, and city officials in Coney Island that helped craft that neighborhood's grand bargain that's still playing out. And they look like every single person who has needed to make a decision: Where will I live, and what will the impact be of that decision? Like all wars, they're hard to sum up easily.[115]

For Brooklyn to thrive as a globalized space, it would help to preserve its cultural resources. Future plans must include more protection for individuals and historic buildings, as well as room for green spaces to help support communities. Recent history helps us understand what kind of a space this will be. The ways the borough coped with Super-Storm Sandy, the focus of the next chapter, suggest the city also has to think more about coping with rising tides.

Chapter seven

Of Tempests and Storms:

Super-Storm Sandy and Climate Chaos in Global Brooklyn

Figure 1: "The morning after the storm."
Photo by Brennan Cavanaugh.

From October 22-31, 2012, Super-Storm Sandy pummeled the East Coast, bringing rising tides, floodwater, and devastation to New York City. Reverend Billy, a.k.a. Bill Talen, a Brooklyn-based performance artist, described the scene as he viewed Frederick Olmsted's majestic Prospect Park the morning after the storm.

I'm standing in our doorway at dusk, looking out at the branches strewn up and down the street, hanging over the edges of the roofs. They look like imploring arms, like veins of dark lightning. With me is our 2-year-old Lena. She hugs my leg and catches my eye with a look from the center of the world.
I live in New York City with my partner Savitri and our Lena. We have our place, near Prospect Park. There are 20 million people around here and some of us are in terrible torment. Regardless of what we're doing, we all have storming going on inside us a week later. It is a strange feeling that our city was swallowed by something so dark and huge, with the name of a 50's teenager. The way the house groaned and whistled.
I can still feel it. Lena? You seem to have moved on.[1]

Many had a much harder time moving on than Lena. The storm seemed to be in all of us. Everyone had stories about their storm night. Some lost homes and livelihoods to the most recent tide that crashed on the shores of this global borough. Eighteen died, while thousands of others were left homeless. Many went for weeks without electricity, living in dark, mold-filled apartments.

In the weeks to follow, many marveled at the ways—both good and bad—that the city responded to the hurricane disaster. Before Sandy, we already knew just how top-down, cold and indifferent the city tends to be to the needs of the disenfranchised; witness the edict by the Bloomberg administration against feeding the homeless (that seemed to have little impact on homeless groups who continued to provide free meals throughout New York). This indifference manifested itself most visibly after the devastation of Hurricane Sandy, as city, state and federal aid lagged behind that of grassroots mutual aid groups, such as Occupy Wall Street's offshoot, Occupy Sandy. The process grew over the next twelve months as New York had its own Katrina moment. From the earliest days of OWS, the movement highlighted the power of mutual aid networks, in which people shared ideas and resources, friendships and material aid. When Occupy was kicked out of Zucotti Park a year prior, it had already been spreading citywide, with working groups reaching out across the city. In the weeks after the storm, local and global movements dovetailed with waves of creative direct action and mutual aid.

Figure 2 and 3: "Kids in Carroll Gardens after the storm." Photos by Benjamin Shepard.

At the end of Shakespeare's *The Tempest*, the storm forces characters to reflect on who they are.

> Our revels now are ended. These our actors,
> As I foretold you, were all spirits, and
> Are melted into air, into thin air:
> And like the baseless fabric of this vision,
> The cloud-capp'd tow'rs, the gorgeous palaces,
> The solemn temples, the great globe itself,
> Yea, all which it inherit, shall dissolve,
> And, like this unsubstantial pageant faded,
> Leave not a rack behind. We are such stuff
> As dreams are made on. And our little life
> Is rounded with a sleep.[2]

The storm brought dissolution of lives and property, as a lack of vision impaired action from those in the halls of government. So many stepped up. With lives and fortunes "melted into air," regular folks responded to New York's tempest, helping us reimagine what a city could look like, the way it could function, the way people could care, the way people could transport themselves, and share what they have.[3] This interconnected "we" is such stuff as dreams are made of. This seventh chapter of *Brooklyn Tides* considers the story of some of the innovative responses of people coping with the rising tides crashing on the city's shores.[4] And this time, it wasn't just metaphorical; the tides were literal.

Immediately after the storm, Occupy started organizing relief efforts, while Time's Up! started Fossil Fuel Disaster Relief bike rides to deliver food, blankets, bike-powered charging stations, and mobile bike-repair units to neighborhoods devastated by Sandy. Time's Up! used its fleet of bike-trailers and cargo-bikes to make such deliveries from Occupy Sandy centers in churches across Brooklyn.

"We believe in the power of the people and we believe in creating a sustainable future without destructive fossil fuels!" explained Monica Hunken, one of the organizers of the relief rides.

*Figure 4. "Monica Hunken involved in relief efforts at an Occupy Sandy station."
Photo by Benjamin Shepard.*

"The idea is to offer relief to people who are cold and hungry today and to address the root cause of this disaster at the same time, so that fewer people will go through this in the future," explained Keegan Stephan, who helped organize the relief rides.[5] "All this devastation is the direct result of burning fossil fuels. We should not ignore this while trying to help those who have been devastated. That is why Time's Up! is offering sustainable alternatives to energy-production and transportation as well as delivering food and blankets."

Throughout November, Time's Up! brought food and supplies out to Rockaway with a hub set up in the empty lot across the street from Veggie Island at Beach 96th Street and Rockaway Boulevard. After the first Saturday ride, Jackie Junttonen, a participant on the ride, wrote: "Thank you, Time's Up!, for organizing a steadfast and well executed show of support to NYC. Today was the first of the Fossil Fuel Disaster Relief Rides. Over 20 cyclists with bike trailers and panniers converged from the five boroughs to deliver Occupy Sandy donations to families without electricity, heat and other basic services. We rode *en masse* from Williamsburg to the Rockaways, offered help with cleanup, distributed food, blankets and necessities, charged many cell phones with pedal power energy, and offered free bike mechanic services."

Sunday, the ride destination was altered, taking riders back to the Rockaways instead of Staten Island. "There are many reasons for this," noted

Keegan. "Bicycles are more useful in the Rockaways than on Staten Island. The Rockaways are gridlocked. It takes cars two hours to make deliveries, whereas bikes can make deliveries in less than 15 minutes. On Staten Island, cars are making deliveries faster than bikes."

I (Ben Shepard) joined the Monday ride, words from *The Tempest* warming my insides. I felt like I was floating. My friend Sarah, from the Occupy Wall Street Sustainability Committee, was there to send us off. She talked about the need for bioremediation. We have tools to clean up and remove pollutants from communities around the city, she explained. Levees and sea walls won't do it, she suggested. We will need to rebuild the marshlands around New York. Wonderful things happen when communities face these challenges. We rebuild cities from the ashes and floodwaters. Kids squatted buildings and rebuilt housing in New Orleans after Katrina. Here in New York, we are already re-imagining what our city could look like.[6]

Much of this was on my mind as we rode our bikes to the Hurricane Sandy Emergency Relief Station. Arriving at the Church of St Luke and St Matthew at 520 Clinton Avenue, in Prospect Heights, the makeshift Occupy Sandy hurricane supply hub, I was greeted by my friend LA Kauffman.[7] She had brought her kids after doing relief work all day long. Kauffman is one of the organizers who helped me see the radical potential of a community garden.[8] Today these spaces are more important than ever. They provide food security and oxygen, while helping us reduce asthma and crime.

In front of the church-turned-relief station, a sign declared "Mutual Aid Not Charity." There, countless activists talked about the idea that recovery had to involve a different model than charity, which seems to put a Band-Aid on the problem, while leaving structures of oppression still in place. Mutual aid involves creating a different set of engagements, which involve connections and networks of support rather than power imbalances or dependencies. Here everyone helps each other.

Figure 5: "'Mutual Aid Not Charity' sign at Occupy Sandy, 520 Clinton Avenue."
Photo by Benjamin Shepard.

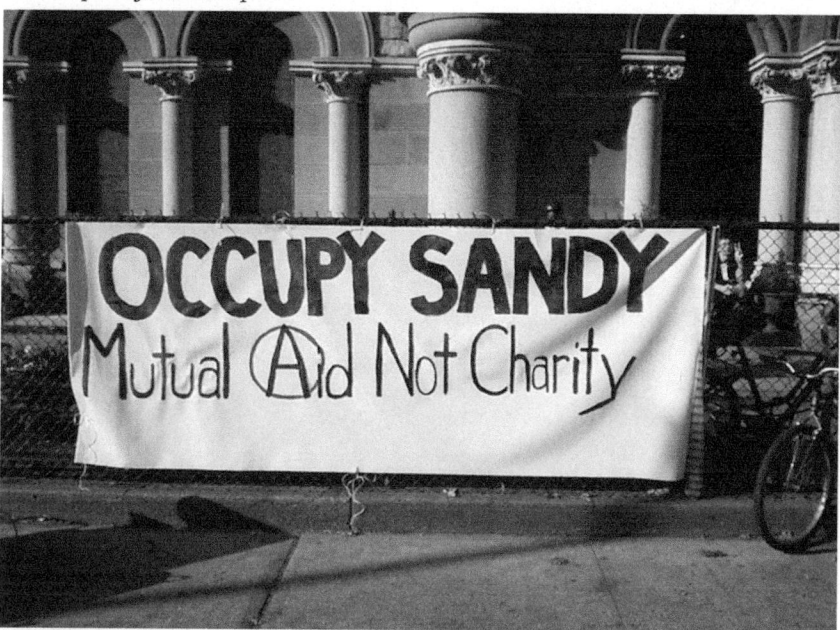

Figure 6: "A well-organized Occupy Sandy relief station."
Photo by Benjamin Shepard.

The Occupy Sandy station inside the church was pulsing with volunteers, pointing people to drop-off areas for new supplies, coordinating supplies for those going out to the Rockaways, Coney Island and Staten Island, and orienting new volunteers. Longtime activists and neighborhood people were there to help, along with kids home for Veterans Day. FEMA (the Federal Emergency Management Agency) was nowhere in sight. As the team rode down Flatbush Avenue to Fort Tilden and the Rockaways, we passed cars parked in bike lanes, waiting for gas.

Figures 7, 8 and 9: "Occupy Sandy relief ride." Photos by Benjamin Shepard.

Chapter seven: Of Tempests and Storms 173

Arriving in the Rockaways, it felt like this part of New York City was a war zone—fire engines and police cars lined streets filled with debris, in front of houses with no electricity. The damage from the storm was only intensifying in areas such as Coney Island, Staten Island and the Rockaways. Two weeks after Super-Storm Sandy, people in Brooklyn and Staten Island were still without electricity or heat. Many relied entirely on grassroots support efforts organized through Occupy Sandy. Countless members of the movement had joined in the people's recovery, offering alternatives to corporate approaches, that seemed to exacerbate the social inequalities exposed by the storm and its aftermath.

Those in public housing in Coney Island were left to make due without electricity as mold started to form. "The buildings didn't look so bad on the outside, but when you opened the door you saw the consequences of what happened and saw what people needed," related Williams Cole, who volunteered with Occupy Sandy and later started the People's Relief Project. Early on, he saw that while FEMA and the Red Cross seemed slow to do outreach to people in these spaces; this was desperately needed. "The stairwells were pitch black and smelled like urine and feces and the apartments had no heat, hot water, power, working elevators, or working septic systems."[9] So Williams and company started organizing outreach to communities in need, delivering supplies. By December the city was putting eviction notices on residents' doors for not paying their rent. (They later relented.) Regardless, the storm had exposed something ugly about the way the city leaves those most vulnerable to fend for themselves.

"After touring only a few of the devastated areas in NYC—the Rockaways, Sheepshead Bay—it is clear that New York is not ready for the devastating effects of extreme weather," argued Josh Fox, director of the documentary film *Gasland* in a post on Facebook:

Seeing Riis Park turned into a massive landfill of rubble, the ruins of houses from Breezy Point, it is almost too much to bear. To think that this type of destruction goes all the way up the East Coast is beyond what any film could encompass. We have to get serious about reducing emissions, folks, or else we will continue to watch our coastal areas damaged beyond recognition. Hats off to the remarkable work that Occupy Sandy is doing to provide mutual aid. Hundreds of thousands of meals provided, tens of thousands of volunteers, medical clinics, relief supply distribution...amazing to see what non-hierarchical leadership can provide. Power to the people y'all. Stop climate change. Prevent the next Hurricane Exxon.

Chapter seven: Of Tempests and Storms   175

Figures 10 and 11: "Rockaway Sandy Relief Supply areas."
Photos by Benjamin Shepard.

Riding past Rockaway Taco, a taco-shack/make shift relief hub, people cheered for the cyclists delivering supplies. Arriving, cyclists canvassed the area, delivering supplies to people's homes. After hugs and thank you's, I had to turn around so I could make it back to Downtown Brooklyn in time to teach my 2:30 pm class. Many of our students at City Tech who live in the Rockaways were impacted; without subway service they had to take shuttles and ferries. Yet they coped, navigating the city through their own networks of support. Somehow, the storm reminded us there are other ways to live; with everyone taking action, we could see there was love among the ruins.

Figures 12 and 13: "The Rockaways felt like ruins after the storm." Photos by Benjamin Shepard.

ENERGY BIKES, MUTUAL AID, AND AUTONOMOUS POWER

More relief rides were scheduled for the next few weekends. Time's Up! built ten energy bikes, which we brought to Veggie Island, where the group stationed themselves. "Not only will we provide relief from this disaster, but we will work to prevent more disasters in the future," said Keegan.

Of course, there were those who questioned the use of bikes to transport or clean up the impacted coasts. "You don't handle a gunshot wound with more guns. You need to inspire people," stated Joe Sharkey, who participated in the rides. "After the blackout, we saw the need for bikes as opposed to cars," explained Joe. "Burning fuel to move a car is not efficient. Bikes are more efficient," he continued, pointing out that the solution had to include a critique of the source of the problem. "We have to go after the fossil fuel companies head on and tell them they cannot destroy the world," noted writer Naomi Klein, after taking part in Occupy Sandy relief efforts.

Gandhi was famous for leading his followers to make salt, even if it meant facing arrest and forcing a change in laws. The campaign, the Salt Satyagraha, challenged a British salt tax, when the English still ruled India with colonial law. The campaign began with the Salt March to the coastal village of Dandi in 1930. It was a vital step in the march to the end of colonial rule in India.[10] Gandhi implored his followers to spin their own fabric and boycott British textiles in defiance of colonial rule. In doing so, he suggested they could create their own power. Energy emanated from spinning their own cotton to create their own clothing. "The spinning wheel represents to me the hope of the masses," stated Gandhi. The same thing happens with people-powered energy—cycling events and energy bikes, recharging people's phones, while sharing our lives with others.

Such gestures propose a different set of expectations; they ask us all to share, to be fully human. "I just really enjoy it," explained one of the riders, after one of the relief rides. "You can't say I am not getting something out of this."

With these expanding mutual-aid networks in mind, Alexandre Carvalho, of the Occupy Revolutionary Games Working Group, sent out a post on the group's listserve:

I really see the advent of Occupy Sandy as the beautiful religare to Occupy's spirit of Zuccotti Park. A relational atmosphere that was missing from the scene in a while and is the cornerstone of what we do—a deep respect and solidarity with human beings in suffering, first and foremost ... meaningful movements have Lost Paradises, certain lost times, which serve as an ethical compass for political dispositions. The park is our Paradise Lost. That eerie smooth human atmosphere that is at the core of what makes us human. The parks and streets and communities of the world are our roving Paradises—this time, Paradises that can be found and built together.

Aristotle once wrote that *poiesis* is to "learn by making." The new Mutual Aid network of Occupy Wall Street should stay even after the destruction of the hurricane is over and done: there will always be natural disasters, and human-caused disasters to struggle side-by-side against, such as poverty, oppression, violence, environmental degradation, labor exploitation, injustice.

Reflecting on the uses of Mutual Aid, Alexandre referred to the absurdist spirit of the Dada movement:

MADA this,
MADA that
NADA this
DADA that!
Mutual Aid as Direct Action is a meme that wants to fly.

Much of this spirit powered our ride down Bergen Street and across Brooklyn on Flatbush Avenue to the Rockaways. "It was a wonderful ride," said my friend JC as we crossed the bridge to Jacob Riis Park, where piles of rubbish filled what was once a putt-putt golf course. "That's so telling of our culture," mused JC.

The rambunctious ride was enjoyed by kids, animal lovers, and cyclists. "Love seemed to emanate from that ride," he added.

Delivering supplies, we found homes covered with sand and houses abandoned—many were forced to leave their homes. Others stayed the course and tried to clean up the mold damaging their homes in the affected areas.[11] Doing so, everyone involved was building a model of sustainable urbanism based on mutual aid, care, non-polluting transportation, wind, solar power, renewables, and people powered energy.[12] The solutions to global warming seemed to be in front of our eyes. These elements could be found where people rode to deliver supplies, planted urban farms, organized and supported each other.

Adapting to Change

In the days after Hurricane Sandy, it became clear that we all had to adapt to a new reality of life in the city. This was not only about a single storm that ruined lives and property, but about life over time—how to sustain it and improve it along a city bracketed by water. Over the next few months, we organized countless relief rides and events to share ideas about the ways the city needed to adjust to the evolving and encroaching realities of climate change. The rides took us through the community gardens, along the waterfront, past locations for sewage overflow, through ways to reimagine what the city would be if sea levels continued to rise. Along the way, we reflected on the steps, stories, and experiences of countless friends throughout the city, as we re-assessed what New York's hyper-development onto marshlands meant, wondering if the city needed to take a different route in which it recognized the city's true ecological footprint.[13]

For December's "Adapting to Change" ride we met in Tompkins Square Park in Manhattan's East Village. Wendy from Green Map was there to greet everyone. We talked about the lessons of the storm waters that surged throughout the city, heralding a new twenty-first-century reality, discussing responses that increase livability, as well as long-term planning options for a more resilient city. She pulled out a 17th-century map of New York City, showing that much of the Lower East Side of Manhattan was once a marshland. We toured along the waterfront, looking at various green projects and buildings, imagining what a more sustainable model of a city would be like, if we had more community gardens to provide natural irrigation systems and more marshes to absorb the storm surge, among other solutions that could mitigate the realities of climate change.

"The Atlantic coastline of the United States is a global hotspot for sea level rise, with predicted rates in some areas more than two times higher than the global average," writes the Nature Conservancy, describing the benefits the tidal marshes Brewer talked about our ride.[2] "Among the most productive ecosystems on earth, tidal wetlands perform many functions that are highly valued by society, called 'ecosystem services.' Wetlands protect coastal water quality by filtering land-derived nutrients and contaminants; they are an important component of the coastal food web; they provide valuable wildlife habitat; and they protect upland and shoreline areas from flooding and erosion associated with storms. In sum, wetlands support the health of our coastal ecosystem and the recreational and economic activities that depend on it."[14]

The tours of the rapidly transforming city would last throughout the spring and summer. On a Friday in the spring of 2013, a group from my college took a trip out to Sheepshead Bay, to check out where the progress of the community was after a rough few months since Sandy. We were there to pilot surveys for disaster-preparedness. Instead of riding a bike, I took the subway from Park Slope to Brooklyn College, where my ten-mile trip dropped me off a few miles short of our destination. Watching the B44 buses pass me by at the connecting stop, the reality of this community's isolation from the rest of the city was daunting. I ran down Nostrand Avenue from Avenue H to Z to the bay, got off, and ran the rest of the way. The 45-minute jog offered ample time to reflect on the limitations of the woefully inadequate transit system out there, which along with many cars, broke down during the storm. We met at a diner, where we paired off with community partners from local organizations. Fran took us down her block where the water rose some four feet during the storm, just gushing down the street to her home. Those who did not leave immediately were left to fend for themselves without electricity for months. While the Federal Emergency Management Agency (FEMA) and Red Cross were nowhere to be found, Occupy Sandy arrived the day after the storm. Most of Fran's street was heightened during construction and repairs in the 1970's. The same could not be said of the Courts, a housing development that runs below street level between streets, and is inaccessible to most automobiles. While water flooded the basements on Fran's street, it ran up to the first and second floors on the Courts, leaving folks stranded for days while their apartments filled with water.

Fran and her neighbors smoked cigarettes and swapped stories. They had been through a lot. Far too many impacted communities were left out in the cold, they recalled, especially during the long cold winter. Most everyone they knew stayed for the storm. What of the weakest, the most vulnerable, the disabled or elderly on the block, where were they to go? Few had any desire to leave, so they survived with the support of their neighbors.

That Fall of 2013, we went for another tour, exploring the ways in which the Brooklyn neighborhood of Red Hook was coping with the storm a year later. We met residents who talked about how useful the hashtag #occupysandy had been for organizing recovery projects, pointing those on Twitter to spaces in need of immediate support, where volunteers could lend a hand. We visited the Red Hook Winery, which was completely demolished by the floodwaters. Several on the tour asked why they planned to stay along the waterfront.

Figure 14: "Water largely flooded the Courts where people were left hoping for assistance." Photo by Benjamin Shepard.

Figure 15: "Red Hook residents sharing food on the street after the storm." Photo by Benjamin Shepard.

My colleague Richard Hanley wrote in an email that he'd talked with the owners after I left. "They had a real Brooklyn tenacity," he related. "They said that they knew that in the long run they would be defeated; they would lose. They also love doing what they are doing where they are doing it, so they will keep fighting until they can't fight anymore—until they can't afford to come back." Richard suggested the interaction conjured up a scene from Yeats's play *On Baile's Strand*. "The play ends with the tragic hero, Cuchulainn, walking into the sea battling the waves with only his sword. They are like Cuchulainn; they will go out battling the waves."

"We're all battling against the tides," I rejoined.

Figure 16: "Red Hook, Brooklyn graffiti: 'Give it your best, Sandy.'"
Photo by Benjamin Shepard.

Years after the storm, impacted communities in the projects and all over Red Hook, in the Rockaways, and on Staten Island are still coping with its ravages. The storm and the city's response to it highlighted a vexing challenge of mixed neighborhoods of people of different classes living together, who are rarely treated equally. The storm impacted far more than a winery; it left people stranded in desolated public housing. And while it might be easy to move a single business, it is not easy to move the Red Hook Houses (or other public housing built along the Brooklyn waterfront throughout the 20th century). The storm reminded everyone that we live in a delicate ecosystem worth protecting and supporting. It also highlighted the need for public commons, the spaces where Occupy Sandy met and organizing took place. Our meetings expanded a conversation about food security and sustainable urbanism which would take place long after the storm. Forcing action, the storm pointed us toward an image of a healthier, more integrated city, driven by civil engagement and the power of organizing. After all, Brooklyn is the globe, the globe is Brooklyn. They cannot be separated.

Figure 17: "Clothes, shoes drop-off in the Rockaways." Photo by Caroline Shepard.

Figure 18: "*The Gateway National Recreation area Fort Tilden, where the beach reclaimed homes after Hurricane Sandy.*" *Photo by Benjamin Shepard.*

Chapter eight

Community Gardening, Creative Activism, and the Struggle for Open Space

Figure 1: No trespassing signs are everywhere in Brooklyn, with public spaces cordoned off. Photo by Benjamin Shepard.

For much of the 19th century, Brooklyn was an agricultural community, transformed by the region's industrial development in the post-bellum period. In recent years, activists and scholars have come to wonder if there is another path for the borough beyond over-development. Gardens are the seminal heterotopias, spaces where people from different places connect, build community, and support a model for what sustainable urban spaces can be.

They are also places where water recedes into the ground after a rain or flooding, providing natural irrigation systems. These are also spaces where those without their own backyards or country homes can share, support each other, grow food, connect with the earth, and create the sort of "eyes on the street" Jane Jacobs said was necessary for healthy neighborhoods to thrive.[1] Here, use is valued over exchange. For this they are viewed as a threat to those who see urban space as something from which to maximize profit by the inch.[2] As necessary as green spaces are, today it is easy to wonder if there is still room for them in this global borough. Throughout this volume we've considered the social, cultural, and ecological costs of Brooklyn's massive redevelopment, while suggesting there could be a different route toward a more ecologically balanced, livable, community-based model for this space. Could there be another story? Will this global borough follow a path toward more ecological disrepair or sustainable urbanism?[3] To consider this question, we consider some of the recent struggles for green spaces here.

Social movements are often sources for solutions. After all, creative activism is fundamentally about telling many different kinds of stories, engaging the polyglot nature of our society rather than submitting to the limitations of a single narrative. Here, the practice of activism aims at transforming urban spaces into living, breathing, mutable works of art.[4] Some look to paintbrushes and graffiti. Others use bodies or public spaces. George McKay and Zack Furness look to gardening and cycling as ways of creating new models of sustainable urbanism. Claire Nettle and McKay fashion gardening as a form of resistance culture, as a model of social action.[5]

These stories point to forms of activism that impact everyday life. One need not purchase a train or airplane ticket or use sick days to participate in these forms of activism, which are transforming cities the world over. Everyone can take part, shaping the spaces where we live as works of art. All you have to do is get on your bike and ride, pull out a can of spray paint, a shovel, or a bolt cutter. This was certainly the point during the months of March, April, and May 2013 when I (Ben Shepard) worked with a group of cyclists and garden activists to create a community garden in Williamsburg, a neighborhood in North Brooklyn where gentrification and over-development has robbed the community of much-needed open space. The aim was to create an open place for dialogue, bicycle repairs, and ecological awareness.

Cyclists and gardeners have long worked with each other. Critical Mass rides themed around the community gardens were popular events throughout the late 1990's in New York City. Through this collaboration, the community gardeners created their own Central Park out of the rubble of New York's fiscal crisis. Thanks to determined advocacy and direct action, they have become a long-term staple of New York City.[6] Along the way, they propelled a new wave of environmental activism in Brooklyn and around New York City.[7] This eighth chapter of *Brooklyn Tides* considers efforts to create this new community garden and defend other green spaces, framing this struggle as part of a larger push to create open spaces for ideas and remediation, as well as a sustainable future in this global borough.

GARDEN PLANNING AND OUTREACH

Figure 2: "Outreach sign for Nothing Yet Garden." Photo by Benjamin Shepard.

The story of the Williamsburg garden began in January 2013 when a group from Times Up! environmental group started making plans to plant in a vacant lot. Over the previous weeks, we'd brought bags of donated dirt from Queens into a garden space, digging out piles of bricks from the rubble of the Lower East Side vacant lot. The goal was to turn this mess into a space where a garden could grow. We then put together a conveyor belt of bodies to move the thousands of pounds of dirt throughout the garden. It felt so good to be part of the process of creating a garden out of nothing. The gardeners later dubbed the space *Siempre Verde* (always green).

Finishing the clean-up, a smaller crew of us rode out to scout out other vacant lots, identified on the 596 Acres organization's watched lot list, to create a new garden in Brooklyn, just as we had done in Manhattan. We rode throughout Williamsburg, down Bedford Avenue to Division Avenue, up Berry Street, and down to the waterfront, searching for the right sweet spot on which to support the ever-mutable, ever-changing work of art which is the city of New York and its pulsing communities full of art, color, murals, storms, people, and big plans.

We climbed through fences locking regular people from the waterfront. Fences are all about capitalism, an attempt to re-make Brooklyn as the "Walled City" it once was. Jumping through and finding secret spots is part of the joy of resisting the privatization of public space. Finishing the tour, we talked about what we hoped to create and which lot seemed most amenable to future gardening. Given that all the lots we'd seen were spoken for in one way or another, by April we decided to start gardening in the space directly below the Williamsburg Bridge on South 5th Street.

Creating the Nothing Yet Garden and the Fight for Green Open Space

For years now, Brooklynites have been enjoying community gardens; though they often found themselves fighting for these pieces of free space in a city of social controls, condos, and developer-driven politics. Every green space seemed to be involved in a fight over what it was going to be, who was to control and profit from it.

My life as a gardener and public-space advocate in New York came in several phases—the first being the period when I initially recognized gardens as vital pieces of public space in the late 1990's when the mayor was planning to auction off and bulldoze gardens, such as Esperanza on East 7th Street and Chico Mendez on 9th Street, both on Manhattan's Lower East Side.[8] Shortly after Esperanza was bulldozed, my girlfriend and I moved to Carroll Gardens in Brooklyn, enjoying a green patch in the back of the house though it was not the same as a community garden. In subsequent years, I enjoyed watching the gardens become a part of life in New York.[9] Unlike Brooklyn Bridge Park, Prospect Park, or Central Park, these are oases in neighborhoods with fewer open spaces, often far from the big parks. They serve lower-income neighborhoods, including immigrants from the Caribbean and migrants from the U.S. South, helping those living in this concrete jungle to connect with the earth, to plant food, and learn about their environment. For many, gardens represent the future of cities. Supporters point to an extraordinary social rate of return for community gardens—reduced crime, increased community cohesiveness, food security, resiliency, and environmental action.[10] Despite this, throughout the last decade, neighborhood after neighborhood in New York has been re-zoned, with developer interests trumping neighborhood needs. All through the process, gardens and green spaces have been replaced by concrete, while countless others face constant threats. When the Brooklyn neighborhood of Williamsburg was re-zoned in 2005, the city ignored the

Community 197A Plan to increase open space, instead favoring 22 40-story condos along the waterfront, with no increased public space, green space, schools, or transportation. "Gentrification on steroids" is how neighborhood members described the plan which mandated no minimum of affordable housing units, privatized access to the waterfront, failed to expand the amount of open space or park space, and increased the population of Williamsburg/Greenpoint by 40,000 without addressing resultant infrastructural needs.

Figure 3: "A crowded Brooklyn Waterfront." Photo by Benjamin Shepard.

Faced with developer-driven planning models transforming the city's distinct neighbor-hoods into retail outlets of "NYC Inc.", residents fought back, with regular people cobbling together plans to build new gardens across Brooklyn and New York.[11] Helping the effort, 596Acres unleashed a powerful weapon as activists throughout the city took to logging onto their website to scour the vacant lots in their neighborhoods in search of potential green spaces.

After the experience at *Siempre Verde*, which quickly won support from the community board,[12] the plan was to do the same thing in Brooklyn. We identified our lot on the 596 Acres list and put out a call for support for the guerrilla gardening action:

Groundbreaking Day Is Tomorrow, Come One Come All!!!
2PM, 99 S 5TH ST, Williamsburg Brooklyn, between Bedford and Berry!

Bring shovels, rakes, hammers, nails, screws, scrap wood, wheelbarrows, plants, paints, brushes, and whatever else you have to beautify a vacant lot! We will be cleaning up trash, clearing the soil, making paths with rocks, setting up composting, painting walls and wood, barbequing, organizing, and so much more. Please join us for this historic day of fun!!!

The day of the guerrilla gardening, I drove up to Friends of Brook Park in the Bronx to pick up supplies. Legendary gardener Harry Bubbins, one of the founders of the More Gardens! coalition was there to greet me. He told me I could use whatever I needed from the Bronx garden to start one in Brooklyn. You are the city, he reminded me; regular people have a right to impact their own spaces. Harry gave our group a few plants with which to get started.

Arriving back at South 5th Street in Brooklyn, volunteers were already filling the garden with energy, cleaning out trash, planting flowers, and organizing. We talked, cleaned, and listened to music as we made a day of guerrilla gardening, dancing as we ran wheel-barrows around the space. Late in the afternoon, we held a small meeting, talking about what we wanted to see happen in the space. Some talked about using the space for a sculpture garden. Others talked about creating a performance space. We agreed we would rather have an open garden than individual plots. And finally, we would meet the following Sunday for another work day, inviting everyone in the neighborhood for a BBQ.

Figures 4 and 5: "The first NOTHING YET meeting and outreach." Photos By Barbara Ross.

Chapter eight: Community Gardening, Creative Activism 191

Throughout the afternoon, I collected signatures from people walking by that we planned to bring to the community board. Almost everyone was excited about the space and our plans to open it for everyone. Others were concerned that Los Sures, a non-profit organization that focuses on affordable housing, had won a bid to build low-income housing there. Housing is a human right, we all know and agree with this. Yet surely there is room for gardens and housing. This is what healthy communities are all about—places for people to hang out, where flowers can grow, and we can nourish ourselves and our neighbors. Everyone talked about how the neighborhood needs more open spaces for everyone, not fewer, more flowers and fewer towers.[13]

LACKING OPEN SPACE: THE CASE FOR NOTHING-YET COMMUNITY GARDEN

Starting a garden is not that complicated. Every city is different, but in New York, the steps include: finding a plot of land, looking into who owns it, researching what plans might exist for it, and connecting with others interested in a particular lot. It is is very much a process of direct action: cutting fences, clearing out the rubble, testing the soil, planting some seeds, watering them, and sharing your love for the space as things start to grow. From the beginning, bring as many people into the process as possible. For community gardens to thrive, they need to be open spaces where everyone feels like they can take part.

So invite people in, collect their signatures, rally, organize supporters, write to the local community board, get on their next meeting's agenda; see if you can impress them with your plans and earn their support.[14] Keeping gardens, on the other hand—now that is a little more complicated.

Figure 6: "Nothing Yet Gardeners in action." Photo by Benjamin Shepard.

When Time's Up! announced plans for the space we called "Nothing Yet Garden" some suggested the group wait to find out what the city planned to do with the lot, and that we should not be surprised if the lot is bulldozed. Yet, playing by the city's rules does not always produce results. For years, open-space advocates played by the rules of the city in Williamsburg and Greenpoint. We created a 197A Community Plan calling for open space, got it approved by the Community Board and it was promptly ignored by the city, which went ahead with its own re-zoning plan in 2005. Yet there was a condition in support of re-zoning—that the city create affordable housing and badly needed open green space. In subsequent years, plans for open space lingered and stalled.

A *Wall Street Journal* article from 2012 concerning this rezoning was aptly titled "Brooklyn Awaits a Park." In it, the city admitted that follow through on commitments to add green space to Williamsburg and Greenpoint had yet to materialize. The article specifically noted that:

A plan to remake Williamsburg and Greenpoint with gleaming luxury apartment towers was sold to a skeptical community seven years ago with the promise of new waterfront parks and 3,500 "affordable housing" units.[15]

But with about 18 months left in Mayor Michael Bloomberg's last term, few of those plans had materialized, and community leaders in North Brooklyn were concerned they were running out of time. "They made these commitments, and as a result we rezoned the last large swath of industrial waterfront," said City Councilman Stephen Levin, who represents the area. "The community wants to know and I want to know, 'What's the plan?'"[16] It has become a familiar scenario across the city, as large developments such as Atlantic Yards in Brooklyn and Willets Point in Queens move forward: the promises made by the city and developers to overcome opposition are delayed long into the future. In northern Brooklyn, community leaders said they were particularly concerned about the status of Bushwick Inlet Park, a proposed 28-acre space that would connect Williamsburg and Greenpoint and feature a running path, playgrounds, and waterfront views. The Bloomberg administration acquired about half of the 28 acres; the rest of the property would not be purchased until November 2016.[17] By the time we started the garden, only a soccer field had been built on the southern tip of the proposed park area. Since the 2004 rezoning we fought, the city failed to follow up on their plans to create open spaces.

In its statement of community needs, Community Board 1 in Greenpoint/Williamsburg noted that expanding parkland was a priority. The Williamsburg/Greenpoint Open Space Plan specifically noted:

Brooklyn Community District One's population is 160,000, equivalent to a small American city, with 38,000 in Greenpoint and 44,000 in Williamsburg living proximate to the waterfront (west of the Brooklyn Queens Expressway). With city-proposed rezoning, massive development will bring the district's total population to as much as 200,000 within the lifetime of today's youth. Community District One currently ranks near the bottom of the list in open space per capita, with .06 acres per 1,000 residents.... [A]fter a population increase of 25 percent and a waterfront newly occupied by 22 high-rise towers the community will be back where it started; seriously underserved for park space.[18]

This is part of why supporters suggested the city should support the Nothing Yet garden with a lease. But over and over, community gardeners are told that the need for affordable housing trumps the need for gardens, as if this is a zero-sum game, an either/or. Most of the housing provided in such projects is for median income, listed in Manhattan as about $75,000 and Brooklyn as about $50,000. NYC as a whole has a median income of about $61,000. This does not constitute housing for lower or even middle-income people. These housing deals are not available to most people who live in Brooklyn.

Figures 7, 8, and 9: "Gardening days at Nothing Yet Garden."
Photos by Benjamin Shepard.

Chapter eight: Community Gardening, Creative Activism   195

At a subsequent garden clean up day at *Siempre Verde* garden, the gardeners shared advice about strategy, experience, as well as wheelbarrows. They are the model for a successful community garden. The gardeners suggested that we reach out the community board and get in their agenda, which we planned to do. After some gardening there, I rode over to Williamsburg to join the garden cleanup which was already going on. Some of the bulbs and bushes from Friends of Brook Park were already planted. And gardeners from all over the neighborhood joined us. Friends from Occupy stopped by, as we planned and planted, sharing sweat equity to support something better for Willaimsburg.

I talked with a hundreds of people on the street about the project. They all said the same thing: Williamsburg needs green space and not more towers.

"Today was next to perfect," Keegan, one of the organizers, posted later, after the work day. "After a scare this morning, our garden clean-up was fantastic, planted a pumpkin patch, started a compost pile, received a wheelbarrow donation, cleaned more dirt, painted a new sign, created a seating area, and had a productive meeting. More neighbors are getting involved every day. We have collected more than 200 signatures. We are looking for donations of a long hose, more shovels and rakes, materials/knowledge for building benches, tables, a tool shed, and more. We really need someone to research our community board meetings so we can start going. We will meet every Sunday from here on out at 2pm!"

The next day, a worker from the city took down our new sign for the garden. It was Earth Day. That evening, we organized a garden ride, throwing seed bombs through fences into gardens and vacant lots throughout the neighborhood. "One, Two, Three, More Gardens!" we screamed, hurling the seeds.

Spring Bulldozers

Things were going well in the garden when I traveled to Prague in May of 2013. Walking through Wenceslas Square, site of the Velvet Revolution rallies, as well as the space where the Soviet tanks rolled during the repression of the Prague Spring in 1968, little did I know that bulldozers were moving in on the Nothing Yet Garden we had created over the previous weeks in Williamsburg. Instead of the tanks which crushed "socialism with a human face," bulldozers destroyed our little garden, where we hoped to bring a little humanity to our capitalist city.[19]

Keegan posted a note at 596 Acres: "On May 22, 2013 HPD [Housing Preservation and Development] announced that North Brooklyn Development Corporation had won the RFP [request for proposals] and would be developing the lot this year. After finding out about the RFP announcement, Time's Up volunteers were eager to talk to North Brooklyn Development Corporation and find out if they would permit the garden until development started, or even include a garden in the plans, since the RFP required open space. Instead, the next day at 7 am the Sanitation Department showed up at the garden with a bulldozer and dump trucks. They said that HPD has asked them to 'clean up the lot.' Two reps from HPD were with them. When we arrived and tried to talk to them, they told us that we had 'been squatting just long enough,' and to call the commissioner. They gave me the phone number we have called and left messages on numerous times, which is still not being answered or returning calls. They destroyed all the planters and benches rather than giving us a chance to move them, and even removed all the rocks we had organized as pathways. When HPD finally returned the calls, we were told that the lot was actually not part of the RFP, it still belonged to HPD, and would remain vacant. HPD came in without any warning, destroyed valuable materials that the organization can never get back, and reversed hundreds of hours of hard work put into cleaning and beautifying this lot. If they would have just given us a reasonable amount of time, we would have moved the raised beds, tables, benches, stage, and beehive to another location."

Dozens of people approached the gardeners as the bulldozers did their work, offering condolences. "I've been watching you guys work on this from my office window, and it looked just great," one person said. "It doesn't make any sense; this lot was full of trash for 20 years and they never cleaned it up until you guys started gardening here." If the garden had been destroyed by the developer who had bought the lot, the gardeners could have understood the impetus to clean the space. But none of us understood why the city spent its own money and resources destroying a project that had extensive community support and no complaints.

Bulldozing the space, one city worker confessed he felt horribly, but he was just following orders. History is really driven by these dialectical forces: build and destroy. We fight for land, but ownership—as the original inhabitants of this land understood so well—is illusory. No one owns it, though the city easily claims it. Still, battles over our commons churn through history. That Spring, Children's Magical Garden on the Lower East Side went through a similar battle, winning their right to remain through the City Green Thumb Program—but even then the owner of the other half of their lot fenced up their half. Some work the inside angle to save gardens, building relationships with those in power; others work outside channels, in the street. Both inside and outside are more than necessary. The struggle for open space continues in Brooklyn.

Figures 10, 11, and 12: "Nothing Yet Garden bulldozed." Photos by Times Up!

HPD List

Over the next two years, countless gardens would find themselves under threat, especially after the city department of Housing Preservation and Development placed 17 active community gardens on a list of sites to be developed for "affordable housing" in 2014. Community leaders and activists know that these gardens are not getting in the way of affordable housing. Quite the contrary, gardens are homes to dreams for a better city that brighten our lives. Gardens support community capacity-building, reduce asthma, increase fitness, support social equity, help cool neighborhoods in the summer, curb greenhouse gases, reduce storm-water overflow, increase biodiversity, provide fresh produce in "food deserts," etc. The benefits are endless. And none of these issues preclude supporting affordable housing. There are vacant lots owned by HPD throughout the city that can become sites for affordable housing. Most garden activists know that supporting rent control is the best way to support affordable housing. More developer giveaways will not support long-term affordable housing. And in this case the short-term trade off will lead to rent increases and displacement all too soon.

Save the Garden, Save New York: Community Gardens in Danger Ride 2015

There's a fence outside of Roger That Garden on 98 Rogers Avenue at Park Place in Crown Heights, that declares: "Save the Garden, Save NYC." The sign says it all. This is a city connected by people and ideas, streets and green spaces, bike lanes and sidewalks, spaces for cars and pedestrians, as well as those who yearn for public spaces where they can actually put their hands in the dirt—everyone sharing delicate community ecology worth preserving and honoring. When we lose a green space, this balance is threatened in a similar way. Everything is interconnected here. On Saturday April 18, 2015 a few of us participated in a bike ride organized by Public Space Party and 596 Acres to visit gardens under threat all over New York City. We planned to ride from Prospect Park to Prospect-Lefferts, on to Crown Heights and Bushwick, and then out to the Lower East Side of Manhattan and Soho, visiting gardens under threat. "[R]ide to small gardens and community parks that add essential depth to New York City's open space network and are in danger of losing their land to private development: Maple Street, Roger That, Eldert Street, Children's Magical, Siempre Verde, and Elizabeth Street", the invite for the ride declared. "These gardens need community support in asking the city to move their land from the private market into the public inventory where they belong. They are small, community spaces that serve as multi-purpose community living rooms year round."

Figure 13: "Route of the Gardens in Danger Ride. Courtesy 596 Acres."

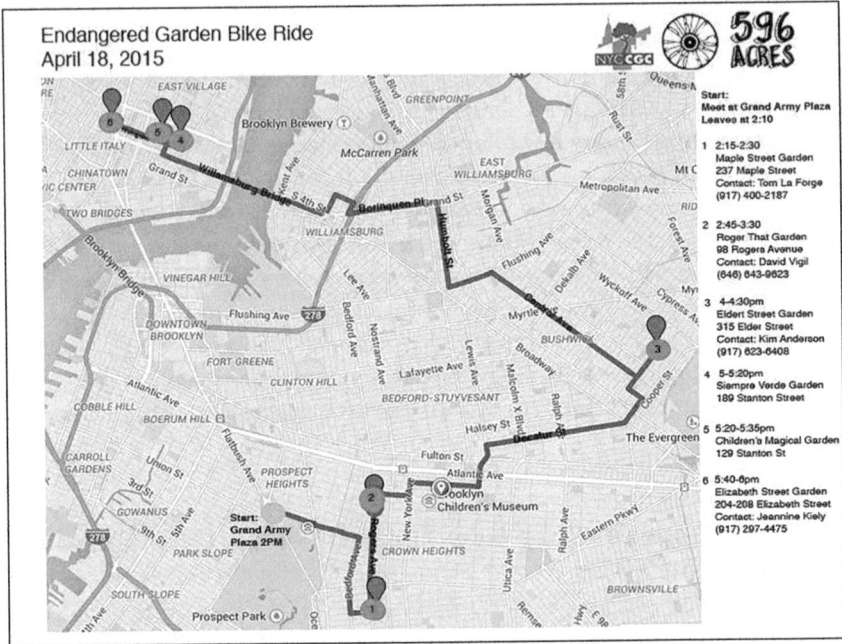

The day of the ride, cyclists met at the Plaza at Grand Army Plaza. Our first stop was Maple Street Garden in Brooklyn's Prospect Lefferts Gardens neighborhood. Kids were playing in a tree when we arrived. It felt as though the whole neighborhood was on hand. Maple Street Garden was formed in 2012 by the Maple 3 Block Association and community members who transformed a trash-strewn vacant lot into a multi-purpose garden and community space. The lot had been vacant and collecting trash for over a decade since its most recent resident and owner passed away and her home burned down. As Ali Jacobs, 31, an active member who lives on Sterling Street stated, "Our neighborhood is beautiful, but very short on public land. Our garden has no gate nor lock, it is accessible by the entire neighborhood, and is used heavily by children and adults as a common outdoor space."

Paula Segal of 596 Acres, who serves as an attorney for several of the gardens under threat from private developers, noted that developers see land as worth more than our lives: "They want to scheme to get our gardens. For two years, this was a garden that increased the property values for the neighborhood. Before that, it was a trash heap. And no one took notice of the space. We want to convince the city to protect it. We want to keep the sheriff from coming."

The Maple Street Community Garden was threatened with demolition by Housing Urban Development LLC, a private development corporation with a history of subprime lending and irregular title transfers. (Its name was obviously chosen to create confusion with the almost identically named city agency.) Gardeners were urging the city to take the property by eminent domain and transfer it to the Parks Department.

Roger That community garden was our next stop. Meeting us when we arrived, David Vigil told the story of the space. "Grown from a crumbling building, this is a community space in Crown Heights, Brooklyn, that stewards native plants, grows edibles, and maintains community compost. Roger That garden is currently under threat of development by a real estate speculator who purchased the deed to the land, subject to hundreds of thousands of dollars in tax debt liens, for $10 from the man who used to own and operate a hardware store on this lot before abandoning the buildings. The developers have attempted to illegally evict the garden through a lock-out. It had been an abandoned space, but now someone wants to make money with it. But we want to preserve it," said Vigil. "We want to save it, preserve it, and have it secured. The paper for the property needs to move to a land trust of the Parks Department."

The next stop for the ride was Eldert Street Garden in Bushwick. To get there, we rode through the lovely Brooklyn day, from Crown Heights to Bushwick. Eldert Street offers vegetable plots, educational programming for kids and adults, composting, and a welcoming public space where folks can relax and connect with the natural world. Developers tried to move in on the space the day before our ride.

Kim Anderson welcomed us and told the story of the space. "Let's start from the beginning," she said. "Originally this space was a pile of rubble from a building in the 1970's. The land was donated to a nonprofit with the expectation that it would become a garden. In 2009, we approached the two owners of the space and told them we'd like to make a garden here. So we got started. They said that was always the intent of the space, to be a garden. This September, we saw folks in the lot saying it had been sold. We checked it out and were told nothing had been sold. But it was. We're still trying to figure out what happened there. In January, we learned it had been sold for $300,000.00. Yesterday, we were trying to have a work day and workers showed up saying they were here to start work on a vacant lot. They were confused. If you want us to move, you have to go through due process, or you are trespassing."

"With those words, we had a standoff," she recalled. "Yet, the garden had community support. We're hoping to keep the lot. The Attorney General's office has not been contacted by the owners who are required to notify them when selling land in a nonprofit. There are restrictions on dispositions for nonprofits, noted one of the lawyers. Yet there is no information on the deed for the garden. It was an illegal sale."

As of the ride, the transfer of the garden to a private for-profit corporation was under investigation by the New York state Attorney General's office. The gardeners were asserting their rights as tenants under New York City law continuing to grow in the face of bullying by the developer, asking that the city halt all construction permits for the property and acquire it for transfer to the Parks Department. Anderson explained what the fight was about: "For those of us without a private garden to grow in, or a forest to walk in, community gardens are all we have. When we work in our community gardens, we *take back* our fundamental right to work the land, and call a piece of earth our own, no matter how small. And we do it together."

From Bushwick, riders rode over to the Williamsburg Bridge and into Manhattan to visit *Siempre Verde* garden, two small parcels of public land on Attorney and Stanton Streets. Riding over, I looked at the lot where Nothing Yet garden was planted, by then two years vacant.

"We are essentially animals, so having access to nature provides creature comforts, soothes the savage soul, and regenerates the weary spirit," says Ann Lee of *Siempre Verde* community garden. "Gardens are a place to pause and find respite from the grind of concrete cities. Gardens are the future for urban people."

"The city needs to take a more active interest in the fates of these properties and affirmatively act to preserve the institutions that New Yorkers love," Segal concluded as we completed our ride. "This isn't about housing versus gardens. This is about living in a city that places the needs of people who live in neighborhoods above the potential for others to make money off those neighborhoods."

The struggle for open space in Brooklyn would ebb and flow for the next few years.

In 2015, two of the gardens we visited on the gardens in danger ride—Maple Street and Eldert Street Garden—won significant legal victories, staving off eviction and paving the way toward permanence.[20]

"It's crazy, all of a sudden my garden docket is clear," said Paula Segal, lawyer for all three gardens."[21]

The following spring, of 2016, we organized another gardens-in-danger ride. I reached out to the gardeners at Roger That, who reported that Roger That had lost its battle after a court ruling allowed the owners to evict the garden. It was closed down.

"Not always winning," their lawyer, Paula Segal, posted on Facebook on May 25.

DNA info reported: "A realty company has closed the Roger That community garden in Crown Heights this week following a ruling earlier this spring that granted the owners permission to evict the group."[22]

Figure 14: "'Stop the Towers' message along the Williamsburg, Brooklyn." Photo by Benjamin Shepard.

"Stop the Towers. Save the Waterfront" declares a mural along the Williamsburg waterfront. Today, the delicate ecology of the city is in danger. The social rate of return for community gardens takes place in countless forms. Gardens support the air, health, sustainability, and beauty of neighborhoods, among countless other benefits of green space in a world facing increasing temperatures and climate chaos. Hopefully, we can support and preserve this delicate ecology. After all, when we save the garden, we save NYC.

Figure 15: "This open space in Bedford Stuyvesant could remain open. It could be a garden." Photograph by Caroline Shepard.

Figures 16, 17, 18, 19 and 20: "Scenes from Bushwick neighborhood in flux." Photographs by Caroline Shepard.

Chapter eight: Community Gardening, Creative Activism 205

Chapter eight: Community Gardening, Creative Activism   207

Figure 21: "Save the Garden, Save the City." Photo by Benjamin Shepard.

Chapter nine

Rethinking Jay Street and the Downtown the City Forgot:
Lost Between Double-parked Cars and Ugly Buildings

"Downtown Brooklyn presents a layered, seemingly impenetrable wall when viewed from Brooklyn Heights. The composition, especially with the oblique view of Borough Hall, seems designated as a purposeful representation of the city while it simultaneously denies continuity and the expansiveness to the neighborhoods beyond."

Figure 1: Photo and caption by Jason Montgomery.

> "It has often been observed that lively downtowns are apt to have dwellings fingering into them and close to them, and night uses these residents enjoy and help support.... [I]n real life where such combinations have vitality the residents are part of a very complex pool of downtown day, night, and weekend uses in reasonable balance.... When a city heart stagnates or disintegrates, a city as a social neighborhood of the whole begins to suffer: People who ought to get together, by means of central activities that are failing, fail to get together."
> Jane Jacobs, The *Death and Life of Great American Cities*, (1961).[1]

In "A Windstorm in Downtown Brooklyn," Robert Sullivan observes:

a lot of people living in New York City don't even know that there is a downtown Brooklyn.... That's because New York's celebrity downtowns are Wall Street and Times Square and maybe even Herald Square. In Brooklyn, downtownness is, generally speaking, dispersed, spread throughout various neighborhoods and downtown Brooklyn, possibly as a result, is, on first glance, less spectacular-seeming, more work-a-day, more middle urban America. In the morning in downtown Brooklyn, into the streets and the triangle of green but mostly cement park around the old classically columned Borough Hall, commuters rise up out of the subways and gently collide...[2]

To Sullivan's observation, we would add that sometimes the colliding of commuters is not so gentle; sometimes it comes with a crash. At least this is the case on Jay Street, where occupants of cars double-park in bike and bus lanes as they text; buses and bikes zoom across traffic; and police make illegal U-turns across the congested, six-lane stretch of road (four for cars, two lanes for bikes).

Just behind Borough Hall runs Jay Street, one of Brooklyn's most dysfunctional corridors. Pedestrians, bicyclists, buses, taxis, and private vehicles all compete for space on this chaotic street, re-zoned for new shiny office towers in 2004, extending through Downtown Brooklyn, roughly between Flatbush and Atlantic Avenues, Adams and Tillary Streets. Unlike the integrated neighborhoods Jane Jacobs describes, Downtown Brooklyn feels isolated, walled off from the rest of the borough. Today, waves of cars zoom or sit clogged in traffic in front of the homogenized office buildings. "Without a strong inclusive central heart, a city tends to become a collection of interests isolated from one another," Jacobs writes. "It falters at producing something greater, socially, culturally, and economically, than the sum of its separated parts."[3]

The roots of the problem here run deep. Between Robert Moses' design for the Brooklyn Queens Expressway and Bruce Ratner's MetroTech Center, Downtown Brooklyn has been forced to contend with years of poor planning. Characterized by too many cars, re-zoned streets, office towers, bland buildings, and unused public space, the corridors down Jay Street are some of the city's least friendly or inviting of spaces. "If Brownstone Brooklyn offered a sense of place, Concord Village, the Civic Center, and urban renewal superblocks represented a landscape of sameness, or simply non-place," notes Suleiman Osman in *The Invention of Brownstone Brooklyn*.[4]

The mismanagement of the space is years in the making. Six decades ago, Robert Moses blocked plans to build a baseball stadium at Atlantic and Flatbush Avenues, preferring plans that allowed more cars to pour through the area. Instead of a destination, it became the opposite. Sixty years later, Bruce Ratner used the same eminent domain Moses was famous for to build Atlantic Yards in the same space Walter O'Malley once planned to move the Dodgers. When plans for the Civic Center were unveiled in 1945, a sprawl of government buildings, research facilities, the college where we teach, and apartment buildings were to stretch from Borough Hall to the Brooklyn Bridge, transforming the area's landscape. "Like a Parisian boulevard, a widened Adams Street would cut through the obsolete street grid, allowing traffic to flow smoothly from the interior of the borough to the Brooklyn Bridge and the new and majestic Brooklyn-Queens Expressway," writes Suleiman Osman.[5] At least that was the plan. "This Civic Center is to Brooklyn what the great cathedral and opera plazas are to European cities," boasted Moses.[6] Seven decades later, few would suggest travel between Fulton and Tillary Streets is a smooth ride. Yet the situation here might be changing. Across the globe, the design of urban centers is evolving, with emphasis on sustainability and energy conservation, the health and welfare of citizens, social vitality and civic involvement, as well as economic development.

Jay Street is where we teach at City Tech, an undergraduate senior college within the City University of New York. The path from neighborhood to subway to the rezoned and rapidly transforming Downtown Brooklyn space where our campus sits can be a precarious one. Just a stone's throw from the Manhattan and Brooklyn Bridges, it connects students' lives from their homes to the bus routes and subway rides. It marks a path between the spatial inequalities of the streets through the cultural and political histories of the residents of our global city, of immigrants and those who have been here for generations. This space is a microcosm of the city, a living lab that stretches from our campus downtown, to Bedford-Stuyvesant, Fort Greene, and Gowanus, as well as beyond the borough where students make their way to and from the Bronx, Queens, and Staten Island. The space around our campus, our students' lives, and their engagement is anything but linear. As a part of a post-welfare neo-liberal city, we are all impacted by the changes taking place involving the campus and community, the city and government, Wall Street and civil society. The what-has-been and will-become of the streets, coffee shops, parks, and classrooms remind us of the possibilities and limits of Global Brooklyn.

Throughout Brooklyn, countless people are taking part in a conversation about what the borough has become. On a Saturday morning in May of 2015, noted sociologist Stanley Aronowitz, for example, kvetched about what he saw happening in Downtown Brooklyn in a class he was running at the Commons on Atlantic Avenue. "Downtown Brooklyn is a massive scandal," he posited, lamenting the skyscrapers and construction cranes he saw everywhere. "No innovation, nor creativity. Standardization creates a system of conformity and authority."

Others in his morning class chimed in. "The function of architecture in Downtown Brooklyn is to make sure the community does not have a voice," added Michael Palias, a lecturer in Philosophy at Long Island College, echoing the point from Marx's *Gundrisse* that the group was reading. "The job of capital is to extract surplus value, not to open space for democracy. The architecture of Downtown Brooklyn seems to be doing just this," he argued.

Across the borough in Windsor Terrace, performance artist Bill Talen, a.k.a. Reverend Billy, was making a similar argument, from the vantage point of a burgeoning anti-consumer movement. "For decades the storm battering New York City was consumerism. The monoculture—the malls and chains and deluxe condos—flooded down into New York's key organisms, our 500 distinct neighborhoods." He laments the latest tide to hit Global Brooklyn: homogenization: "Tens of thousands of family businesses and complex laughing and dancing societies on street corners have been drowned in a sea of identical details. We have lost our soul to an invasive species."[7]

Others hold out hope that something else can be born of the downtown that the city forgot, even as the cranes and bulldozers remake it in front of our eyes. This ninth chapter of *Brooklyn Tides* considers what might become of this downtown space. It reviews the ten years since its most recent re-zoning and the ways we make our way through this space, as bodies and ideas collide. If we read this urban space as a text, the question is: what might it tell us?[8]

Figure 2: "Construction in Dumbo." Photo by Caroline Shepard.

THE REZONING OF DOWNTOWN BROOKLYN

If you look at Jay Street, you see a street in transition, with universities, economic development, double-parked cars, unused public spaces, a bike share station, and other experiments. [9] From the vantage point of a bike or train stop, getting here can be tricky, involving navigating between a condensed field of bodies, cars, and crowded space. For those who drive, park at Concord Village, and walk to their destination, their experience is no better.

Few feel satisfied with Jay Street and the sprawling office complex of the MetroTech Center stretching from Tillary to Fulton Streets. From 2014-15, Transportation Alternatives worked to make Jay Street a safer place to walk and ride, envisioning a future without double-parked cars, constant illegal U-turns, and chronically obstructed bus stops and bike lanes. The efforts of TA were just the beginning, as countless players participated in conversations and panels to rethink this space, its traffic and zoning, hoping to implement a new vision for the area.

In April 2015, Jason Montgomery (a City Tech architect), Eric McClure (an organizer with Park Slope Neighbors), and I (Benjamin Shepard) organized a panel at the Brooklyn Historical Society on the topic of the re-zoning of Downtown Brooklyn. Montgomery introduced our session, reviewing the aims of the rezoning that displaced historic businesses to make way for skyscrapers, luxury towers, and a more polished view of urban life. "Downtown Brooklyn is evolving and changing rapidly with a surge of new development," he stated. "But will these changes give us the downtown we all desire? What is the future of Downtown Brooklyn since the 2004 Special Purpose District Zoning Resolution?"

"The point of the rezoning was to establish a comprehensive plan for strong and diverse commercial markets, bringing business to downtown," Montgomery continued.[10] "Through the rezoning, Downtown Brooklyn was promoted as a third business district in New York, after Lower and Midtown Manhattan. The planning challenges for the space, including poor streetscape and an isolated downtown core, were many. Still, the city moved on a zoning plan for a business district. Ten years later, we wondered what had happened to Downtown Brooklyn."

Figure 3: Image of Downtown Brooklyn by Jason A. Montgomery NCARB LEED AP. He writes: "The map is a figure ground, showing buildings in black. This shows the lack of a clear pattern of the downtown fabric after urban renewal, resulting in a confusing and disorienting place."

"Today, you can't count the cranes," said Professor Michael Duddy, commenting on the horizontal changes to the landscape. "This includes a swathe of residential buildings that have gone up in the last decade, skyscraper after skyscraper, as Downtown Brooklyn evolved with a developer-friendly agenda, without complimentary public infrastructure of schools or transportation." The recent redevelopment of the neighborhood has gone through several stages. 1985-2005 witnessed Forest City's MetroTech. This was a space few used or enjoyed. 2004 ushered in a new phase of development: new towers, City Tech, and NYU anchoring this as a student space. Today, it strives to link educational, residential, and cultural resources, as well as the neighborhoods of Boerum Hill, Brooklyn Heights, and Fort Greene, each of these neighborhoods disconnected and separate from downtown and each other. The problem is that Brooklyn's downtown has rarely related to these other neighborhoods. The most natural integration moves from south to north, from Boerum Hill to Atlantic Avenue; others are less smooth, with the core isolated from the rest of the city. The barriers, congestion, cars zooming down Flatbush, seem to demarcate the space from the rest of the borough. "Getting from Fulton to Jay Street, one sees no smiling faces," confessed Duddy.

Comparing glossy photos of plans for glitzy streets without cars to images of gridlock along Flatbush, Hilda Cohen (a transportation advocate with Make Brooklyn Safer and Families for Safe Streets) offered a telling observation: "In between planning and construction is 15 years of change. Within remains a vast gap between the 'bold new ideas' and the reality. Where are the bold new ideas for streets?" she wondered. "Our streets are for us, not for cars. What are the ways to improve? How can we market streets for people to linger, to share space? How can we reimagine Jay Street, making this street usable for multiple users, while doing away with barriers. If Brooklyn wants to be a cutting-edge space, our streets must reflect this; it must realize that shared space is necessary. We need bold new designs."

Downtown Brooklyn is the third largest "business district" in New York City after the Financial District and Midtown Manhattan. The 2004 Development Plan promoted Downtown Brooklyn as a key location for back-office space. With Brooklyn's evolution and technology boom, the planning for Downtown Brooklyn likely now needs to achieve different goals. What should be changed in the planning for Downtown Brooklyn to adapt to these new conditions? Is there a model urban "character" that should guide the development of Downtown Brooklyn?

Kevin Hom (an architect and Dean at City Tech) suggested that Brooklyn, itself, could be a source for insight. "Brooklyn was once one of the great cities in the U.S.," he argued. "Ocean Parkway is a great model of a street, as an open thoroughfare, offering rapid transit, supported by both practical and elegant design. Downtown Brooklyn, surrounded by water and industrial sites, could be an ideal urban space. Manhattan, in contrast, is saturated with little to no room for further development. Some parts of Brooklyn have been a model for design for 100 years. Take the Brooklyn Academy of Music (BAM), for example. Good planning makes BAM thrive. It has an active theater and restaurants and an open streetscape that could be extended downtown, adding vibe. This is Brooklyn's Carnegie Hall, which helps connect a whole neighborhood of mixed uses that Jane Jacobs praises."

Hilda Cohen concurred, adding that the social impact of new development in Brooklyn must be accounted for. "We have to rethink the streets here as other cities have." She pointed to the example of Portland, Oregon, where buses run for free downtown. "There people use the buses, instead of cars, and gridlock is reduced. We have to rethink how we get around. How can Downtown be connected with the Navy Yards, Dumbo, and the Brooklyn Strand? How can this city enhance the changes that have already happened and support the need for connection between disparate neighborhoods, downtown, and the waterfront?"

While Downtown Brooklyn is an economic hub, it is missing needed infrastructure, noted several of the audience members, with frustration in their voices. While 10,000 new residential units have been created, supporting schools, libraries, and hospitals have not been developed. It is the responsibility of government and community pressure to create such things. Over and over, the crowded audience called for halting the residential development until attendant needs are addressed. "It's like an ocean liner with no rudder crashing onto the coast," reflected one audience member.

Rethinking Jay Street

On October 8, 2014 downtown re-zoning panel was an extension of a conversation started the year before with Rethinking Jay Street. There, we held another session at 300 Jay Street considering issues related to remaking streets, urban accessibility, sustainable modes of transportation, place-making, social vitality, civic involvement, and a lack of amenities drawing students after classes. We argued that a rapidly developing hub—located in the downtown of a global borough—can and must do better.

Figure 4: "Building along Jay Street and Tillary Street." Photo by Benjamin Shepard.

On the way to Rethinking Jay Street, cycling advocate Barbara Ross found herself blocked by a police car parked within a bike lane on Jay Street. Of course, this is the crux of the problem on Jay Street, and throughout New York.

Jay Street is a critical connector to the Brooklyn and Manhattan bridges, but it lacks the bicycle and pedestrian infrastructure needed to protect New Yorkers from dangerous traffic. Before our session, Transportation Alternatives,' Brooklyn Activist Committee held their own event with the community board, inviting residents to weigh in with ideas about how to fix the space. Those in attendance suggested the city end car parking on Jay Street; add protected bike lanes, pedestrian plazas, bike corrals, and other traffic-calming measures to reduce dangerous speeding and double-parking; and encourage healthy transportation choices for more New Yorkers. Their ideas lay the groundwork for a formal request for these improvements to the Department of Transportation. Rethinking Jay Street would continue the process, inviting audience members and panelists to dream about what they would like to see here.

At the 2014 session, Councilman Stephen Levin offered preliminary remarks, suggesting the city fix many of the obvious problems with traffic flow along Jay Street. Ryan Grew, the deputy director of operations for the Downtown

Brooklyn Partnership, noted that there was so much to do to better utilize the public spaces along the street. The question was: how to connect people with the oddly designed, car-centric space from the Manhattan Bridge Plaza to the Brooklyn Bridge Promenade and Cadman Plaza?

Figure 5: "Police car parked in bike lane on Jay Street. November 5, 2014."
Photo by Benjamin Shepard.

Caroline Samponaro (Director of Bicycle Advocacy for Transportation Alternatives) spoke about cycling and efforts to make streets all over New York safer. She described the Transportation Alternatives plans for the re-imagining of Jay Street. "For as long as I've been here, Jay Street has been a mess," she related. "But there are things we can do. Today, we passed legislation reducing the speed limit in New York. It came through a lot of mobilization. This came from the grassroots. This is a grassroots problem and opportunity to do better."

Mike Lydon (a principal of the Street Plans Collaborative), concurred, calling for a redesign of Jay Street to make U-turns impossible. "Let's do better," he concluded. "The sense of place is missing." (He would later submit plans as part of a proposal to stop double-parking on Jay Street). Jessica Daley (a senior editor at *Curbed NY*) pointed out the structural problems. "The 2004 re-zoning did not include support for infrastructure, including transportation." She argued the neighborhood would need a new re-zoning, as well as better connection between Jay Street and Dumbo.

Figure 6: "Street memorial for Matthew Brenner, killed by a car, off Jay Street."
Photo by Benjamin Shepard.

Jason Montgomery, in turn, argued that Jay Street is well-positioned to be a Main Street of Downtown Brooklyn, the north/south spine tying into the east/west spines of Atlantic Avenue and Fulton Street. He then recounted the different eras of development from the 18th century to the 20th-century redesign of Cadman Plaza. "Could the current zoning strategy give us a vibrant urban community in Downtown Brooklyn?" he wondered. "Do we need an alternative planning strategy that goes beyond the limits of use-based zoning? Would a special mode of public transit (bus rapid transit, streetcar, or light rail) make sense to help connect the neighborhoods within the borough to the downtown? Do the colleges along Jay Street require a greater dedication of pedestrian open space than a typical New York City street? How can the student use of Jay Street be part of the solution? And should the Mayor's initiative for the Strand, a proposed greenway stretching from Cadman Plaza to the waterfront, be broadened to address the larger structural issues of the neighborhood?[11] How do we make this a more people-friendly place?"

"There should be more required of developers," noted Jessica Daley.

The best public spaces are well-used public spaces, the American urbanist William H. Whyte used to explain. Today, the spaces around the Ratner-designed MetroTech feel dead, austere, unused, the result of poor design.

Figure 7: "Street memorial by Right of Way." Photo by Benjamin Shepard.

The gaps between plans and reality, between users and the space's design are many. Jane Jacobs would suggest that city spaces succeed to the extent that they emphasize multiple uses, bottom-up planning, local economies, and ecosystems with cultural resources which draw people in, connecting a broad range of uses. "Old ideas can sometimes use new buildings," Jacobs explained. "New ideas must use old buildings."[12] In Downtown Brooklyn's case, there are too many new buildings and not enough new ideas.

"Yet this might be changing," suggested Mike Lydon.[13] "Put the public space where the students are rather than vice versa", he concluded.

Several of the students on hand pointed out that there was more that had to be done to cope with the secondary harmful effects of development, including gentrification and displacement. What are the social impacts? How do we keep Brooklyn diverse and inclusive?, asked others in attendance, raising the bigger question about what Brooklyn is going to become. Who was going to stay and who was being pushed out? How do we make this a Brooklyn everyone can live in over the long haul?

"Get involved," Caroline Samponaro responded. "We have to do more to get more people involved in the planning process. Connect the streets to public space. Design can lead to that outcome. Make this a more open plaza-like space. Eighty percent of the public space in the city is streets and sidewalks. It's where we connect. We need to do more." Her point was that cities need to create ways of encouraging people to connect. "It is B.S. that public space means more people have to leave, have to move. I've been to cities around the world where this is not the case. If Brooklyn is to develop, we need to look at ways to have more people stay instead of getting pushed out."

Others in the audience were more frank about the need to remove the cars from the space. Yet this involves moving away from Robert Moses' vision of cities as locomotive spaces, accommodating the car, at the expense of other uses. "The presence of curbside parking on Jay Street between Willoughby and Tillary is the root cause of 80 per cent of the dysfunction there," noted transportation advocate Eric McClure, of Park Slope Neighbors. "Eliminating curbside parking and relocating it to leased spaces inside the Marriott garage, where there's routinely excess capacity, would free up space for dedicated bus lanes and a physically protected cycle track. This possible solution just makes too much sense not to explore."

Looking back at the Rethinking Jay Street Symposium, Jason Montgomery noted that "the consensus emerged that Downtown Brooklyn needed a new round of study and planning. The planning that is needed is not merely an updated zoning document, but a streetscape and place-making design that ties together and connects the disparate parts of the district into a cohesive whole and transforms Downtown Brooklyn into a destination rather than a traffic corridor. This process needs to consider all forms of movement and accessibility through the district and reduce the overwhelmingly dominating and intimidating presence of private vehicular traffic on Downtown Brooklyn's streets."

The state of Jay Street and its connection to Downtown opens up a number of questions. If Jay Street were a text, what would it tell us—that traffic lights should be ignored and buildings should be made to repel people? Or is there another storyline? Today, reimagining Downtown Brooklyn means rethinking the very nature of this urban space.

While the authors were writing this chapter, messages calling for the city to "#fixJayStreet" flooded twitter. Many residents have taken to social media, others to the streets, universities, and/or City Hall, calling for a different kind of street. This flurry of activism has already borne fruit, with calls for a redesign of the street, featuring shared space for pedestrians as well as lanes dedicated to bikes and buses, public transportation, and fewer double-parked cars.[14] For this plan to succeed, it must reconsider what has happened to downtown and throughout Brooklyn, extending from the center to the periphery of this borough of hundreds of neighborhoods. Can this be a borough where people have an impact over the elites, the developers, where the streets feel connected with neighborhoods as Jane Jacobs imagined? Or will the unelected Robert Moses and Forest City Ratner dominate what the street will feel like? Can Brooklyn be a space that is different and open to all its different uses and needs? In our view, a Jay Street that is simultaneously car, bike, and pedestrian friendly is absolutely consistent with what a reimagined global city can be.

***

In 1939, James Agee wrote in "Southeast of the Island: Travel Notes" how Brooklyn could only be understood in relation to mighty, vertical Manhattan. In comparison to the world renown financial and cultural industries across the river, Brooklyn lacked an individual identity. It was a farm whose crops were "far less industrial or industrial or notable or in any way distinguished or definable." While Manhattan was a destination for those looking to get ahead, Brooklyn was "a pulsing mass of scarcely discriminable cellular jellies and tissues; a place where people merely 'live.'"[15] In Agee's view, Brooklyn, in comparison to Manhattan, just prior to WWII, was provincial, without a center. Today, however, the tides have changed, for Brooklyn has risen to be an equal. But, like Manhattan, it now needs to define *its* center.

To create a vital downtown space, over 40 stakeholder groups have aligned with Mayor Bill De Blasio to establish the Brooklyn Strand.[16] This massive project aims to increase pedestrian access in and around Brooklyn Bridge, make improvements to a number of local parks, realign the on/off ramps of the Brooklyn-Queens Expressway, re-open the Brooklyn War Memorial, create open markets, and bring in more public art. The problem with this and similar well-meaning endeavors such as High Line park in Manhattan, however, is that they tend to be monuments of super-gentrification, that cater to the interests of the well-off and result in blandness. Critiquing the High Line, Christoph Lindner (Professor of media and culture at the University of Amsterdam), for example, spoke of how the park at first promised to exhibit "the wild beauty of the self-seeded landscape." Ultimately, it became an overly planned, "fairly stifling" experience. Too often, especially on weekends, the High Line is overcrowded, recalling "airport security lines" visiting tourists had just left.[17]

To create a bustling, vital Jay Street and environs rather than a blandified tourist attraction, we suggest offering reasons for the local community and residents across Brooklyn, to linger and mix. Let's start by putting the cars underground making the entire area a walking/biking zone. Add historical trolleys (or modern light rail trains) that link to the Navy Yard, Plymouth Church, the Underground Railroad Museum, Fort Greene Park, and the new Waterfront Barge Museum. Help to retain local businesses and restaurants like Los Papis, a cheap and delicious Spanish eatery near DUMBO, rather than bringing in the chain operations that have begun to flood Adams Street and the Fulton Mall. Fight to keep open The Commons on Atlantic Avenue, a space that allows local residents to congregate and discuss cultural and urban matters. Keep the handball courts open along Jay Street and encourage similar open space activity areas over condo construction. Be more inviting to all of Brooklyn's residents of all ages and walks of life. Let's especially think about the rising generation of young Brooklynites.

Up and down Jay Street are new businesses and two new universities (NYU-Poly Tech and NYU's Tandon School of Engineering) looking to take advantage of what has come to be known as the Technology Triangle. Somewhat overlooked as a potential player, however, is New York City College of Technology. Like other CUNY campuses it has long been underfunded and under-staffed. For six years (2010-2016), CUNY faculty worked without a contract or a raise. Even with our hard-fought, newly-won contract, faculty salaries have not kept up with the high cost of living in New York, and most classes are still taught by part-timers who earn approximated $3,500 per course and have no job security. While almost 500,000 students attend CUNY (18,000 at City Tech), tuition is constantly rising making staying in school difficult for them. Many must also work multiple jobs to make ends meet and, for some, support young children. For many New Yorkers from low-income backgrounds, gaining a degree is often life-changing, a chance to enter America's general prosperity. When Michelle Obama gave her commencement address at City College in 2016, she rightly identified CUNY students as "living, breathing proof that the American dream endures."[18]

Just as public education needs to be put at the center of America's attention, City Tech too needs to take its rightful spot as a central part of Brooklyn's development. For too long downtown Brooklyn and the waterfront area have catered to the middle and upper classes. Public education is the central proven path toward economic and social upward mobility. As such, City Tech—and CUNY more broadly—should be adequately funded and viewed as engines of change rather than burdens on state budgets. Relatedly, the spaces surrounding our public institutions of higher education should feel accessible and welcoming to our students. With a vision of inclusivity and prosperity for all, Jay Street and the surrounding waterfront district can be made into a model for all global cities, in which the needs of the majority are viewed as central.

Figures 8, 9 and 10: "Empty spaces and transition in Downtown Brooklyn, Atlantic Ave and DUMBO." Photos by Caroline Shepard.

Chapter nine: Rethinking Jay Street and the Downtown the City Forgot

Epilogue
The Global Street

Figures 1, 2, and 3: "Skateboards and street scenes along on Atlantic Avenue, Coney Island and throughout the borough. The streets of Brooklyn offer a panorama." Figure One by Benjamin Shepard, Two by Brennan Cavanaugh, and Three by Caroline Shepard.

Epilogue: The Global Street   229

> "I once started out
> to walk around the world
> but ended up in Brooklyn.
> That Bridge was too much for me."
> Lawrence Ferlinghetti, "Autobiography,"
> *A Coney Island of the Mind* (1958)[1]

On October 1, 2011, some 770 people involved with the Occupy Wall Street movement were arrested as they walked from Manhattan across the Brooklyn Bridge. The arrests catapulted what had felt like a local movement into a global phenomenon, with word about the protests heard around the world. Far from slowing the momentum of the movement, the scene of the clash of bodies and ideologies on the iconic bridge seemed to kick it up a gear, as its message reverberated around the globe.[2]

Figure 4: "Occupy Brooklyn."

Figure 5: "Arrests on the Brooklyn Bridge." Photo by Brennan Cavanaugh.

Looking at Global Brooklyn, the street tells us a lot. We see protests and art, street parties and lost characters, developments rising and brownfields paved over, an eternal cycle of restaurants opening and closing, and bike lanes and street signs shifting in the contours of the night. In *The Death and Life of Great American Cities*, Jane Jacobs suggests that the pulse of urban space is often found in just these sorts of dramas of the street.[3]

What is remarkable about Brooklyn's streets is who walks on them and where they take us. Many are lined with newsstands with papers reporting on hospital closures, street occupations, anti-police-brutality rallies, cultural events, and other developments. What is also remarkable is what is absent. We see fewer ships embarking from the place that Whitman once deemed the "City of Ships." What remains in these streets are the tides.

> City whose gleeful tides continually rush or recede, whirling in and
>   out, with eddies and foam!
> City of wharves and stores! city of tall façades of marble and iron!
> Proud and passionate city! mettlesome, mad, extravagant city!
> Spring up, O city! not for peace alone, but be indeed yourself,
> warlike![4]

There is a delight in Whitman's words about his beloved city written during the Civil War, but also a recognition of the paradoxes in this space, pregnant in its opposites.

Throughout this book, we've reviewed some of these various tides and their rumbling dialectics of peace and war, open space and hyper-development, immigrant flows and parochial resistance, gardens rising, bulldozers razing, of stories and storms churning through the Brooklyn streets. Without sufficient open space is there still room for this to be an "other space?" Without its ships, is Brooklyn destined to become just another blandified same-space? After all, cities across the globe seem to be increasingly mimicking each other. With ubiquitous shops like H&M, GAP, Shake Shack, Starbucks, McDonald's, IKEA, places like Zurich, Brussels, Tokyo, and Paris are losing individual identity to a sea of identical details.[5] Yet might there be a different story, a different way of creating a city by and for everyone. Throughout these cases, we've considered the stories of people comprising a city of friends, who dream as Whitman once dreamed. Here people imagine another city which finds itself by slowing down, opening spaces for bikes and pedestrians and sustainable urbanism. Throughout these stories, we've asked if there is another story of Global Brooklyn? Reflecting on the campaigns and stories reviewed in these chapters, one sees a series of contested spaces and struggles, as well as the possibility for agency in a globalized world. People can create gardens, bike lanes, and impacts on cities, including affordable housing for the majority of lower and middle-class residents.

It's hard to walk or ride through the streets without feeling some of that energy. On a spring day in May 2015, my wife (Caroline) and I (Benjamin Shepard) rode all afternoon, biking up to Red Hook, back to Gowanus, through Clinton Hill to Bed-Stuy and Bushwick, through Greenpoint, along the waterfront, and back downtown. In Red Hook, we stumbled upon an image of a wave crashing on the beach painted on a wall. It was an astonishing rendition of Hokusai's "The Great Wave of Kanagawa" painted next to the words, "Injustice anywhere is a threat to justice everywhere."

Along the way, every unspoken-for lot or open wall space seemed to be transformed into a community garden, local park, or mural; each open space had become a canvas for a work of art in this ever-evolving, transforming borough.

Later that month, Monica, a stalwart of the public activism traced throughout this volume, wrote an invitation for a Public Space Party for the group's June 4, 2015 ride:

Discover new public spaces all along the Brooklyn waterfront ... We'll check out the changing landscape, from the blight of the high-rise condos in Williamsburg, to the last shreds of the Domino Sugar Factory, to the Brooklyn Navy Yard's Admiral Row before their imminent destruction, to the new beaches, BBQs and soccer fields in Brooklyn Heights, to a neighborhood hit hard by Sandy—Red Hook—finding its way back. How can we develop in a way that is equitable? Where have we come from and where are we going? Lots to think about...

As we finished the ride, our group sat at Sunny's bar in Red Hook and talked about policies that could help Brooklyn survive rising sea levels and other changes challenging it. We reviewed the plans for the waterfront for coping with rising tides. "With polar ice caps melting at such an alarming rate, more will be necessary," one woman argued. The majestic new Brooklyn Bridge Park boasts of salt marshes to protect the waterfront tidal ecosystem from rising waters. Yet is this enough to save this global waterfront from another Super-Storm Sandy? None of us were convinced. "The biggest tide hitting the shore is hyper-development," another contended. Through rides such as this, a different city feels possible. Leaving the bar, we noted how the sun was setting on the waterfront, illuminating the Statue of Liberty in the distance. This borough is still a thrilling home for many, even as it transforms. It still offers all sorts of openings and opportunities. In between the ebbs and tides crashing on the shores, there arise lessons worth considering. This epilogue highlights a few, from voices across the borough.

Figure 6: "Red Hook Tides." Photo by Caroline Shepard.

BEYOND GENTRIFICATION

Figure 7: "Night of Fire 2007, Sarah Sparkles."

"When gentrification swept through Manhattan like a wave, its effect across the East River in Brooklyn was felt initially as little more than a ripple," notes Colin Moynihan in Todd Seale's book *Bright Lights: Photographs of Another New York*.[6] This book suggests there is still a little boogie-woogie left in these streets; there are still adventures and stories in the nooks and crannies. "With the turn of the century, there came a major shift of focus in the underground art scenes in New York from Manhattan to Brooklyn," writes Sto Len.[7] "It was a natural evolution, one spurred by economics and real estate. When I moved here, I couldn't afford to live in the Lower East Side, so I naturally ended up sleeping on a couch in my friend's kitchen in Greenpoint."[8] And that bit of squatting changed everything. "Brooklyn turned out to be more fun anyhow," he conceded. "It felt freer and ripe with possibility. All of a sudden, I wasn't going to Manhattan anymore. I wasn't even going to clubs because the best shows were happening in parking lots, junkyards, warehouses, and people's lofts.... Bands played in people's basements and backyards. It felt like home because it was someone's home," he wrote.[9]

Upon completing his Ph.D. in American Studies, author Mark Noonan moved out of Manhattan to settle in Brooklyn, where he now teaches. In 2003, his new neighborhood of Boerum Hill, in contrast to the Upper East Side, offered a more livable community. He participated in block parties and came to know several of his neighbors on a first-name basis. Just around the corner from his apartment was Brawta Café celebrated by many as the best Caribbean eatery in the borough, famed for its curried goat, oxtail stew, and chicken roti. On sunny summer weekends, he drank beers with friends at picnic tables in front of Fish Restaurant on Smith Street as parades of pedestrians passed by. In addition to enjoying the neighborhood's wide array of culinary offerings and quirky hangouts, Noonan also took note of Brooklyn's cultural and historical richness. Soon, his research and teaching interests turned to the authors and artists of the borough.

The Brooklyn waterfront has long been awash in great writers. On 70 Willow Street, Truman Capote rented a basement apartment to finish *Breakfast at Tiffany's* and write *In Cold Blood*. Arthur Miller had once lived nearby and, for a short while, right below Norman Mailer on 102 Pierrepont Street. For the *Mailer Review*, Noonan wrote of the successive Brooklyn apartments Mailer lived in and how he drew inspiration from them. Mailer's Brooklyn accents, he argued, appear prominently in many of his works including *The Naked and the Dead*, *The Barbary Shore* (set in Brooklyn Heights), and *Ancient Evenings*. Noonan also taught and wrote about contemporary works such as Jonathan Lethem's *Motherless Brooklyn* and *Fortress of Solitude*, Paul Auster's *Sunset Park*, Jennifer Egan's *Manhattan Beach* and Edwidge Danticat's *Krik? Krak!*, in which Brooklyn serves as an important setting.

In the last decade, however, Boerum Hill, like so much of Brooklyn has transformed. Rents have skyrocketed driving many long-term tenants away. Many family-owned businesses have also come and gone. Fish Restaurant is now a stationary store. Brawta is now Steven Alan Woman's Shop, a clothing boutique where shoes sell for $350. Gentrification has even had an effect on some of the neighborhood's famed literary landmarks. Mailer's family, for example, could not afford to hold onto their father's nautically-themed "writer's nest" on 142 Columbia Street, where the Norman Mailer Society often hosted events. First sold in 2011 for 2.5 million, as of 2017, it is again on the market, this time for an astonishing 16 million dollars. What's good for speculators is obviously less good for the artists. In yet another cycle, it's clear that the great writers of tomorrow will be hailing from edges of the borough, far away from the waterfront that once inspired so many classic works of art.

Countless people have embraced the distinct pleasures of Brooklyn but are fearful of the incoming tides. "I don't know how to feel about the changes taking place in Brooklyn," says City Tech student Kenneth Pimental in an essay about how gentrification is transforming neighborhoods of this global borough.

Part of me is proud and excited that others see in Brooklyn what I always saw in it: the fun, the beauty, and the diversity of people in its neighborhoods. Yet, I'm sad because some will never know about just hanging on a stoop with your friends and laughing till the sun went down and sometimes till the sun went back up. Opening the fire hydrant on a hot summer day and buying home-made ice pops from the lady across the street. Impromptu BBQ's. Throwing a party in a vacant apartment. Hopping turnstiles on our way to Rockaway Beach...

I am also excited to see the changes happening right before me. I don't have to tuck in my chain or hide my cell phone on the train while I'm headed to eat Thai food at Sea restaurant. I see new green spaces and watch as kids and adults enjoy them without any fear whatsoever. I'm hopeful that we can find a balance of the new and old, that to rebuild doesn't mean to destroy, and that future generations won't have to get their Brooklyn edge from a website.[10]

Another City Tech student, Keith Haly, shares similarly mixed sentiments. A resident of East Flatbush, Haly writes how "what was formerly called Vanderveer Projects is now called Flatbush Gardens Estates. Unfortunately, landlords are raising rents forcing tenants to give up their apartments as people from higher income brackets move in." Such developments have stirred racial resentment amongst some of the residents. As Haly explains, "on various subway platforms, one will see anti-white gentrification graffiti."[11]

As Pimenthal and Haly suggest, both the negative and positive effects of Brooklyn's changing neighborhoods must be given serious consideration. Others, meanwhile, embrace these changes, as Whitman always suggested, by singing. Current borough president Eric Adams praised the students taking part in the economically and socially diverse Brooklyn Youth Chorus, noting the practice of singing together helps us see and be in a different way together. "When children sing together, they can live together. As we approach the uncertainty of direction for the borough, many may find the unfamiliar sounds, and faces and styles frightening," Adams elaborated. "When our children sing together, it turns the question mark of uncertainty into an exclamation point: We are going to be all right!"[12]

There is a mutable quality to the life and pulse of the streets in this global borough that might have something to teach observers about democracy and globalization. From Jackie Robinson, who broke baseball's color line with the Dodgers in 1947, to Jason Collins, who became the first openly gay player in U.S. professional sports with the Brooklyn Nets in 2014, Brooklyn is a place where people sometimes beat back seemingly inevitable trends and create something different. Together, we share space, fighting to create open spaces for a different kind of sustainable urbanism.

Slow Down Brooklyn

Slowing down Brooklyn means multiple things. At least that's how it felt on a cold night in November of 2013 when I (Ben Shepard) joined a group of cyclists to install 20 mph signs all along Prospect Park West after the City Department of Transportation refused.

Figure 8: "Twenty is plenty sign." By Right of Way.

The pedestrian rights group Right of Way installed the signs on Prospect Park West, in part because the Park Slope Civic Council's application for a Slow Zone was rejected by city officials in 2012. The death of 12-year-old Park Slope resident Sammy Cohen-Eckstein by a driver doing 30 mph was the prime impetus for the action.[13] This street is directly adjacent to a park where children play and then cross the road to go home. There is no reason drivers need to go 30 mph here, or on any residential street in New York City.

Figure 9: "Right of Way installed 20mph speed limit signs of the same size, shape, and material as official DOT signs, at regulation height, on every other block along Prospect Park West."
Photo by Benjamin Shepard.

According to the U.S. Department of Transportation, pedestrians have only a slightly better than an even chance of surviving being struck by a vehicle going 30 mph, compared to a 95 per cent chance of surviving when struck by a vehicle going 20 mph.

"This is not enough," said Keegan Stephan, another organizer with Right of Way. "We need complete street redesigns, speed and red light cameras, and vigilant law enforcement to eliminate traffic deaths. But even signs alone can save lives," he added. "According to state law, the city could lower the speed limit on most of New York City's streets tomorrow. This would inevitably slow down traffic, allowing the NYPD to focus on people who continue to speed and engage in other life-threatening criminal driving, such as failure to yield. While these signs are not permanent," said Stephan, "we have put them up to show the city just how easy it is." Over the next few weeks, the city would move ahead to slow the speed limit.

Many of us in Right of Way and the broader traffic and environmental justice movement saw the "20 is Plenty" signs as emblems of a city in transition, moving toward human-scale issues. The signs served as a direct-action strategy, a policy solution and a plea for the city to embrace a slow-growth approach toward development. Slow down, we were asking. For us, slowing down means both traffic and development. This plea also speaks to the global challenge of our era: the changes in the environment. With recent years only continuing to break temperature records, unfettered capitalism seems to have brought the world dangerously close to a precipice.[14] To counter these trends, environmentalists, we argue have to slow down development in order for the city to sustain itself. To do so, we would need to support a de-growth model challenging conventional capitalist development approaches and favoring sustainable development strategies involving less consumption, effective struggles against inequality, including equitable distribution of resources, as well as an environmental paradigm shift. Lena Dominelli suggests urban inhabitants can address the problem of climate chaos in a number of distinct ways, including reducing harms to the planet, reducing greenhouse gases through alternative models of development, lobbying for preventative local measures, advocating for green technologies, equitable sharing of resources regardless of country boundaries, mobilizing communities to reduce carbon emissions, and by working with scientists and policy-makers, as well as using media to change policies at local, national and international levels.[15]

Many of the activists involved with Right of Way traced throughout this book took part in Occupy Sandy relief efforts, which looked to mutual-aid models for community support. In a world coping with floods and droughts, water shortages, tsunamis, and hurricanes, none of us know where the next disaster will strike. But we do know we need to support each other. A city of friends depends on such efforts. It also depends on effective public policy.

Figure 10: "A crowd of over 200 met to implore the state to give NYC home rule so New York can make its own choices. Slow down, implored the crowd of activists from all over Brooklyn. Image of Sammy Cohen-Eckstein at bottom right." Photo by Benjamin Shepard.

"This is a crucial step in Mayor de Blasio's push toward Vision Zero," said Keegan Stephan, referring to the mayor's initiative to reduce traffic fatalities to zero. "Drivers going 20 miles per hour have more time to react in the event of the unexpected, reducing the frequency of crashes," added Hilda Cohen, founder of Make Brooklyn Safer. Elaborated Stephan, "There is no reason drivers need to be going faster than that on our residential streets, in the nation's most pedestrian-rich city."

Those in the traffic justice movement called for "home rule" to shape our own model of urbanism in Brooklyn. The state would later approve the move, and the city voted to reduce the speed limits city-wide. Despite the difficulties, individuals and groups can impact this global city. A lesson of Brooklyn's recent lived experience is that there is still space for individual social actors in an increasingly globalized world. There is still room for regular people to have an impact on our neighborhoods, at least in some spheres.

Figures 11 and 12: "Street stencil for Puran, killed by car on Myrtle Avenue in Brooklyn in January 2013, and a subsequent street action placing signs along Prospect Park West imploring cars to slow down in November of 2013." Photos by Benjamin Shepard.

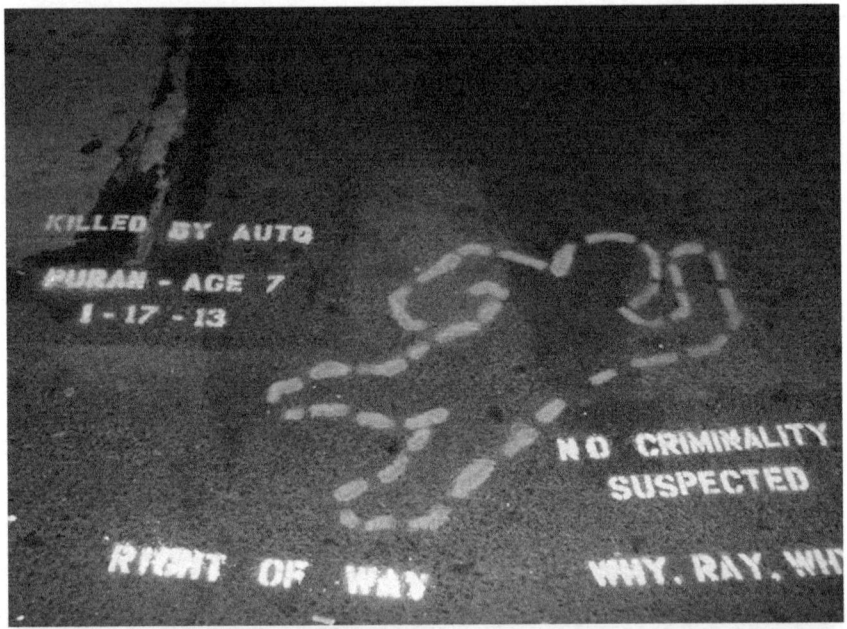

Throughout these chapters, we've explored the tensions between workers and global capital, neighborhoods and toxic social relations, patterns of migration, community-building and displacement, the way the city copes with neighborhood threats, police brutality, housing, super-storms, climate chaos, struggles for open space, and safe streets. Throughout them all, regular people have been able to demonstrate a degree of agency. While Downtown Brooklyn offers challenges, other streetscapes, such as Prospect Park West—where a bike lane and 25 mph speed limit transformed the space—suggest this is a sphere where regular people can create change.

Gregory Pardlo addresses some of the messy dynamics of the space and the people who gather here, in his poem "Marginalia."[16]

...Olmsted's signature
archways and meadows. Kite
strings tensing the load of a saddle-
backed wind. This is Prospect Park,
Brooklyn, where limbs tickle
and jounce as if ice cubes shiver....[17]

People from all over the world converge "on the uneven playing fields" in this park.[18] People are drumming there. "Orthodox women walk powerfully by, jogging."[19] In between it all, everyone in the park seems to:

... Take heart in the percussion
Structuring the distance like prophetic
weather, a shelter of vibrations[20]

The whole world seems to be here.[21] In this city, we are all:

perpetual stranger[s] with a fork
in the socket of life's vivid grid...
you're thinking: not the brick and mortar, but
the quickening backfill of belonging, the stranger
facing, the neighbor knowing confidence and ease
with the ripple that diminishes as it extends
over the vast potential immovable thirst.
You are home now, outsider, for what it's worth.[22]

In Pardlo's hopeful narrative, the "outsider," the "perpetual stranger," is home here. From Iranian punk musicians playing in Williamsburg, Jamaicans in Church Avenue, Italians in Carroll Gardens, or Russians in Brighton Beach, there is space for countless people to become a part of this city of friends.

Figure 13: "Signs of the times in Greenpoint. Overdevelopment and fears for the last of the blue skies along the Williamsburg waterfront."

The tides crashing onto these shores pour in from countless directions. In the fourth act of Shakespeare's *Julius Caesar*, Brutus declares:

There is a tide in the affairs of men.
Which, taken at the flood, leads on to fortune;
Omitted, all the voyage of their life
Is bound in shallows and in miseries.
On such a full sea are we now afloat,
And we must take the current when it serves
Or lose our ventures.[23]

There's a time to act and rise and resist—before the chance goes by. The weeks after the 2016 presidential election offered ample testament that there are times to rise up and take the offensive. While we were completing this book during the last week of January 2017, people around the city stood up for each other, in solidarity, converging at John F Kennedy airport in opposition to the "Muslim ban" instated by Donald Trump and his Cabinet. On January 28th 2017, we joined a large crowd as it celebrated in front of Brooklyn's Borough Hall after a federal judge granted a stay against the order.

On January 30th, the borough president's office, along with students and members of CUNY's Professional Staff Congress, condemned the administration's Muslim ban—which was keeping one CUNY student from returning to school for the semester. CUNY doctoral student Saira Rafiee was also denied entry into the U.S. as a result of Trump's executive order barring entry for legal, documented immigrants from seven Muslim-majority countries. Saira was traveling back from Iran, where she is a citizen, to resume her studies at the CUNY Grad Center. She was in transit by way of Abu Dhabi when she was forbidden to board a plane to New York and was detained for almost 18 hours. She flew back to Tehran, but was still barred from re-entry to the U.S. Instead of cultural exchange, the administration was promoting xenophobia. But the people were pushing back.

On February 2, 2017 Yemeni grocery store owners across New York closed over 1,000 stores from noon to 8 pm in response to the "Muslim Ban" executive order. This shut-down was a public show of the vital role these grocers and their families play in New York's economic and social fabric. During this period, grocery store owners spent time with their families and loved ones to support each other; many of these families have been directly affected by the ban.

Later in the day, at 5:15 pm, at Brooklyn Borough Hall, the borough's Yemeni community held a rally. The program began with a public sundown prayer by Muslim rally participants. The prayer was followed by several Yemeni merchants and their families sharing personal stories of how their lives and families had been impacted by the ban, as well as stories read on behalf of families who are afraid to come forward. Showing up after teaching classes, we observed kids wrapped in American flags and women in hijabs chanting "This is what America looks like, this is what democracy looks like." Others cried "Immigrants in, Trump out!" "We're all Muslim," another sign read.

On February 4th, 2017, news emerged that Saira Rafiee had been allowed to return to Brooklyn from Iran. Borough president Eric Adams tweeted out, "I'm excited to share Saira Rafiee is coming home to Brooklyn! She has landed in Boston safe and sound. #NoBanNoWall!"

These latest tides of resistance show that in a place like Brooklyn, we can still beat back inevitable trends. The residents of global Brooklyn are standing strong, pushing back, insuring they do not lose their rights. In Shakespeare's illustrious language, they ride the currents to secure their "ventures" and win their well-deserved good "fortune."

Figure 14: "NYC Yemeni Grocery Stores Shut Down in Response to 'Muslim Ban'. Yemeni and US Flags Fly at Rally at Borough Hall, February 2, 2017." Photo by Benjamin Shepard.

A Return to the Water

On the first day of the year, 2017, it seemed like all of New York made their way to Coney Island, to take part in the New Year's "polar bear" swim. Riding there, several of us made fast friends on the subway, talking about finding something better in our lives here, beyond the 9-to-5 jobs. People from around the borough were there. The city wanted people to wait in line and sign in, but most of us just jumped in rather than ask for permission. In and out of the water, giddy bodies were everywhere, talking and high-fiving each other, celebrating the event and just being alive.

"I can't find Caroline," I (Benjamin) told Reverend Billy, drying off after the plunge.

"I'll wait for them a Ruby's. And beg for beer. It wouldn't be the first time."

"Here take a ten," Billy smiled.

Caroline eventually joined us and then walked out to the Wonder Wheel, which we rode with our friends. The famed ferris wheel ascended, aching into the sky. This was it. Life was over. We felt as if the wheel was going to leap out into the sky and tumble back into the boardwalk below. That would be a poetic ending.

Epilogue: The Global Street 245

"Look out over the horizon," Caroline advised. So we looked past the rides into the water.

Figure 15: "On the Wonder Wheel on New Years Day, Coney Island!" Photo by Benjamin Shepard.

Back up, around, down,—somehow, we survived. We then made our way down the boardwalk. We talked about activism and poetry, kids growing up and rock climbing. The kids ran into the distance as we walked toward Brighton Beach to get Russian food. We walked with our friend, Savitri D, who talked about being Mermaid Queen back in 2008 and how she went on a hunger strike to stop the horrible plans for redeveloping Coney Island. Those plans for a "gentrification apocalypse" were stopped in their tracks.[24] And we agreed that Coney Island was as great as ever. Magic light from the setting sun was everywhere. Looking around, we found our kids playing along with the beach, by a secret door they discovered below the boardwalk. It was a relic from the overflow sand from Hurricane Sandy. Watching them play, I was reminded of a scene from *The Little Fugitive*, the 1953 black-and-white film by Morris Engel about a boy lost for days in Coney Island. The film inspired François Truffaut to make *The 400 Blows* in 1959.[25] Looking out at the water along the boardwalk, the relics of the old cascaded along the new within a panorama of what our global borough could be, as we all enjoyed a moment in time, the Brooklyn tides crashing on the beach for a new year.

Figures 16-22: "*Scenes from Global Brooklyn. January 1, 2014 and 2017 polar bear swims on the beach, with New Yorkers converging to enjoy being alive together for just a moment. Some just swim and run to grab a pint at Ruby's, still alive and thriving. And kids discover secret places along the shore.*" *Photos by Benjamin Shepard.*

Doors to secret places.

Endnotes

Prologue

1 | Allen, W. (1977): Annie Hall.
2 | Whitman, W. (1945/1865): "City of Ships," in: The Portable Walt Whitman. New York: Viking, 217.
3 | See Metropolitan Avenue. (1988): A POV film by Christine Noschese and Brooklyn Dodgers: Ghosts of Flatbush. (2007): Produced by R. Greenberg. HBO Sports. Written by A. Cohen and C. Oliver.
4 | Kazin, A. (1951): A Walker in the City. New York: Haughton Mifflin, 8-12.
5 | Foucault, M. (October 1984): "Of Other Spaces, Heterotopias," in: Architecture, Mouvement, Continuite (5) 46–49. Translated by J. Miskowiec.
6 | Roma, T. (2015): The Vale of Cashmere. New York: Powerhouse Books.
7 | Barron, J. (2016): "The Battle of Brooklyn: A Loss That Helped Win the Revolution." New York Times. 26 August. http://www.nytimes.com/2016/08/27/nyregion/the-battle-of-brooklyn-a-loss-that-helped-win-the-revolution.html. Alexiou, J. (2015): Gowanus: Brooklyn's Curious Canal. New York: New York University Press.
8 | Recent books on Brooklyn include S. Osman, The Invention of Brownstone Brooklyn: Gentrification and the Search for Authenticity in New York (New York: Oxford UP, 2011) and J. N. DeSena, Gentrification and Inequality in Brooklyn: The New Kids on the Block (Lanham, Md: Lexington Books, 2009). Notable ethnographies of Brooklyn include T. M. Brown, Raising Brooklyn: Nannies, Childcare, and Caribbean's Creating Community (New York: New York University Press, 2011); N. Marwell, Bargaining for Brooklyn: Community Organizations in the Entrepreneurial City (Chicago: University of Chicago, 2007); J. Rieder, Canarsie: The Jews and Italians of Brooklyn Against Liberalism (Cambridge, MA: Harvard University Press, 1985); I. Susser, Norman Street: Poverty and Politics in an Urban Neighborhood (New York: Oxford University Press, 1982).
9 | Relevant literature on global cities includes J. Abu-Lughod, New York, Chicago, Los Angeles: America's Global Cities (Minneapolis: University of Minnesota Press, 1999); A. D. King, Global Cities: Post-Imperialism and the Internationalization of London (New York: Routledge, 1990); M. Castells, The Informational City (Cambridge, MA: Blackwell, 1989); S. Sassen. The Global City: New York, London, Tokyo. (Princeton: Princeton University Press, 2001); J. Friedmann/G. Wolff, "World City Formation: An Agenda for

Research and Action," International Journal of Urban and Regional Research 6, no. 3 (1982). Less theoretical work on New York's place in the neoliberal global economy includes D. G. Gladstone, S. S. Fainstein, "The New York and Los Angeles Economies," in New York & Los Angeles: Politics, Society, and Culture, A Comparative View, D. Halle (ed) (Chicago: University of Chicago Press, 2003); K. Moody, From Welfare State to Real Estate: Regime Change in New York City, 1974 to the Present (New York: New Press, 2007).

10 | Vitale, A. (2008) : City of Disorder: How the Quality of Life Campaign Transformed New York Politics. New York: New York University Press, 14.

11 | Ibid.

12 | Ibid, 14.

13 | With a nod to works such as G. Woods' Homintern: How Gay Culture Liberated the Modern World (New Haven: Yale University Press, 2016), which looked to literature as evidence, this work leans heavily on the use of literature to help illustrate and support claims. This approach is supported within a larger triangulation of multiple forms of data, including interviews, other secondary sources, and ethnographic observations of our ever-changing borough where we've lived and taught for nearly two decades. An observing participant informs this discussion.

14 | Sites, W. (2003): Remaking New York. Minneapolis, Minnesota: University of Minnesota Press.

15 | Butters, S. (1983). "The Logic of Inquiry of Participant Observation," in Resistance through Rituals, S. Hall/T. Jefferson (eds). London: Hutchinson University Library, 253-73. Lichterman, P. (2002): "Seeing Structure Happen: Theory Driven Participant Observation," in: Methods of Social Movement Research, B. K.andermand/S. Staggerborg (eds). Minneapolis: University of Minnesota Press, 118-145. Tedlock, B. (1991): "From Participant Observation to Observation of Participation: The Emergence of Narrative Ethnography." Journal of Anthropological Research, 47, 69-94.

16 | Hamill, P. (1986): "A New Day Dawns," New York Times, 21 April, 35.

17 | Hevesi, A. G. (2004): "Brooklyn: Economic Development and the State of Its Economy" (New York Office of the State Comptroller). http://www.osc.state.ny.us/press/releases/feb04/bkln2050rpt.pdf. Freeman, J. (2000): Working-Class New York: Life and Labor Since World War II. New York: Free Press. Levinson, M. (2008): The Box: How the Shipping Container Made the World Smaller and the Economy Bigger. Princeton, NJ. Princeton University Press.

18 | Zukin, S. (2010): Naked City: The Death and Life of Authentic Urban Spaces. New York: Oxford University Press.

19 | Marilyn J. (2003): Street Justice: A History of Police Violence in New York City. Boston: Beacon Press. Vitale, A. (2008): City of Disorder: How the Quality of Life Campaign Transformed New York Politics. New York: New York University Press. Wilder, C. (2000): A Covenant with Color: Race and Social Power in Brooklyn. New York: Columbia University Press.

20 | Vitale, 25.

21 | Smith, N. (1984): Uneven Development: Nature, Capital, and Production of Space. Athens, Georgia: University of Georgia Press.
22 | Freeman.
23 | Zukin.
24 | Berman, M. (2007): "Introduction." New York Calling: From Blackout to Bloomberg. Marshall Berman and Brian Berger, eds. London: Reaktion Books. Levinson.
25 | Linder, M./Zaccarias, L. (1999): Of Cabbages and Kings County: Agriculture and the Formation of Modern Brooklyn. Ames, Iowa: University of Iowa Press.
26 | "Brooklyn Rooftop Farm In Sunset Park Will Be The World's Largest." (2012) Huffington Post. 6 April. http://www.huffingtonpost.com/2012/04/06/brooklyn-rooftop-farm-brightfarms_n_1408045.html.
27 | Schneider, K. (1999): "The Farmer and the Urb: Only Yesterday, Almost, Brooklyn was an Agricultural Heavyweight." New York Times. 24 October. https://www.nytimes.com/books/99/10/24/reviews/991024.24schneit.html.
28 | "A City Reshaped Under Bloomberg." (2013): New York Times. 18 August. A1.
29 | Berman, M. (1982): All That is Solid Melts into Air. New York: Penguin.
30 | Merrifield, A. (2002): Metromarxism: A Marxist Tale of the City. New York: Routledge.
31 | Osman, S. (2011): The Invention of Brownstone Brooklyn: Gentrification and the Search for Authenticity in New York. New York: Oxford.
32 | Benjamin, R. (1982): My Favorite Year. Brooksfilms.
33 | Foucault.
34 | Roma T. (2015): The Vale of Cashmere. NY: Powerhouse Books. Seelie, T. (2013): Bright Nights: Photographs of Another New York. Prestel USA.
35 | Coscarelli, J. (2014): "Spike Lee's Amazing Rant Against Gentrification: 'We Been Here!'" New York Magazine. 25 Feb. http://nymag.com/daily/intelligencer/2014/02/spike-lee-amazing-rant-against-gentrification.html.
36 | Hughes, E. (2011): Literary Brooklyn: The Writers of Brooklyn and the Story of American Life. New York: Henry Holt.
37 | Municipal Arts Society. "The Red Hook Graving Dock." http://saveindustrialbrooklyn.org/red_hook.html.
38 | Oliver, C. (2007): Brooklyn Dodgers: The Ghosts of Flatbush. HBO Sports.
39 | Nolan, K. (2014): "Prince William and Pregnant Kate Middleton Set to See Brooklyn Nets take on LeBron James, and the Cleveland Cavaliers." 14 November. New York Daily News. http://www.nydailynews.com/entertainment/gossip/prince-william-kate-middleton-set-nets-game-visit-article-1.2011183.

CHAPTER ONE

1 | Muir, J. (1938): John of the Mountains: The Unpublished Journals of John Muir. L.M. Wolfe (ed). Boston: Houghton Mifflin, 89.
2 | Robertson, R. (1992): Globalization: Social Theory and Global Culture. London: Sage, 29.
3 | Roberston, R. (1995): "Glocalization: Time-Space and Homogeneity-Heterogeneity," in: M. Featherstone, S. Lash, and R. Robertson (eds), Global Modernities. London: Sage, 25-44.
4 | Yee, V. (2014): "Junior's Brooklyn Site Will Be Sold to Developer, but Restaurant Will Return." New York Times. 20 Feb.
5 | Stiles, H. (1870): A History of Brooklyn. Volume II. Brooklyn, NY: Octavo.
6 | McCully, B. (2007): City at the Water's Edge: A Natural History of New York. New Brunswick: Rutgers University Press, 37.
7 | McCully, 47.
8 | For more on each of these tribes, see E. Pritchard (2007) Native New Yorkers: The Legacy of the Algonquin People of New York. San Francisco: Council Oak Books, 283-303.
9 | McCully, 55.
10 | Van der Donck, A. (2008): A Description of New Netherland. C. Gehring and W. A. Starna (eds). Translated by D. W. Goedhuys. Lincoln: University of Nebraska Press, 98.
11 | Ibid.
12 | Abu-Lughod, J. L. (1999): New York, Chicago, L.A.: America's Global Cities. Minneapolis-London: University of Minnesota Press, 7-10.
13 | Verrazzano, G. (1524): "Letter to King Francis 1 of France." 8 July. nationalhumanitiescenter.org.
14 | Ibid.
15 | Elliman, D. (2009): Half Moon: Henry Hudson and the Voyage That Redrew the Map of the New World. NY: Bloomsbury Press, 170.
16 | Ibid, 30.
17 | Jacobs, J. (2009): The Colony of New Netherland. Ithaca: Cornell.
18 | O'Callaghan, E. B. (1948): History of New Netherland: Or, New York Under the Dutch. NY: Appleton.
19 | Burrows, E. G./Wallace, M. (2000): Gotham: A *History* of New York to 1898. NY: Oxford University Press, 35. This figure was calculated in the 1900s. Historians James and Michelle Nevius posit that, in today's currency, the figure would be between $2,600 and $15,600. See (2009) Inside the Apple: A Streetwise History of New York City. NY: Simon and Schuster.
20 | Stiles, 49.
21 | Shorto, R. (2009): The Island at the Center of the World: The Untold Story of Dutch Manhattan and the Founding of New York. New York: Transworld Publishers Limited.
22 | Van der Donck, 103.

23 | Kraft, H. (2000): The Lenape or Delaware Indian Heritage: 10,000 BC to AD 2000. Delaware: Lenape Lifeways, 413.
24 | Ibid.
25 | Wilder, C. (2000): A Covenant with Color: Race and Social Power in Brooklyn 1636-1990. New York: Columbia University Press.
26 | "Deed for Manhattan & Long Island 1645 & 1649." (1961). Translated from the original Dutch manuscripts. Historical Documents Company.
27 | According to Patric Verell, "The origins of the name Gowanus are disputed. Although it most likely comes from 'Gowane,' a leader of the Canarsee Indian tribe that lived in Brooklyn; it has also been pegged to the Dutch word Gouwee, which means bay." The Gowanus Canal: A Waterway Steeped in History. http://thesixthborough.weebly.com/the-history-of-gowanus.html.
28 | Marzulli, J. (2014): "Gang leader at Brooklyn Housing Project Brought Down by Littering, YouTube videos," New York Daily News. 6 April.
29 | Environmental Protection Agency. Record of Designation Gowanus Superfund Site. (September 2013): http://www.epa.gov/region2/superfund/npl/gowanus/ri_docs/692106_gowanus_canal_rod_9_27_13_final.pdf.
For a general overview of this space, see J. Alexiou (2015) The Gowanus: Brooklyn's Curious Canal. NY: NYU Press.
30 | Livingston. E.A. (2012): Brooklyn and the Civil War. NY: The History Press, 22.
31 | Ibid.
32 | Jea, J. (2009): The Life, History and Unparalleled Sufferings of John Jea, the African Preacher. NY: Dodo Press, 4.
33 | Ibid.
34 | Wilder.
35 | Wellman, J. (2014): Brooklyn's Promised Land: The Free Black Community of Weeksville, NY. NY: NYU Press.
36 | Du Bois, W. E. B. (1935/1999): Black Reconstruction in American 1860-1880. New York Free Press. For an elaboraton on Black counterpublics, see N. H. Singh (2005) Black a Country: Race and the Unfinished Struggle for Democracy. Cambridge, MA: Harvard University Press.
37 | Livingston, E.A., 27.
38 | Ibid.
39 | Ibid, 16.
40 | Ibid, 21.
41 | Simon, M. (Fall 2010): "'The Walled City': Industrial Flux in Red Hook, Brooklyn, 1840-1920," Buildings & Landscapes: Journal of the Vernacular Architecture Forum (17) 2.
42 | Ibid.
43 | Qtd. in T. Steinberg. (2014): Gotham Unbound: The Ecological History of Greater New York. New York: Simon and Schuster, 85.
44 | "Slavery in New York." http://slavenorth.com/newyork.htm.

McManus, E.J. (1966): A History of Negro Slavery in New York. Syracuse: Syracuse University Press.
45 | "Professor James Brings Wealth of Experience To Discussion of African Americans' Role In Brooklyn Waterfront Development." http://www.citytech.cuny.edu/aboutus/newsevents/archivednewsevents/2008-2009news/james/index.shtml.
46 | Linder, M./Zacharias, L. (1999): Of Cabbages and Kings: Agriculture and the Formation of Modern Brooklyn. Iowa City: University of Iowa Press.
47 | Ibid.
48 | Scientific American. (May 14, 1898): 1.
49 | Ibid.
50 | Harper's Weekly. (February 26, 1898): 2.
51 | Ibid.
52 | Ibid.
53 | Ibid.
54 | Qtd. in E. G. Burrows and M. Wallace. (1999): Gotham: A History of New York to 1898, 1233.
55 | Ibid.
56 | Burrows, E.G./Wallace, M. (1999): Gotham: A History of New York to 1898.
57 | Haw, R. (2005): The Brooklyn Bridge: A Cultural History. New Brunswick: Rutgers UP.
58 | Harper's Weekly. (Feb. 2, 1895).
59 | Whitman, W. (2002): "Crossing Brooklyn Ferry," in: Leaves of Grass and Other Writings. M. Moon (ed). New York: Norton.
60 | Brown, J./Ment, D. (1980): Factories, Foundries, and Refineries: A History of Five Brooklyn Industries. New York: Brooklyn Educational and Cultural Alliance.
61 | See A. Mindlin (2008) "On the Waterfront, Locked Gates and Grumbling." *New York Times*, 8 June, 6CY. Also see B. Shepard and G. Smithsimon. (2011): The Beach Beneath the Streets: Contesting New York's Public Spaces. New York: State University Press of New York.

CHAPTER TWO

1 | Whitman, W. (1865): "I Hear America Singing". https://www.poets.org/poetsorg/poem/i-hear-america-singing.
2 | Snyder-Grenier, E. M. (1996): Brooklyn! An Illustrated History. Philadelphia: Temple UP, 124.
3 | Freeman, J. (2000): Working-Class New York: Life and Labor Since World War II. New York: Free Press.
4 | Freeman, 164.
5 | Abu-Lughod, J. L. (1999): New York, Chicago, L.A.: America's Global Cities. Minneapolis-London: University of Minnesota Press, 7-10.

6 | Aronowitz S./DiFazio W. (1995): The Jobless Future. Second Edition. Minneapolis:University of Minnesota Press.
7 | Villarosa, L. (2012): "Group Helps You Find Mr. Wright." New York Times. 12 March. http://fort-greene.thelocal.nytimes.com/2012/03/20/group-tries-to-help-you-find-mr-wright/#more-72421.
8 | Hughes, E. (20110: Literary Brooklyn. The Writers of Brooklyn and the Story of American City Life. Holt: New York.
9 | Styron, W. (1976): Sophie's Choice. New York: Vintage International, 3.
10 | Styron A. (2007): "Reading My Father. A Writer's Triumphs and His Torments." The New Yorker. 10 December. http://www.newyorker.com/magazine/2007/12/10/reading-my-father.
11 | Coates T. (2016): "On Homecomings," Atlantic Magazine. 9 May. Also see A. Kuban (2011) "Brooklyn Literary Walking Tour." http://www.nycgo.com/articles/brooklyn-literary-tour-nyc.
12 | Aronowitz, S. (1991): False Promises: The Shaping of American Working Class Consciousness. Revised Edition. Duke University Press. Durham, NC. Also see S. Wilentz (2004) Chants Democratic: New York City and the Rise of the American Working Class, 1788-1850. 20th Anniversary Edition. New York: Oxford University Press.
13 | Poole E. (1915): The Harbor. New York: The Macmillan Co., 103.
14 | Ibid, 107.
15 | Ibid, 7.
16 | Ibid, 188.
17 | Ibid, 306.
18 | Winslow, C. (2003): "Italian Workers on the Waterfront: The New York Harbor Strikes of 1907 and 1919," in: The Lost World of Italian-American Radicalism. P. Cannistraro/G. Meyer (eds) Westport: Praeger, 102-103.
19 | Winslow, 103.
20 | Poole, 317.
21 | Ibid, 386.
22 | Du Bois, W.E.B.. (1935/1999): Black Reconstruction in America 1860-1880. NY: New York Free Press. For a history of racism in the labor movement, see S. Aronowitz (1973) False Promises: The Shaping of Working Class Consciousness. NY: McGraw Hill. For Black social and cultural influences on work in New York, see C. Wilder (2001) In the Company of Black Men: The African Influence on African American Culture in New York. New York. NYU Press. For a history of the struggles for community control in Brooklyn, see C. Taylor (1994) Black Churches of Brooklyn. Columbia University Press. For an elaboration on Black counterpublics, see N. Singh (2005) Black Is a Country: Race and the Unfinished Struggle for Democracy. Cambridge: Harvard University Press. On "underpaid and overworked" black workers see, Associated Press (2014) "Art Installation at Old Domino Sugar Refinery Honors Black Workers." 17 May. Daily News http://www.nydailynews.com/life-style/domino-sugar-refinery-art-instillation-honors-black-workers-article-1.1796419.

23 | Winslow.
24 | History of International Workers of the World. http://www.u-s-history.com/pages/h1050.html.
25 | Center for Constitutional Rights. Sacco and Vanzetti were two innocent men executed. Bill of Rights in Action (Summer 2007). Volume 23, No. 2. http://www.crf-usa.org/bill-of-rights-in-action/bria-23-2-a-sacco-and-vanzetti-were-two-innocent-men-executed. Also see F. Russell (1971) Tragedy in Dedham: The Story of the Sacco and Vanzetti Case. New York: McGraw-Hill and M. Topp (2005) Sacco and Vanzetti Case: A Brief History With Documents. New York: Palgrave MacMillan.
26 | Hugle, P./Schulman, N. (2005): Wobblies: A Graphic History of the Industrial Workers of the World. New York: Verso, 109, 160-61.
27 | Baker, K. (2013): "City of Water." New York Times. 12 October.
28 | Ward, N. (2010): Dark Harbor: The War for the New York Waterfront. New York: Farrar, Straus, and Giroux, 507.
29 | Ibid.
30 | Budd Schulberg screenplay for E. Kazan (1954) On the Waterfront. http://www.imdb.com/title/tt0047296/quotes. Also see J. Rapf (2003) On the Waterfront. Cambridge, UK: Cambridge University Press.
31 | Smith, B (1943): A Tree Grows in Brooklyn. New York: Harper Collins, 20.
32 | Ibid, 192.
33 | Ibid, 364.
34 | Snyder-Grenier, E. (2004): Brooklyn!: An Illustrated History. Philadelphia: Temple University Press, 129.
35 | Ward.
36 | Miller, A. (1977 reissue): A View From the Bridge. New York: Penguin Books.
37 | Miller.
38 | Schulberg, B. (1955): Waterfront. New York: Donald I. Fine, 5.
39 | Ibid. 308.
40 | Levinson, M. (2008): The Box: How the Shipping Container Made the World Smaller and the World Economy Bigger. Princeton: Princeton University Press.
41 | Lethem, J. (1999): Motherless Brooklyn. New York: Random House.
42 | Hellman, C. (Oct. 2013): "'A Walker in the City.' Lee's Native Speaker, Lethem's Motherless Brooklyn, and Whitman's Cartograhic Legacy." Studies in American Culture, 82.
43 | Ibid., 86.
44 | See T. Kushner (2011) The Intelligent Homosexual's Guide to Capitalism and Socialism with a Key to the Scriptures. NY: Public Theater. For more on gentrification in Brooklyn, see S. Osmond (2011) The Invention of Brownstone Brooklyn: Gentrification and the Search for Authenticity in Postwar New York. New York: Oxford University Press.
45 | For more on the fate of the old International Longshoreman's Association building on Court Street, see T. Whitman (2008) "The Clarett Group Unveils Plans for Carroll Gardens Development Site" 4 April. http://www.brooklyneagle.com/archive/category.

php?category_id=5&id=19765. Biuso, G. (2011): "Clarett Group Closures Makes Court Street Site a Hole Lot of Nothing." 15 March. The Brooklyn Paper. http://www.brooklynpaper.com/stories/34/11/cg_claretthole_2011_3_18_bk.html?utm_source=feedburner&utm_medium=feed&utm_campaign=Feed%3A+TheBrooklynPaper-FullArticles+%28The+Brooklyn+Paper%3A+Full+articles%29
Curbed (2011) "#240 Court Street." Curbed NY. 12 June. http://ny.curbed.com/tags/340-court-street. For more on containerization, see M. Levinson (2008) The Box: How the Shipping Container Made the World Smaller and the World Economy Bigger. Princeton: Princeton University Press.

46 | ILA. Ud. "Rebuilding the ILA." Accessed 5 June 2011 from http://ilaunion.org/history_rebuild.html. Russell, M. (1966): Men Along the Shore: The I.L.A. and Its History. New York: Brussel & Brussel.

47 | Erikson, E. (1967): Identity and the Life Cycle. NY: WW Norton.

48 | Rockville Center Teacher's Association. (Undated): "Learning about the Triborough Agreement and the Taylor Law." http://rvcta.ny.aft.org/about-us/learning-about-triborough-amendment-and-taylor-law.

49 | For more on the sociology of paying for sex, see E. Bernstein (2007) Temporarily Yours: Intimacy, Authenticity, and the Commerce of Sex. Chicago: University of Chicago Press.

50 | T. Kushner (2011) The Intelligent Homosexual's Guide to Capitalism and Socialism.

51 | Ibid.

52 | Ibid.

53 | See A. Berube (2011) My Desire for History: Essays in Gay, Community, and Labor History. Chapel Hill: University of North Carolina Press. Also see KQED (Undated) "Hope Along the Way, the Life of Harry Hay." Accessed 5 June 2011 from http://www.harryhay.com/AH_labor.html.

54 | MadebyHand. "The Beekeeper." http://www.designindaba.com/videos/creative-work/made-hand-beekeeper.

55 | MadebyHand. Made by Hand is a short film series celebrating the people who make things by hand—sustainably, locally, and with a love for their craft. http://thisismadebyhand.com/about/.

56 | Curan, C. (2014): "Made in Brooklyn Brands See a Major Boom." New York Post. 28 June. http://nypost.com/2014/06/28/made-in-brooklyn-brands-see-major-boom/.

57 | Styron, 48.

CHAPTER THREE

1 | "Lynch Law in America." https://courses.washington.edu/spcmu/speeches/idabwells.htm.

2 | Payne, C. (1996): I've Got the Light of Freedom. Berkeley: University of California Press.

3 | English, T.J. (2011): Savage City: Race: Race, Murder and a Generation on the Edge. New York: Harper Collins, xiii.
4 | Jacobson, M. F. (1999): Whiteness of a Different Color: European Immigrants and the Alchemy of Race. Cambridge, MA: Harvard University Press.
5 | English, xiii.
6 | Ibid, xiv.
7 | Ibid, xiv.
8 | Crichlow, M.E. (2014): Staging Migrations toward an American West: From Ida B Jones to Rhodessa Jones. Boulder: University Press of Colorado, 19-20.
9 | Ibid.
10 | Miller, R./Miller, R./Karp, S. (1979): "The Fourth Largest City in America—A Sociological History of Brooklyn," in: R. Miller (ed) Brooklyn USA: The Fourth Largest City in America, 7.
11 | Ibid.
12 | Shepard, B. (2014): Community Projects as Social Activism. Thousand Oaks, CA: Sage.
13 | For examples of regular people defending their homes against eviction, see K. Chernin (1983) In My Mother's House: A Daughter's Story. San Francisco: Harper Collins and M. Naison (2005) Communists in Harlem During the Depression. Urbana: University of Illinois Press.
14 | Sanneh, K. (2016): "Is Gentrification Really a Bad Thing." The New Yorker. 11 and 18 July. http://www.newyorker.com/magazine/2016/07/11/is-gentrification-really-a-problem.
15 | Marshall, B. (1982): All That is Solid Melts into Air. New York. Penguin.
16 | Metropolitan-Avenue-with-christine-noschese. http://www.uniondocs.org/2013-02-03-metropolitan-avenue-with-christine-noschese/ Also see R. Shaw (2013) The Activist's Handbook Winning Social Change in the 21st Century. Berkeley, CA: University of California Press and J. Freeman (2000) Working-Class New York. New York: Free Press.
17 | O'Donoghue, L. (2014): "Don't Call it Gentrification." Salon.com http://www.salon.com/2014/11/02/don%E2%80%99t_call_it_gentrification/.
18 | Tracy, J. (2014): Dispatches Against Displacement. Oakland: AK Press, 18.
19 | Ibid, 34-5.
20 | O'Donoghue.
21 | Tracy, J. (2014): Dispatches Against Displacement. Oakland: AK Press, 95.
22 | Ibid., 96.
23 | Ibid.
24 | Ibid.
25 | Perelman, M. (2013): "A Short History of Primitive Accumulation." Counterpunch. 16 April. http://www.counterpunch.org/2013/04/16/a-short-history-of-primitive-accumulation/ Also see K. Marx. Capital. Volume One, Part Eight. https://readingcapitalsydney.wordpress.com/2010/04/26/capital-1-part-8-so-called-primitive-accumulation/.

26 | Ibid.
27 | Ibid.
28 | Ibid.
29 | Marx, K. (1906): Capital: A Critique of Political Economy. Trans. by S. Moore and E. Aveling. New York: The Modern Library, 784.
30 | Ibid., 784.
31 | Sites, W. (2003). Remaking New York. Minneapolis, Minnesota: U of Minnesota Press, 12-3.
32 | Perelman, M. (Nd). The Theory of Primitive Accumulation. http://www.csuchico.edu/~mperelman/primitive_accumulation.htm.
33 | Marx, K. (1906): Capital: A Critique of Political Economy. Trans. by S. Moore and E. Aveling. New York: The Modern Library, 787.
34 | Writers for the 99%. (2011): Occupying Wall Street. New York: OR Books.
35 | Lennard, N. (2011): "Community Stands Strong to Block Eviction." New York Times. 19 August. http://cityroom.blogs.nytimes.com/2011/08/19/community-stands-strong-to-block-a-foreclosure/?_r=0.
36 | Holman, R. (2011). "Great-grandmother Fighting Eviction Becomes Symbol of Bank Lending Crisis." France 24 International News. 1 September. http://observers.france24.com/content/20110901-usa-new-york-brooklyn-neighbourhood-fights-eviction-great-grandmother-alleged-victim-predatory-lending-bedford.
37 | Aronowitz, S. (2003): How Class Works. New Haven: Yale University Press, 58.
38 | Willams, S. Facebook post. 21October. http://www.wherevent.com/detail/Black-Autonomy-North-DEFEND-OUR-STREETS-RALLY-MARCH-FOR-AKAI-GURLEY.
39 | "Fires, Vandalism, Gunfire Follow Grand Jury Decision in Ferguson." (2014): CBS/AP. 24 November. http://www.cbsnews.com/news/ferguson-decision-grand-jury-decides-not-to-charge-police-officer-darren-wilson-in-michael-brown.
40 | "Family of Kyam Livingston, Dead in Police Custody, To Sue City. Kyam Livingston Died Three Months in Brooklyn Central Booking. Her family is Demanding Answers." (2013): Metro New York. 21 October. http://www.metro.us/local/family-of-kyam-livingston-dead-in-police-custody-to-sue-city/tmWmju---b3XA6ANnSb54I/.
41 | Ibid.
42 | Statement of Governor Andrew Cuomo. (2013): http://www.brooklyneagle.com/articles/subpoena-issued-against-brooklyn-landlord-accused-harassing-tenants-2013-10-10-180000. October 10.
43 | Ibid.
44 | Lawhead, C. (2014): "There's Nothing Hip or Cool Happening in Brooklyn. It's a War." HTTP://BROKELYN.COM/FIGHT-GENTRIFICATION-BROOKLYN-BATTLEGROUND/. OCT. 28.
45 | Ibid.

46 | Ibid.
47 | Lawhead.
48 | Crichlow, 19-20.
49 | Tracy, J. (2014): Dispatches Against Displacement. Oakland: AK Press.

CHAPTER FOUR

1 | Warshawer, G. (2007): "Close Up Gowanus Brooklyn." The Village Voice. Accessed 28 Feb 2014 from http://www.villagevoice.com/2007-01-02/nyc-life/close-up-on-gowanus-brooklyn/full/ See also: United States Environmental Protection Agency. (2013): "EPA Finalizes Cleanup Plan for Gowanus Canal Superfund Site in Brooklyn, New York; $506 Million Cleanup Will Remove Contaminated Sediment and Create Jobs." 9 September.
http://yosemite.epa.gov/ Alexiou, J. (2015): The Gowanus: Brooklyn's Curious Canal. New York: New York University Press.
2 | Michals, R. (2009): "Notes on the Brooklyn Brownfields." Also see R. Michals (2009) "Toxi City: Brooklyn's Brownfields." Exhibit at the Brooklyn Lyceum, 227 4th Avenue, Park Slope, Brooklyn (October 25-November 8).
3 | Ibid.
4 | McCully, B. (2007): City at Water's Edge: A Natural History of New York City. New Brunswick, NJ: Rivergate Books.
5 | Waldman, J. (2012): Heartbeats in the Muck: The History, Sea Life, and Environment of New York Harbor. NY: Oxford University Press, 110.
6 | Kurlansky, M. (2006): The Big Oyster: History on the Half Shell. NY: Random House, 277.
7 | Wilder, C. (2000): A Covenant with Color: Race and Social Power in Brooklyn. New York: Columbia University Press.
8 | My Brooklyn. (2012): Directed by K. Anderson. http://www.mybrooklynmovie.com/.
9 | Gregor, A. (2014): "A Brooklyn Artery in Transition." New York Times. 31 January.
10 | My Brooklyn.
11 | I credit Professor Caroline Hellman for coming up with the term "East River School" and allowing my use of it in this book.
12 | Miller. A. (1998): Death of a Salesman. NY: Penguin Books, 165.
13 | Selby, H. (1964): Last Exit to Brooklyn. New York: Grove Press.
14 | Ibid., 19.
15 | Ibid., 252.
16 | Bennets, L. (1988): "'Last Exit' Brings Pleasant Moments at Last." New York Times. 4 August. http://www.nytimes.com/1988/08/04/movies/last-exit-brings-pleasant-moments-at-last.html.
17 | Selby, H. (1978): Requiem for a Dream.

18 | Shepard, B. (2014): Community Projects as Social Activism. Thousand Oaks California: Sage Press.
19 | Hamil, D. (2012): "Jay-Z's Hardknock Life in Marcy Projects Paves Way to a Better Life for Daughter Blue Ivy Carter." 10 January. New York Daily News. http://www.nydailynews.com/new-york/jay-z-hardknock-life-marcy-projects-paves-better-life-daughter-blue-ivy-carter-article-1.1003633.
20 | Carter, S. (2010): Decoded. New York: Random House, 176.
21 | Hamil.
22 | Jay-Z. (1997): "Where I'm From," http://genius.com/Jay-z-where-im-from-lyrics.
23 | Walker, K. (2014): "A Subtlety," Domino Sugar Factory in Williamsburg, Brooklyn. creativetime.org/projects/karawalker/.
24 | Als, H. (2014): "The Sugar Sphinx." New Yorker. 8 May.
25 | Michals, R. (2009): "Notes on the Brooklyn Brownfields."
26 | Campo, D. (2013): The Accidental Playground: Brooklyn Waterfront Narratives of the Undesigned and Unplanned. New York: Fordham University Press.
27 | Zukin, S. (2010): Naked City: The Death and Life of Authentic Urban Spaces. New York: Oxford University Press.
28 | Jensen, K./ Bland, B./ Manthorne, K. (eds) (2014): Industrial Sublime: Modernism and the Transformation of New York's Rivers. New York: Fordham University Press, ix.
29 | Crane, H. (1930): "The Bridge." http://macaulay.cuny.edu/eportfolios/smonte10/files/2010/08/To-Brooklyn-Bridge.pdf.
30 | Ibid.
31 | Hughes, E. (2011): "The Strange, Great History of Norman Mailer's $2.5 Million Penthouse." May 9. Also see E. Hughes (2011) Literary Brooklyn. New York: Henry Holt.
32 | Mailer, N. (1983): Ancient Evenings. New York: Little, Brown, and Company.
33 | Barney, M. Dir. (2014): River of Fundament.
34 | Parla, J. (2014): "Hot Gowanus. " https://www.artsy.net/artist/jose-parla.
35 | Hartman, S. (1900): Camera Notes. No. 4. October, 91-97.
36 | Ibid.
37 | Despite assurances, the fate of the Gowanus Canal Superfund Cleanup is uncertain. Albrecht, L. 2017. Trump Can't Stop Gowanus Canal Superfund Cleanup, EPA Official Says. *DNA Info.* 24 January. https://www.dnainfo.com/new-york/20170124/gowanus/how-trump-affects-gowanus-canal-cleanup-superfund-epa.
Albrecht, L. 2017. Gowanus Canal Superfund Cleanup Could Run Out of Money Next Month, Official Warn. *DNA Info.* 30 March. https://www.dnainfo.com/new-york/20170330/gowanus/trump-gowanus-canal-superfund-cleanup

CHAPTER FIVE

1 | Rankine, C. (2015): Citizen. quoted in Edward Ball. "Slavery's Enduing Resonance." New York Times. 15 March, 5.

2 | On November 20, 2014, Akai Gurley was killed by the police in a hallway in the public housing where he lived. See A. Baker and D. Goodman (2015) "New York City Police Officer Is Said to Be Indicted in Shooting Death of Akai Gurley." 10 Feb. http://www.nytimes.com/2015/02/11/nyregion/akai-gurley-shooting-death-officer-indicted.html?_r=0

3 | Abu-Lughod, J. (1999): New York, Chicago, Los Angeles: America's Global Cities. Minneapolis, Minnesota: University of Minnesota Press. Gladstone, D./ Fainstein, S. (2003): "New York and Los Angeles Economics," in Halle, D.. (2003): New York and Los Angeles: Politics, Society and Culture: A Comparative View. Chicago: University of Chicago Press, 79-98. Sassen, S. (2001): The Global City: New York, London, Tokyo. Princeton: Princeton University Press. Zukin, S. (2010): Naked City. New York: Oxford University Press.

4 | Wilder, C. (2000): A Covenant with Color. New York: Columbia University Press. Witt, S.. (2006): "Ground Zero for Foreclosures." Brooklyn Heights Currier. 26 September, 2.

5 | Klein, N. (2003): "Reclaiming the Commons," in Movement of Movements. T. Mertes (ed). New York: Verso, 219-29. See also N. Smith (1990). Unequal Development. Boston: Blackwell.

6 | Lennard, N. (2011): "Community Stands Strong to Block Eviction." New York Times. 19 August. http://cityroom.blogs.nytimes.com/2011/08/19/community-stands-strong-to-block-a-foreclosure/. Osman, S. (2011): The Invention of Brownstone Brooklyn. New York: Oxford. Shepard, B./Smithsimon, G. (2011): The Beach Beneath the Streets: Contesting New York's Public Spaces. New York: State University New York Press.

7 | Butters, S. (1983): "The Logic of Inquiry of Participant Observation," in Resistance through Rituals: Youth Subcultures in Post-war Britain. S. Hall and T. Jefferson (eds). London: Hutchinson University Library.
Lichterman, P. (2002): Seeing Structure Happen: Theory Driven Participant Observation. B. Klandermans/Staggenborg, S. (eds). Methods of Social Movement Research. Minneapolis: University of Minnesota Press. Tedlock, B. (1991): "Participant Observation to Observation of Participation: The Emergence of Narrative Ethnography." Journal of Anthropological Research. (47), 69-94. This chapter borrows from Benjamin Shepard's first person observations, some of which first found expression in his blog, "Play and Ideas." http://benjaminheimshepard.blogspot.com/2014/12/strange-fruit-hanging-in-trees-laying.html.

8 | Vitale, A. (2008): City of Disorder. New York: NYU Press.

9 | Johnson, M. (2003): Street Justice. Boston: Beacon Press.

10 | McArdle, A./Erzen, T. (eds) (2001): Zero Tolerance. New York: NY University Press.

11 | Sites, W. (2003): Remaking New York. Minneapolis: U of Minnesota Press.

12 | Harvey, D. (2005): A Brief History of Neoliberalism. New York: Oxford. Shepard, B./ Smithsimon, G. (2011); Vitale, A. (2008).

13 | Gane-McCallaj, C. (2008): "Top 5 Worst NYPD Brutality Moments." News One. 8 December. http://newsone.com/52571/top-5-worst-nypd-brutality-moments/. Yakas, B. (2013): "Kimani Gray Shot 7 Times by NYPD, 3 Times in The Back." Gothamist. http://gothamist.com/2013/03/13/kimani_gray_shot_7_times_by_nypd_3.php.

14 | (2014): "NYPD Investigates Alleged Police Brutality in Sunset Park. The NYPD is Reportedly Investigating an Alleged Incident of Police Brutality that took Place Sunday in Sunset Park." 17 September. Brooklyn Daily Eagle. http://www.brooklyneagle.com/articles/2014/9/17/nypd-investigates-police-brutality-sunset-park. (2013). "Medical Examiner Rules Death of Man Shot by Police in Brooklyn Stairwell a Homicide." 24 November. http://www.nbcnewyork.com/news/local/Akai-Gurley-Peter-Liang-NYPD-Pink-Houses-Shooting-Homicide-Ruling-283696031.html.

15 | Many in the Black Lives Matter movement echo Angela Davis' call to abolish the prisons entirely, arguing "we do not need police." See A. Davis. (2003) Are Prisons Obsolete? New York: Seven Stories Press. For an overview of the Black Lives Matter movement, see K. Taylor (2016) From #BlackLivesMatter to Black Liberation. Chicago: Haymarket Books.

16 | Herbert, B. (2007): "Arrested While Grieving." New York Times. 26 May. Accessed 2010 from http://query.nytimes.com/gst/fullpage.html?res=9F0DEFDD1730F935A15756C0A9619C8B63&sec=&spon=&pagewanted=all.

17 | Quoted in B. Herbert (2009) "No Cause for Arrest." New York Times. 18 April.

18 | Ibid.

19 | Ibid.

20 | Trymaine, L. (2007A): "Arrest of 30 Leads Youths to Organize in Brooklyn." New York Times, 6 June. Accessed on 12 October 2009 from www.nytimes.com/2007/06/06/nyregion/06arrests.html?fta=y. Lee Trymaine. (2007B.) "Mass Arrest of Brooklyn Youths Spotlights Tactics." 24 June. New York Times.

21 | Alexander, M. (2010): The New Jim Crow: Mass Incarceration in the Age of Colorblindness. New York: New Press.

22 | In his 2008 essay, "The Right To the City," David Harvey posits: "We live, after all, in a world in which the rights of private property and the profit rate trump all other notions of rights. I here want to explore another type of human right, that of the right to the city. New Left Review. September-October, 53: 23-40. See also H. Lefebvre (1996) Writing on Cities. NY: Wily Blackwell and D. Harvey (2013) Rebel Cities: From the Right to the City to the Urban Revolution. NY: Verso.

23 | Herbert, B. (2009).

24 | McArdle, A./Erzen, T. (eds) (2001): Zero Tolerance. New York: NYU Press.

25 | Vitale, A. (2008): City of Disorder. New York: NYU Press.

26 | Harvey, D. (2005): A Brief History of Neoliberalism. New York: Oxford, 48.

27 | Logan, J.R./Molotch, H. (1987): Urban Fortunes: The Political Economy of Place. Berkeley, CA: University of California Press.

28 | Kauffman, L.A. (2015): "A Love Note to Our Folks: Alicia Garza on the Organizing of #BlackLives Matter." Accessed 6 May 2015 from https://nplusonemag.com/online-only/online-only/a-love-note-to-our-folks/.

29 | Wilkerson, I. (2015): "When Will the North Face its Racism?" New York Times. 11 Jan., 6.

30 | Effinger-Crichlow, M. (2014): Staging Migrations Toward an American West. From Ida B Jones to Rhodessa Jones. Boulder: University Press Colorado.

31 | Kauffman,L.A. (2017): Direct Action: Protest and the Reinvention of American Radicalism. NY: Verso.

32 | Effinger-Crichlow.

33 | Hall,.S., et al.. (1978): Policing the Crisis: Mugging, the State, and Law and Order. New York: Holmes and Meier Publishers, Inc. Also see B. Shepard (2007) Moral Panic in the Welfare State Journal of Sociology and Social Welfare 34 (1), 155-172 and A. Michelle (2010).

34 | Singh, N. (2004): Black is a Country. Race and the Unfinished Struggle for Democracy. Cambridge: Harvard University Press.

35 | Goodman, David 2013. Anger in East Flatbush Persists Over Teenager's Killing by the Police New York Times. 13 March http://www.nytimes.com/2013/03/14/nyregion/teenager-killed-by-new-york-police-was-shot-7-times.html?pagewanted=all&_r=0.

36 | 'I can't breathe': Eric Garner put in chokehold by NYPD officer—video. The Guardian. 4 December. https://www.theguardian.com/us-news/video/2014/dec/04/i-cant-breathe-eric-garner-chokehold-death-video.

37 | Michael Levitin. 2015. The Triumph of Occupy Wall Street. 10 June. http://www.theatlantic.com/politics/archive/2015/06/the-triumph-of-occupy-wall-street/395408/.

38 | LA Kauffman. 2015.

39 | Keeanga-Yamahtta Taylor. 2016. From #BlackLivesMatter to Black Liberation haymarketbooks p. 165.

40 | LA Kauffman. 2017 Direct Action Verso New York.

41 | LA Kauffman. 2014. The Disruption This Time. The Baffler. 8 December http://thebaffler.com/blog/disruption-time.

42 | Ibid.

43 | MLK quoted in Taylor.

44 | Gregory Smithsimon. 2015. Disarm the Police. 29 September. http://www.metropolitiques.eu/Disarm-the-Police.html.

45 | LA Kauffman. 2015.

46 | John Marzulli , Thomas Tracy , Oren Yaniv . 2015. Cop involved in fatal shooting of Akai Gurley has been indicted on manslaughter charges: source Rookie cop Peter Liang was indicted Tuesday by a Brooklyn grand jury for the deadly shooting in November in an unlit stairwell in the Pink Houses, the Daily News has learned. He'll face criminal charges that can send him to prison for up to 15 years. New York Daily News. February 10, http://www.nydailynews.com/new-york/nyc-crime/involved-fatal-shooting-akai-gurley-indicted-article-1.2109892 Liang was eventually convicted. But fa-

ced no prison time. Associated Press. 2016. http://www.kmtv.com/news/national/no-prison-time-for-nypd-cop-who-shot-unarmed-man-in-stairwell.

CHAPTER SIX

1 | Sites, William. 2003. Remaking New York. University of Minnesota Press. Minneapolis.
2 | Gladstone, David G. and Fainstein, Susan S. 2003. New York and Los Angeles Economics. In Halle, David. New York and Los Angeles: Politics, Society and Culture: A Comparative View. Chicago: University of Chicago Press. p. 79-98.
Sassen, Sakia. 2001. The Global City: New York, London, Tokyo. Princeton, NJ: Princeton University Press.
3 | Castells, Manuel. 1996. Rise of the Network Society (Information Age) New York: Wiley. Sites, 2003.
4 | Demause, Neil. 2016. The Brooklyn Wars. Second System Press.
5 | Sites, 2003.
6 | Brown, Kevin. 2007. A Letter from the Editor. Brooklyn Tomorrow.
7 | Brown. 2007.
8 | Peterson, Luca. 2016. Brooklyn's Frugal Soul, On a search for the essence of the real borough, I found a bona fide cultural capital, at prices I could afford. New York Times. 6 November. P.1 6.
9 | Ibid.
10 | Zukin, Sharon. 2010. Naked City. New York: Oxford University Press. p.50.
11 | Zukin, 2010. Brown 2016.
12 | Gladstone, David G. and Fainstein, Susan S. 2003. P. 85.
13 | Kreda, Allan 2016. Islanders Moved to Brooklyn, but the Players and Their Dogs Stay on Long Island. New York Times. 25 November. (https://www.nytimes.com/2016/11/25/sports/hockey/new-york-islanders-play-in-brooklyn-stay-on-long-island.html).
14 | Gross, Matt. 2010. Celebration on the Edge of Decay. New York Times 3 June. E1,6.
Mooney, Jake. 2011. Finding the Borough behind the Brand: Brooklyn Today. City Limits. March 1. Accessed 3 September 2011 from (http://www.citylimits.org/news/article_print.cfm?article_id=4287).
15 | Ouroussoff, Nicolai. 2010. The Greening of the Waterfront. New York Times 2April, c23.
16 | Campo, David. 2013. The Accidental Playground: Brooklyn Waterfront Narratives of the Undesigned and Unplanned. New York, NY Fordham University Press.
17 | McArdle, Andre and Erzen, Tonya eds. 2001. Zero Tolerance. New York: NY University Press.
Vitale, Alex. 2008. City of Disorder. New York: NYU Press.
Wilder, Craig. 2000. A Covenant with Color. New York: Columbia University Press.

18 | Levinson, Marc. 2008. The Box. Princeton, NJ: Princeton University Press.
19 | Farkas, Ava and Newman, Sara 2015. Rezoning Plan Will Cause More Displacement in New York. People's World. 19 November.
20 | Glasser, Edward. 2010. Triumph of the City. New York: Penguin Press.
21 | Smith, Neil. 1990. Unequal Development. Boston: Blackwell.
22 | Hamill, Pete. 2008. Brooklyn Revisited. New York Magazine. October 6. P. 164-70
Hughes, Evan. 2011. Literary Brooklyn. New York: Henry Holt.
23 | Marx. Karl. 1867. Capital: A Critique of Political Economy. Volume One. (https://www.marxists.org/archive/marx/works/1867-c1/).
24 | Eviatar, Daphne. 2007. The Ooze. Ten million gallons of toxic gunk trapped in the Brooklyn aquifer is starting to creep toward the surface. New York Magazine. Jun 4. Also see Smith, Neil. 1990
Witt, S. 2006. Ground zero for foreclosures. Brooklyn Heights Currier. 26 September. P. 2.
25 | Hammett, Jerilou. and Hammett, Kingsly. 2007. The Surbanization of New York: Is the World's Greatest City Becoming Just Another Town? Princeton, NJ: Princeton Architectural Press.
26 | Rem Koolhaas. 1994 Delirious New York.Monacelli Press. New York, NY.
27 | Pogrebin, Robin. 2007. Brooklyn Waterfront Called Endangered Site. New York Times. 14 June El.
28 | Campo, David. 2002. Brooklyn's Vernacular Waterfront. Journal of Urban Design 7, 2:171-99.
29 | Mindlin, A. 2008. On the Waterfront, Locked Gates and Grumbling. New York Times, June 8 6cy.
30 | Economopoulos, Beka. 2005a. [awag] reminder: emergency arts mtg tomorrow 3-5pm. 27 Feb. 2005b. [RTSNYC] Save our 'hoods 3/14 and 3/17. 10 March.
31 | Ibid.
32 | Williamsburg Waterfront 197-A-Plan, (www.nyc.gov/html/dcp/html/pub/197will.shtml).
33 | Silverman, J. R. 2005. Brooklynites give council an earful over zoning changes. amNY 5 April.
34 | Bleyer, Jennifer. 2005. "To the Ramparts, Hipsters." New York Times 6 March. Padalka, Alex. 2005. The Williamsberg Warriors, Dancing Against Rezoning, Drinking for Affordable Housing. Block Magazine. (http://www.blockmagazine.com/the_you.php?title=lstrongglet_the_bidding_begin_l_strongg&more=1&c=1&tb=1&pb=1).
35 | Levin, E. (2005). Email: G.D. Stop Bloomberg's Plot to Sohoify Williamsburg. 2 April.
36 | Bahney, Anna. 2005. Williamburg Reinvented. New York Times. March 20 LI. Cardwell, David. 2005.City Backs Makeover for Decaying Brooklyn Waterfront. New York Times 3May A1. Keller, Emily. 2005. Pols Gush, Nabes Grumble over Rezoning. Greenpoint Star. 5 May. Moses, Paul. 2005. A New Colony. Village Voice. 18-25 May. P. 25.

37 | Jacobs, Jane. 2005. Letter to Mayor Bloomberg and the City Council. Brooklyn Rail. (http://brooklynrail.org/2005/5/local/letter-to-mayor-bloomberg/).
38 | Buettner, Russ and Ray. Rivera 2009. A Stalled Vision: Big Development as the City's Future. Sweeping Rezoning and Billions in Cash Yield Uneven Results. New York Times, October 29, A1.
39 | Osman, Suleiman. 2011. The Invention of Brownstone Brooklyn. New York: Oxford.
40 | Osman, 2011.
41 | Bagli, Charles. 2009. Developer Drops Plan for Gehry's Design for Brooklyn Arena. New York Times. 4 June. (http://www.nytimes.com/2009/06/05/nyregion/05gehry.html).
42 | Maniscalco, Joe. 2007. Stop Him Now. Carroll Gardens Cobble Hill Courier. 20 July. P. 1.
43 | Maniscalco, Joe. 2008. Much too Large. Carroll Gardens Cobble Hill Courier. 25 April. P. 1.
44 | Berman, Marshall. 2007. Introduction. New York Calling: From Blackout to Bloomberg. Edited by Marshall Berman and Brian Berger. Reaction Books, NY NY.
45 | Pratt Center for Community Development. 2008. July 31 Downtown Brooklyn's Detour: The unanticipated Impacts of Rezoning and Development on Residents and Business (http://prattcenter.net/research (downtown-brooklyns-detour).
46 | Mooney, Jake. 2007. Carroll Gardens, Twilight for the Trainspotters. NY Times Sec.14 p. 1.
47 | Biuso, Gary. 2009. Zoning Plan OK'ED. The Carroll Gardens Courier. 30 October. 1 Feedblitz. 2008. Democracy at Work: Carroll Gardens gets a zoning text agreement. July 24.
48 | Kral, Georgia. 2011. City Council Votes to Approve Boerum Hill Rezoning. Carroll Gardens Patch. www.CarrollGardensPatch.com) While certainly, historic districts are anything but populist, they do help put the breaks on forms of development impacting neighborhoods. Certainly many such as Jane Jacobs (1961) were not opposed to large buildings, dense neighborhoods, as long as they were not over crowded, the accompanying infrastructure, schools and transportation, needed to help these spaces thrive seemed to be missing with the Bloomberg era plans. See Jacobs, Jane. 1961. The Life and Death of Great American Cities. New York: Random House.
49 | Mielach, Dave. 2012. What It Really Costs When Walmart Comes to Town. Business News Daily (http://www.businessnewsdaily.com/2405-real-cost-walmart.html). The literature on opposition to Walmart is vast. Lisa Featherstone (2004) argues its bad for workers, for women. Others suggest it expands inequality. Consider the net wealth of the inheritants of the Walmart fortune. At $144 billion, they own more than the other 42% of us workers combined. See Featherstone, Lisa. 2004. Selling Women Short: The Landmark Battle for Workers' Rights at Wal-Mart. New York: Basic Books
The Walmart 1%. http://walmart1percent.org/family/.

50 | Fishman, Charles. 2006. The Wal-Mart Effect. New York: Penguin. Neumark, David; Zhang, Janfu and Ciccarella. Stephen. Zang, 2005. "The Effects of Walmart on Local Labor Markets." Public Policy Institute of California.

51 | Stone, Kenneth 1988. The Effect of Walmart on Businesses in Host Towns and Surrounding Towns in Iowa. Iowa State University. November 1988. (http://www2.econ.iastate.edu/faculty/stone/Effect%20of%20Walmart%20-%201988%20paper%20scanned.pdf).

52 | Hammett, Jerilou. and Hammett, Kingsly. 2007. The Surbanization of New York: Is the World's Greatest City Becoming Just Another Town? Princeton, NJ: Princeton Architectural Press.

53 | Talen, William. 2003 What Should I Do If Reverend Billy Is In My Store? New York: New Press. New York Communites for Change. A Walmart in Brooklyn. No Thanks. (http://nycommunities.org/walmart) Zukin, Sharon. 2004. Point of Purchase: How Shopping Changed American Culture. New York Routledge. Talen, William. 2003. What Should I Do If Reverend Billy Is In My Store? New York: New Press.

54 | Gladstone and Fainstein, 2003. Sassen, Sakia. 2001. The Global City: New York, London, Tokyo. Princeton University Press.

55 | Brecher, Jeremy. 2011. Save the Humans: Common Preservation in Action. : London: Pardigm Publishers.

56 | Jenny Brown. 2011. Strong Words Against Wal-Mart at New York Rally. Labor Notes. 3 February. (http://www.labornotes.org/blogs/2011/02/strong-words-against-wal-mart-new-york-rally).

57 | Silverman. 2000. Judge Strikes Down Rule Limiting on City Hall Park Protests. New York Times 7 April. (http://www.nytimes.com/2000/04/07/nyregion/judge-strikes-down-rule-limiting-city-hall-protests.html
Over and over the "the city had unfairly restricted access to a favored spot for everything from demonstrations to news conferences," notes Silverman. The Walmart hearing was another example of this.

58 | Kelley, Lauren. 2011. "Walmart Protesters Greatly Outnumber Walmart Supporters at NYC Hearing. Change.org. 10 February. (http://news.change.org/stories/walmart-protesters-greatly-outnumber-walmart-supporters-at nyc-hearing).

59 | Ryan, Matt. 2011. Don't Be Related to Walmart. Huffington Post. 13 April. (http://www.huffingtonpost.com/matt-ryan/new-york-city-walmart-related_b_848736.html).

60 | Fukushima on the Globe. Nd. What Happened? (http://fukushimaontheglobe.com/the-earthquake-and-the-nuclear-accident/whats-happened).

61 | Reverend Billy. 2011. Field of Change. Blog. 22 March. Accessed 28 March, 2011 from (http://www.revbilly.com/chatter/blog/2011/22/field-of-change).

62 | Ibid.

63 | Harvey, David. 2008. Forward. Neil Smith. Unequal Development. 3rd ed. Boston: Blackwell. P. viii.

64 | Ibid.

65 | Yakas, Ben. 2012. Walmart Admits Defeat: Mega Retailer Won't Build a Brooklyn Store. Gothamist.15 September. (http://gothamist.com/2012/09/15/walmart_admits_defeat_mega-retailer.php).
66 | Shepard, B. 2011B. In Defense of the Silly: From Direct Action to the Pies of March. Huffington Post. March 23, 2011. (http://www.huffingtonpost.com/benjamin-shepard/times-up-nyc-pies-ofmarch_b_839389.html).
67 | Seaton, Matt. 2011. How one New York bike lane could affect the future of cycling worldwide. A much more significant story than the future of one bike lane in Brooklyn, a great deal hangs on the lawsuit filed against the city. The Guardian UK Bike Blog. 9 March. (http://www.guardian.co.uk/environment/bike-blog/2011/mar/09/new-york-bike-lane-cycling)
68 | Crowley, Michael. 2009. Honk, Ho.nk, Aaah. New York Magazine, May, 17. (http://nymag.com/news/features/56794).
Furness, Zack. 2010. One Less Car. Bicycling and the Politics of Automobility. Philadelphia PA: Temple University Press.
69 | Leopold, Les. 2007. Globalization is Fueling Global Warming. Alter Net. 28 December.
(http://www.alternet.org/environment/71873/globalization_is_fueling_global_warming/).
70 | BrooklynNews12. 2017. Residents: NYPD blocks bike lane in Clinton Hill (http://brooklyn.news12.com/news/residents-nypd-blocks-bike-lane-in-clinton-hill-1.12843035).
71 | Nelson, Katie. 2009. Hunter College Survey Finds Car Drivers Block Bicycle Lanes in Manhattan. New York Daily News. 3 December.
72 | Muessig, Ben. 2008A. Hasids: We'll block the bike lanes. Brooklyn Paper. 26 November. (http://www.brooklynpaper.com/stories/31/47/31_47_bm_wb_meeting.html).
73 | For more on the insular quality of this community in Brooklyn, see Rachel Aviv. 2014. Outcast, After a Hasidic man exposed child abuse in his tight-knit Brooklyn community, he found himself the target of a criminal investigation. The New Yorker. November 10. (http://www.newyorker.com/magazine/2014/11/10/outcast-3).
74 | Fitch, Robert. 1993. The Assassination of New York. New York: Verso
Harvey, David. 2005. A Brief History of Neoliberalism. New York: Oxford.
Moody, Kim. 2007. From Welfare State to Real Estate: Regime Change in New York City, 1974 to the Present. New Press, New York City.
75 | Signore, John Del. 2008. Bunch of Clowns Rally for Kent Ave Bike Lane. 17 December. (http://gothamist.com/2008/12/17/bunch_of_clowns_demonstrate_for_ken.php#photo-1).
76 | Abu-Lughod, Janet L. 1999. New York, Chicago, Los Angeles: America's Global Cities. Minneapolis, Minnesota: University of Minnesota Press.
77 | Muessig, Ben. 2008B. A Bunch of Clowns. Brooklyn Paper. 8 December. (http://www.brooklynpaper.com/stories/31/50/31_50_bm_bike_clowns.html).
78 | Benjamin Shepard. 2017. Sustainable Urbanism. Roman and Littlefield. London.
79 | Osman, 2011.

80 | Rosenthal, Elizabeth. 2011. Green Development: Not in My (Liberal) Backyard. New York Times. (http://www.nytimes.com/2011/03/13/weekinreview/13nimby.html?pagewanted=all).
81 | Olshan, Jeremy. 2009. Biker Brawl goes global. New York Post. 10 Dec. Access 2 Sept 2011 http://www.nypost.com/p/news/local/brooklyn/biker_brawl_goes_global_nhyHe5xds9YB17OsTwblLJ#ixzz1WospozsB.
82 | Bernstein, Andrea. 2011. Community Board Unanimously Supports Prospect Park Bike Lane. WNYC. Transportation Nation. 14 April (http://www.wnyc.org/story/283878-community-board-unanimously-supports-prospect-park-west-bike-lane-with-changes/).
83 | Ibid.
84 | Kazis, Noah. 2012. The NBBL Files: PPW Foes Pursued Connections to Reverse Public Process. Streetsblog. 20 December.
(http://www.streetsblog.org/2012/12/20/the-nbbl-files-ppw-foes-pursued-connections-to-reverse-public-process/).
85 | Lander, Brad. 2010. Prospect Park Reconfiguration Community Survey Results.
NY Department of Transportation. 2011. Prospect Park Bicycle Path and Traffic Calming Update Results. Accessed 25 January 2011.
86 | Shepard, Benjamin. 2011A. New Yorkers: Fight the Bike Lane Backlash. Huffington Post. January 31, 2011. (http://www.huffingtonpost.com/benjamin-shepard/fight-the-bike backlash_1_b_815632.html).
87 | Charles Montgomery. 2013. Happy City: Transforming Our Lives Through Design. Farrar, Straus, Giroux. New York, NY.
88 | Bicyclist Fatalities and Serious Injuries in New York City 1996-2005 A Joint Report from the New York City Departments of Health and Mental Hygiene, Parks and Recreation, Transportation, and the New York City Police Department (http://www.nyc.gov/html/dot/downloads/pdf/bicyclefatalities.pdf).
89 | Flegenheim, Mat and Baker, Al. 2012. Officer in Bell Killing Is Fired; 3 Others to Be Forced Out. New York Times 23 March. (http://www.nytimes.com/2012/03/24/nyregion/in-sean-bell-killing-4-officers-to-be-forced-out.html).
90 | Chung, Jen. 2008. Sharpton Joins Critical Mass to Protest Police Issues. Gothamist.
91 | Sadik-Kahn, Janette and Solomonow, Seth. 2016. Streetfight: Handbook for an Urban Revolution. New York NY. Penguin Publishing Group.
92 | O'Neill, Natalie. 2011. Ride On! City Wins Prospect West Bike Lane Suit. Brooklyn Paper. 17 August. (http://www.brooklynpaper.com/stories/34/33/all_bikelanewin_2011_8_19_bk.html).
93 | Brooklyn Paper. 2011. Editorial: Enough is Enough. 26 August. (http://www.brooklynpaper.com/stories/34/34/34_34_editorial.html). Of course, the Neighbors for Better Bike Lanes appealed. Many hope the group will let it go (Karen (2014).
Karen. 2014. People are Still Fighting the Prospect Park Bike Lane. Seriously. Fucked in Park Slope. 7 January. (http://www.fuckedinparkslope.com/home/people-are-still-fighting-the-ppw-bike-lane-seriously.html).

94 | Ben Fried. 2016. Good Riddance to the Prospect Park West Bike Lane Lawsuit. Streetsblog. 22 September. (http://nyc.streetsblog.org/2016/09/22/good-riddance-to-the-prospect-park-west-bike-lane-lawsuit/).
95 | Levin, Bruce. 2011.The Abuse of Eminent Domain: The Battle of Brooklyn. Counterpunch. 6 September (http://www.counterpunch.org/2011/09/06/the-battle-for-brooklyn/).
96 | Rem Koolhaas. 1994 Delirious New York.Monacelli Press. New York, NY. P. 30-35.
97 | Coney Island Comprehensive Rezoning Plan. 2009. (http://www1.nyc.gov/assets/planning/download/pdf/plans/coney-island/coney_island.pdf) Also see (http://www.nyc.gov/html/oec/downloads/pdf/dme_projects/08DME007K/DEIS/08DME007K_DEIS_00_Executive_Summary.pdf).
98 | Santos, Fernanda. 2007. Coney Island's Astroland Closes. NY Times 10 September. P. B3.
99 | Bush, Daniel. 2009. Coney Takeover. City buys prime Coney Island Acres. Deal pushes revitalization plans forward. Brooklyn Downtown Star. 19 November. P. 1, 24
McLauphlin, Mike. 2008. Freak show! City's Coney plan is dissed by locals. The Brooklyn Paper. 28 June. (http://www.brooklynpaper.com/stories/31/26/31_26_freak_show_citys_coney.html).
Register, Woody. 2001. The Kid of Coney Island. New York: Oxford University Press.
100 | Horan, Kathleen. 2010. Coney Island Businesses Banding Together to Take On Landlord. WNYC. 19 December. (http://www.wnyc.org/story/104617-coney-island-businesses-banding-together-take-landlord/).
101 | Marx, Rebecca. 2011. The Coney Island Eight Will Get One More Summer Reprieve. Village Voice Blog. 8 March. (http://blogs.villagevoice.com/forkintheroad/2011/03/the_coney_islan.php).
102 | Baker, Kevin. 2007. Paving over Fun. New York Times. 12 August. P.c9.
103 | Baker, 2007.
104 | Horan, Kathleen. 2010.
105 | Jonathan Sederstrom. 2008. Mermaid Queen on Hunger Strike. New York Daily News. June 21. (http://www.nydailynews.com/new-york/brooklyn/mermaid-queen-hunger-strike-article-1.293954).
106 | Bush, Daniel. 2011. Brooklyn Reborn: Borough Businesses Back on the Boardwalk. Brooklyn Daily. 12 December. (http://www.brooklyndaily.com/stories/2011/50/all_brooklynbackonboardwalk_2011_12_16_bk.html).
107 | Tricia. 2011. Paul's Daughter Signs 8-Year Lease for Coney Island Boardwalk. December 9. Amuzing the Zillion. (https://amusingthezillion.com/2011/12/09/pauls-daughter-signs-8-year-lease-for-coney-island-boardwalk/).
108 | Agnotti, Tom. 2008. New York for Sale. Cambridge MA: MIT Press.
109 | Kral, 2011.
110 | Jacobs 1961. For more on participatory budgeting used in Brooklyn and elsewhere see:

Lerner, Josh. 2014. Making Democracy Fun: How Game Design Can Empower Citizens and Transform Politics. MIT Press: Boston, MA.
111 | Agnotti, Tom. 2008.
Logan, John. R. and Harvey L. Molotch. 1987. Urban Fortunes: The Political Economy of Place. Berkeley, CA: University of California Press.
Moody, 2007.
112 | Biuso, Gary. 2011. Carroll St. 'hell' house cut down. The Carroll Gardens Courier. 8 April 1,6. Its hard to call this a populist victory, given the rising rents in the neighborhood and the historic district. But it is still a win against a landlord who had repeatedly flaunted local laws and zoning codes.
113 | Not An Alternative. 2011. Email o: reclaimnyc@lists.aktivix.org Subject: [Reclaimnyc] Some Sad News About NO↔SPACE.
114 | Short, Aaron. 2011. Galleries abandoning North Brooklyn for cheaper pastures. The Brooklyn Paper. 14 September. (http://www.brooklynpaper.com/stories/34/37/dtg_williamsburggalleries_2011_9_16_bk.html).
115 | Jeremiah's Vanishing New York. 2017. The Brooklyn Wars. January 18. (http://vanishingnewyork.blogspot.com/2017/01/the-brooklyn-wars.html).

CHAPTER SEVEN

1 | Talen, Reverend Billy. (2012): The End of the World. NY: Stop Shopping Publishing.
2 | Shakespeare, W. The Tempest. http://shakespeare.mit.edu/tempest/full.html.
3 | Both Karl Marx and Marshall Berman paraphrased this line from The Tempest, reminding the world that "all that's solid melts to air."
4 | Barber, B. (2014): Democracy or Sustainability? The City as Mediator. Minding Nature 7(1), 1.
http://www.humansandnature.org/democracy-or-sustainability-the-city-as-mediator-by-benjamin-r.-barber.
5 | Time's Up! "New York City's direct action environmental organization." http://times-up.org/.
6 | In the wake of the storm, Dutch engineers were engaged to help the city rebuild marshlands around Manhattan and Brooklyn. See Tollefson, J. (2013): "Natural Hazards; New York Versus the Sea. In the Wake of Sandy, Scientists and Officials are Trying to Protect the Largest U.S. City from Future Floods." Scientific American. 13 February.
7 | Abruzzo, S. (2012): "Sandy, Brooklynites Come Together." Brooklyn Courier. 16-22 Nov.
8 | Kauffman, L.A. (2017): Direct Action. New York: Verso. Also see Shepard, B. (2017) Sustainable Urbanism: Roman and Littlefield.
9 | Cole, W. (2012): "After Sandy, the People's Relief Grows in Coney." Brooklyn Rail. December, 2.

10 | Ackerman, P./DuVall, J. (2001). A Force More Powerful: A Century of Non-violent Conflict. NY: St. Martin's Press.
11 | Cole, W. (2012).
12 | Abruzzo, P. (2012). Also see: Occupy Sandy. Mutual Aid: Not Charity. http://www.imdb.com/video/wab/vi2723129113.
13 | Steinberg, T. (2014): Gotham Unbound. New York: Simon and Schuster.
14 | The Nature Conservancy. (n.d.). http://coastalresilience.org/project/new-york/.

Chapter Eight

1 | Jacobs, J. (1961): The Death and Life of Great American Cities. New York: Vintage.
2 | Logan, J./Molotch, H. (1987): Urban Fortunes: The Political Economy of Place. Berkeley: University of California Press.
3 | Shepard, B. (2017): Sustainable Urbanism. London: Roman and Littlefield.
4 | Balmori, D and Morton, M. 1993. Transitory Gardens, Uprooted Lives. New Haven: Yale University Press.
5 | Mckay, G. (2011): Radical Gardening: Politics, Idealism, and Rebellion in the Garden. London: Frances Lincoln. Furness, Z. (2010): One Less Car: Bicycling and the Politics of Automobility. Philadelphia: Temple University Press. Nettle, C. (2014): Community Gardening as Social Activism. London: Ashgate.
6 | Shepard, B./Smithsimon, G. (2011): The Beach Beneath the Streets: Exclusion, Control and Play in Public Space. New York: State University Press of New York. Shepard, B. (2011): Play, Creativity and Social Movements: If I Can't Dance It's Not My Revolution. New York: Routledge.
7 | Shepard, B. (2013): "Changing seasons and garden." Blog post. http://benjaminheimshepard.blogspot.com/2013/03/changingseasons-.
8 | For more on the battle of Esperanza, see B. Shepard (2011) Play, Creativity and Social Movements: If I Can't Dance, It's Not My Revolution. New York: Routledge. Also see B. Shepard (2000) Esperanza, Garden of Hope Tenant. http://www.tenant.net/tengroup/Metcounc/Mar00/Esperanza.html.
9 | Shepard, B. (2012): "Community Gardens, Creative Community, Organizing & Environmental Activism," in: M. Gray, J. Coates, & T. Hetherington Environmental Social Work. London: Routledge, 121-134.
10 | Eizenberg, E. (2013): From the Ground Up. Community Gardens in New York City and the Politics of Spacial Transformation. London: Ashgate.
11 | Shepard, B. (2012).
12 | Siempre Verde Garden (2013): Website. http://svgarden.org/.
13 | For more on the plans and thoughts about the new garden, see B. Shepard (2012) Reimagining City Through Direct Action. Blog post. http://benjaminheimshepard.blogspot.com/2012/12/reimaginingcity-through-direct-action.html. B. Shepard (2013a) "Changing seasons and garden." Blog post. http://benjaminheimshepard.blogspot.

com/2013/03/changingseasons-and-garden.html. B. Shepard (2013b) "Staycation in holy Brooklyn." Blog post. http://benjaminheimshepard.blogspot.com/2013/04/staycationin-holy-brooklyn-between.html. Time's Up! (2013) "Community Garden Created from Vacant Lot." Web video. http://youtu.be/UW4b5L4LUPI.
14 | Green Thumb NYC. Partner Links. Website. http://www.greenthumbnyc.org/links.html.
More Gardens (2013) Website. http://www.moregardens.org/landing/. NYC.Gov (2013a) Website.
15 | Kusisto, L. (2012): "Brooklyn Waits on Promise of a Park." The Wall Street Journal. http://www.wsj.com/news/articles/SB10001424052702303734204577464874189536572.
16 | Ibid.
17 | "City Delivers Promised Bushwick Inlet Park City Reaches Deal with Holdout Landowner." (2016). New York Times. 22 Nov. State Assemblyman Joe Lentol and City Councilperson Steve Levin were instrumental in bringing the City and the property owner to the negotiations and keeping them there until the deal was reached. Every elected official from the area joined the community over the past 18 months to push for the delivery of this vital park space, including Congresswoman Carolyn Maloney, Borough President Eric Adams, Deputy Borough President Diana Reyna, State Senators Daniel Squadron and Martin Dilan, Councilmember Antonio Reynoso, and Public Advocate Letitia James. There was also an enormous amount of grassroots, community support, without which none of this would have happened. Thanks to all of the volunteers, rally goers, sign makers, sidewalk campers, fence decorators, flash-mobbers, signers, tweeters and FB posters who worked so hard to keep the City honest, and to Brooklyn Community Board #1 and all of the other community organizations that supported us over the past 11 years.
18 | NYC.gov (2013b): Williamsburg/Greenpoint Open Space Plan. Web document. http://www.nyc.gov/html/bkncb1/downloads/pdf/greenpoint_williamsburg_open_space_plan.pdf. Also see Olechowski, T. and Esposito (2012) Brooklyn Community Board One: Statement of Community District Needs. Web document. http://www.nyc.gov/html/bkncb1/downloads/pdf/district_needs_statement_upt.pdf. Open Green Map (2013). Web page. http://OpenGreenMap.org/nyc-gctour.
19 | Velsey, K. (2013): "City Selects Developer for Affordable Housing Slated to Rise on Williamsburg's Architectural Graveyard." Observer.com. http://observer.com/2013/05/city-selects-developerfor-affordable-housing-slated-to-rise-on-williamsburgsarchitectural-graveyard/.
20 | Tempey, N. (2015): "Three Beloved Brooklyn Community Gardens Win Important Victories." The Gothamist. 18 November. http://gothamist.com/2015/11/18/community_gardens_ftw.php.
21 | Ibid.

22 | Smith, R. (2016): Roger That Garden Closed by Realty Group After Court Upholds Eviction. DNA Info. 25 May. https://www.dnainfo.com/new-york/20160525/crown-heights/roger-that-garden-closed-by-realty-group-after-court-upholds-eviction.

Chapter Nine

1 | Jacobs, J. (1961): The Death and Life of Great American Cities. New York: Vintage, 164-5.
2 | Sullivan, R. (2008): "A Windstorm in Downtown Brooklyn," in: Brooklyn Was Mine. V. Knutsen and C. Knutsen (eds). New York: Riverhead Books, 147-8.
3 | Jacobs, 165.
4 | Osman, S. (2011): The Invention of Brownstone Brooklyn: Gentrification and the Search for Authenticity in Postwar New York. NY: Oxford University Press, 57.
5 | Osman, 55.
6 | Ibid.
7 | Reverend Billy Talen. (2012): The End of the World. NY: Stop Shopping Publishing, 39.
8 | de Certeau, M. (1984): The Practice of Everyday Life. Translated by Steven Rendell. Berkeley, CA: University of California Press.
9 | While cars double-park throughout the bike lanes across Jay Street, in the fiscal year 2014, only 432 of these cars received parking tickets for parking in the bike lanes. See T. Swanson (2014) "NYC Bike Lane Violation Parking." http://29degreesnorth.blogspot.com/2014/02/nyc-bike-lane-violation-parking.html.
10 | For an overview of the limits of the 2004 rezoning, see My Brooklyn, Kelly Anderson (Director). http://www.mybrooklynmovie.com/.
11 | Curbed. (2015): "First Renderings of Downtown Brooklyn's Greenway, Revealed!" 18 March. http://ny.curbed.com/2015/3/18/9979674/first-renderings-of-downtown-brooklyns-greenway-revealed.
12 | Jacobs, J. Quoted in the Project for Public Spaces. http://www.pps.org/reference/jjacobs-2/.
13 | Miller, S. (2014): "Reimagining Jay Street With Shared Space and Protected Bike Lanes." Streetsblog. 21 November. http://www.streetsblog.org/2014/11/21/shared-space-protected-bike-lanes-on-the-table-in-downtown-brooklyn/.
14 | Ibid.
15 | Agee, J. (1994): "Southeast of the Island: Travel Notes," in The Brooklyn Reader. Andrea Wyatt Sexton and Alice Leccese Powers (eds). New York: Random House, 5.
16 | Curbed. (2015): "Brooklyn Strand: First Renderings of Downtown Brooklyn's Greenway, Revealed!" http://ny.curbed.com/tags/brooklyn-strand.
17 | High, R. (2015): "Talk Examines Negative Repercussions of New York's High Line Project." Brown Daily Herald. 30 September.

18 | Bencivenni, M. (2017): "CUNY and the Erosion of Public Higher Education." Academe. Jan-Feb., 15.

Chapter Ten

1 | Ferlinghetti, L. (1958): A Coney Island of the Mind. New York: New Directions, 96.
2 | Baker, A./Moynihan, C./Nir, S. (2011): "Police Arrest More Than 700 Protesters on the Brooklyn Bridge." New York Times. 1 October. http://cityroom.blogs.nytimes.com/2011/10/01/police-arresting-protesters-on-brooklyn-bridge/?_r=0. For a narrative of the movement drafted by members themselves, many of whom recall the Brooklyn Bridge arrests, see "Writers for the 99%" (2011) Occupying Wall Street. New York: OR Books.
3 | Jacobs, J. (1992): The Death and Life of Great American Cities. New York: Vintage.
4 | Whitman, W. (1891): "City of Ships," in: Leaves of Grass. http://etcweb.princeton.edu/batke/logr/log_147.html.
5 | Reverend Billy. (2012): The End of the World. New York: Stop Shopping Publishing, 39.
6 | Moynihan, C. (2013): "A Ferrell Underground Paradise," in: T. Seelie. Bright Nights: Photographs of Another New York. NY: Prestel USA, 113-32.
7 | Len, S. (2013): "Brooklyn Was More Fun," in: Tod Seelie. Bright Nights: Photographs of Another New York. New York: Prestel USA, 133-52.
8 | Ibid.
9 | Ibid.
10 | Pimental, K. (2015): "Reflection on Brooklyn Gentrification." City Tech Writer. Vol 10, 110.
11 | Haly, K. (2017): "Flatbush: Where I'm From." Essay written for Professor Noonan's Composition I course.
12 | Bratburd, R. (2015): "The Future Maestros of Brooklyn." The Wall Street Journal. 21 May.
13 | Musumeci, N. (2013): "Twelve-year-old Hit, Killed by Van on Prospect Park West. Brooklyn Paper. 9 October. http://www.brooklynpaper.com/stories/36/41/dtg_carkillsboyinslope_2013_10_11_bk.html.
14 | "2014 Breaks Heat Records, Challenging Global Warming Skeptics" (2015) New York Times. 17 January.
15 | Dominelli, L. (2012): Green Social Work: From Environmental Crises to Environmental Justice. New York. Wiley. Dominelli, L. (2014): "(Re)Imagining Communities in the Context of Climate Change: A Saving Grace or the Evasion of State Responsibilities During (Hu)Man-Made Disasters?" in: Larsen, A.K./Sewpaul, V./Oline, G. (eds). Participation in Community Work, International Perspectives. New York: Routledge, 175-187. Dominelli, L. (2014): "Learning from our Past: Climate Change and Disaster Interventions in Practice," in: . Noble, C./Strauss, H./Littlechild, B. (eds). Global Social

Work Crossing Borders, Blurring Boundaries. London: Ashgate, 341-352. Bastasch, M. (2014): Environmentalists Champion Economic Degrowth. The DC. http://dailycaller.com/2014/02/27/environmentalists-champion-economic-de-growth/.
16 | Paraldo, G. (2014): Digest. NY: Four Way Books, 71.
17 | Ibid., 4.
18 | Ibid.
19 | Ibid.
20 | Ibid.
21 | Ibid., 5
22 | Ibid.
23 | Shakespeare, W. Julius Caesar. Act 4, Scene 3, 218-224.
24 | Back in 2008, a June 19th letter from the Church of Stop Shopping declared: "Mermaid Queen Declares Hunger Strike! Reverend Billy and Savitri D have been named King Neptune and Queen Mermaid of the 2008 Coney Island Mermaid Parade, this Saturday June 21st. And so it is our freaky-monarchial DUTY to use this power to SAVE Coney Island from the gentrifying apocalypse of RETAIL ENTERTAINMENT HELL! The Queen Mermaid will refuse to go back in the ocean! She will initiate a hunger strike during the parade, and will live in a window on Surf Ave and West 12th from the Mermaid Ball until the critical scoping meeting on June 24th at 6 pm. She is fasting to draw attention to a destructive scheme to reduce 60 acres of amusements to 9. She is fasting so YOU will come to this meeting..." Rev. Billy and Church of Stop Shopping Mailing List (2008) "'08 Mermaid Queen Savitri D Declares Hunger Strike." 19 June. http://community.coneyisland.com/cgi-bin/yabb/YaBB.pl?num=1213880179/3.
25 | Sterritt, D. "Lovers and Lollipops." TCM.com. Turner Classic Movies.

The Authors

By day, Benjamin Shepard, PhD, LMSW, works as Professor of Human Services at New York City College of Technology (CUNY). By night, he battles to keep New York from becoming a giant shopping mall. To this end, he has done organizing work with the AIDS Coalition to Unleash Power (ACT UP), Sex-Panic!, Reclaim the Streets, Times Up, the Clandestine Rebel Clown Army, Absurd Response, CitiWide Harm Reduction, Housing Works, More Gardens Coalition, Time's UP!, Right of Way, Occupy Wall Street, Occupy the Pipeline, Resist AIM, Public Space Party, and the Professional Staff Congress of the City University of New York, where he is a chapter chair at City Tech. He is also the author/editor of ten books including: *White Nights and Ascending Shadows: An Oral History of the San Francisco AIDS Epidemic* (1997), *From ACT UP to the WTO: Urban Protest and Community Building in the Era of Globalization* (2002), *Queer Political Performance and Protest* (Routledge, 2009) *The Beach beneath the Streets: Contesting New York's Public Spaces* (with Greg Smithsimon, SUNY Press), *Play, Creativity, and Social Movements: If I Can't Dance, Its Not My Revolution* (Routledge, 2011), *Community Projects as Social Activism* (Sage, 2014), *Rebel Friendships:"Outsider" Networks and Social Movements* (Sage, 2015), *Sustainable Urbanism* (Roman and Littlefield, 2017), and *Narrating Perspectives on Childhood and Adolescence* (Columbia University Press, 2018). Today, he remains involved in organizing efforts around transportation, HIV/AIDS, labor, public spaces, environmental policy and sustainability.

Mark J. Noonan is Professor of English at New York City College of Technology (CUNY). He is the author of *Reading the Century Illustrated Monthly Magazine: American Literature and Culture, 1870-1893* (Kent State UP, 2010) and co-editor of *The Place Where We Dwell: Reading and Writing About New York City* (2012). He serves on the Advisory Board of *American Periodicals* and is President of the Research Society of American Periodicals (RSAP). He has written extensively on the literature and history of New York and Brooklyn, including "Brooklyn Accents and the Paradox of Ambition in Norman Mailer and Arthur Miller" in *The Mailer Review* (Fall 2013) and "Campus Without Borders: The Brooklyn

GreenWalk" in *Making Teaching and Learning Matter: Transformations in Higher Education* (2011). In June 2015, he served as Director of the NEH Summer Institute, "City of Print: New York and the Periodical Press," which is also the focus of his next book project.

Gregory Smithsimon, whose thoughts inform the preface of this volume, is professor of sociology at Brooklyn College, City University of New York, and the CUNY Graduate Center. He is the author of the book *Cause: And How it Doesn't Always Equal Effect* (Melville House, 2018), of *September 12: Community and Neighborhood Recovery at Ground Zero* (New York University Press, 2011), and co-author, with Benjamin Shepard, of *The Beach Beneath the Streets: Contesting New York City's Public Spaces* (SUNY Press, 2011). He is an editor of the online urban *Metropolitics*, and has written for the *Village Voice*, *Dissent*, *In These Times*, and the *Wall Street Journal online*. He lives in Brooklyn.

Photographer

Caroline Shepard's photo essay of a rapidly transforming global borough accompanies this project. www.carolineshepard.com. Additional photographs by Brennan Cavanaugh, Erik R McGregor, Robin Michals, José Parlá, and Barbara Ross.

Social Sciences

Alexander Schellinger, Philipp Steinberg (eds.)
The Future of the Eurozone
How to Keep Europe Together:
A Progressive Perspective from Germany

October 2017, 202 p., pb.
29,99 € (DE), 978-3-8376-4081-6
E-Book
PDF: 26,99 € (DE), ISBN 978-3-8394-4081-0
EPUB: 26,99€ (DE), ISBN 978-3-7328-4081-6

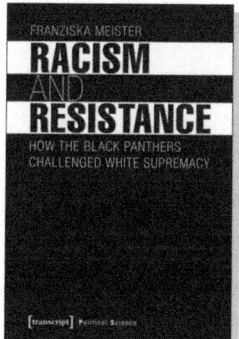

Franziska Meister
Racism and Resistance
How the Black Panthers Challenged White Supremacy

April 2017, 242 p., pb.
19,99 € (DE), 978-3-8376-3857-8
E-Book: 17,99 € (DE), ISBN 978-3-8394-3857-2

Maik Fielitz, Laura Lotte Laloire (eds.)
Trouble on the Far Right
Contemporary Right-Wing Strategies
and Practices in Europe

2016, 208 p., pb.
19,99 € (DE), 978-3-8376-3720-5
E-Book
PDF: 17,99 € (DE), ISBN 978-3-8394-3720-9
EPUB: 17,99€ (DE), ISBN 978-3-7328-3720-5

**All print, e-book and open access versions of the titles in our list
are available in our online shop www.transcript-verlag.de/en!**

Social Sciences

James Morrow
Where the Everyday Begins
A Study of Environment and Everyday Life

October 2017, 220 p., hardcover
99,99 € (DE), 978-3-8376-4077-9
E-Book: 99,99 € (DE), ISBN 978-3-8394-4077-3

Cameron Harrington, Clifford Shearing
Security in the Anthropocene
Reflections on Safety and Care

August 2017, 196 p., hardcover
79,99 € (DE), 978-3-8376-3337-5
E-Book: 79,99 € (DE), ISBN 978-3-8394-3337-9

Ilker Ataç, Gerda Heck, Sabine Hess, Zeynep Kasli, Philipp Ratfisch, Cavidan Soykan, Bediz Yilmaz (eds.)
movements. Journal for Critical Migration and Border Regime Studies
Vol. 3, Issue 2/2017: Turkey's Changing Migration Regime and its Global and Regional Dynamics

November 2017, 230 p., pb.
24,99 € (DE), 978-3-8376-3719-9

All print, e-book and open access versions of the titles in our list are available in our online shop www.transcript-verlag.de/en!

Printed by Printforce, United Kingdom